ENGAGING IRAN

ENGAGING IRAN

THE RISE OF A MIDDLE EAST POWERHOUSE AND AMERICA'S STRATEGIC CHOICE

Nathan Gonzalez

PRAEGER SECURITY INTERNATIONAL

Westport, Connecticut • London

Library of Congress Cataloging-in-Publication Data

Gonzalez, Nathan, 1979–
Engaging Iran : the rise of a Middle East powerhouse and America's strategic choice /
Nathan Gonzalez.
    p. cm.
  Includes bibliographical references and index.
  ISBN-13: 978–0–275–99742–7 (alk. paper)
  1. United States—Foreign relations—Iran.   2. Iran—Foreign relations—United States.
  I. Title.
  E183.8.I4G56   2007
  327.73055—dc22   2007020608

British Library Cataloguing in Publication Data is available.

Library of Congress Catalog Card Number: 2007020608
ISBN-13: 978–0–275–99742–7
ISBN-10: 0–275–99742–1

First published in 2007

Praeger Security International, 88 Post Road West, Westport, CT 06881
An imprint of Greenwood Publishing Group, Inc.
www.praeger.com

Printed in the United States of America

The paper used in this book complies with the
Permanent Paper Standard issued by the National
Information Standards Organization (Z39.48–1984).

10 9 8 7 6 5 4 3 2 1

For Tamara

my soulmate, my inspiration

CONTENTS

PREFACE: IRAN THROUGH OUR EYES

Sitting on an airplane bound for Tehran, I open the pages of a respected American magazine to a short article about state-sponsors of terrorism. The picture featured in the article is meant to rouse passions: A turbaned Iranian cleric stares angrily at the camera, flanked by a woman in a black *chador* (the long garb worn by conservative Iranian women, which covers all but the face and hands). In the background of the picture is perhaps the most famous of anti-American murals, which shows a revolver pistol made of the Stars and Stripes, as it was painted by the Islamic Republic of Iran on the grounds of the former U.S. embassy in Tehran. This is the Iran we know: anti-American and angrily Islamist.

I look carefully at the picture and come to think that it must have been staged. Even if it wasn't, the photographer had to have stood in place for several hours (if not days) to capture such an image. Where are the women not wearing a chador? Where are the men in Levis frantically rushing off to work, daydreaming of visiting their relatives in California? Where are the young people (two thirds of Iran's population is under thirty), making an off-handed remark about the cleric behind his back, laughing at the ridiculous mural? Where is the soldier on guard, looking at his watch, waiting to get off duty so he can help his parents move into a smaller, less expensive apartment, all while fuming about the government's wasted petrodollars on the Lebanese Hezbollah? Where are the men and women being bussed into Tehran to scream "Death to America" on cue at a staged government rally, since the clerics who rule the country couldn't find enough people in a city of 10 million to protest free of charge?

When I set off to write a book about Iran and its impact on American interests, I knew the most difficult aspect of the project would be to dispel popularly held beliefs about the country. After all, like most people, I am annoyed with researchers and opinion makers who seek to debunk common sense just to get attention, like new studies that show coffee can help you sleep. I drink coffee and I know that coffee doesn't help me sleep. But then there are those popularly held beliefs that are simply wrong, despite how logical they appear to be. Why should anyone have believed Eratosthenes when he claimed the Earth to be a sphere? Common sense alone would dictate that the Earth is flat, just as it would dictate today that Iran is the greatest enemy and most difficult strategic challenge to the United States. It's obvious, but it isn't true.

Any American fortunate enough to visit Iran quickly learns the difference between that country and most any other. In Western Europe and in "moderate" Turkey, I have been subjected to countless unsolicited lectures on American greed, warmongering and even the greatness of Osama bin Laden. But not in Iran. There, the image that Americans would like their country to represent still holds ground. "Freedom" and "America" are still mentioned in the same sentence by Iranians of all walks of life, and partly embarrassed taxi drivers, conservative bazaar merchants and wealthy liberals, all remind you that what their government says about America is not what the people believe. More importantly, there is a strong movement, both within Iranian power circles and those in America, which seeks to turn a new page in U.S.-Iranian relations after nearly three decades of name-calling and mutual distrust.

During one of Tehran's uncompromising traffic jams, I asked my friend at the wheel what he thought about al-Qaeda's rising power in Iraq, and America's imminent departure from that country: Would that increase the terror threat against neighboring Iran? Knowing full well that the U.S.- and Iranian-backed Shi'ite government in Iraq was in peril, my friend gave a typically optimistic Iranian answer: "I'm not worried. The important thing is that the Iraq war has brought us closer together. America and Iran will join forces, because there really is no other way." In that phrase lies the essence of this book.

The ideas found in these pages have benefited from over six years of research. It should be noted that while the views of many people I've quoted at times overlap with mine, the central thesis of this book, along with any shortcomings that may be found, are entirely my own.

While countless notes of gratitude are due in relation to this book, space permits me only to mention a few. I would like to thank Dr. David C. Rapoport for his continued support and encouragement since my time as an undergraduate student at UCLA. His friendship and insights are very dear to me. Also of incredible impact was Dr. Jalil Roshandel's class on Iran and the Greater Middle East, which more than anything else started my journey as an observer of Iranian politics.

Needless to say, this book would not have been possible without the active support of my editor, Hilary Claggett, who had the foresight and open-mindedness to consider engaging Iran in dialogue, even before the Baker-Hamilton Commission broke the taboo in late 2006. I am also grateful to Capt. Chris Danbeck and Capt. Dan McSweeney, both dear friends and graduate school classmates, who provided me with useful contacts for my research. Dr. Gary G. Sick and Dr. Lawrence G. Potter of Columbia University were kind enough to grant interviews for this book, as were

Maj. Abigail Linnington and Maj. Richard Wrona of the United States Military Academy, who kindly expressed their personal views (and not necessarily those of the U.S. Army) regarding Iran, Hezbollah, and the general situation in the Middle East.

I cannot thank my mother and father enough for their support throughout my life and especially my studies. This book could not have been written without their investment in my development as an individual and for that I will always be grateful. Most of all, I thank my wife Tamara, whose incredible patience and support throughout the writing of this book is just another testament to her love and unrelenting kindness.

INTRODUCTION: AMERICA'S CHOICES

There is no security on this earth, only opportunity.
—General Douglas MacArthur

The image must have been haunting to the seasoned Iraqi soldier. A wave of children approaching the front, armed only with religious zeal and plastic keys hanging from the neck to open the doors of Paradise. These "martyrs," as they would be known in the Islamic Republic of Iran, were eager volunteers sold on the idea that this war was between righteousness and evil, apostasy and Islam. They would be expected to pick up rifles from dead soldiers, or simply meet their fate on the vast minefields to allow the tanks behind them to pass.

To many, the human wave attacks during the bloody Iran-Iraq war of 1980–1988 were an ominous sign of Iran's weakness following the politically isolating revolution of 1978–1979—the world ganging up on Iran's leader, Ayatollah Ruhollah Khomeini and his firebrand style of Islam. For others, the martyrs represented sheer power: the ability to draw from countless volunteers to serve as sacrificial lambs that would protect the territorial integrity of their homeland, and the political independence of the emerging Islamic Republic.

Power is defined by Max Weber as the possibility that an actor "will be in a position to carry out his own will despite resistance."[1] For military theorist Carl von Clausewitz, power is present in all relationships, even if not stated outright. That is, all relations among states occur over a backdrop of power relationships, which are either clear and telling, or vague and implicit. The more vague they are, the more likely they are to invite aggression. It is that question mark associated with power that has kept theorists of war and peace awake for countless nights. For some, a proven recipe for peace is a balance-of-power world system that ensures no single country or alliance can exercise overwhelming strength. If one nation becomes too powerful in the eyes of its neighbors, others will form mutual security alliances, therefore balancing the other's strength, and making a war of conquest less likely. It was this balance of power that brought relative peace to Europe throughout much of the nineteenth century, bookmarked only by the devastating Napoleonic Wars that ended in 1815 and World War I. Peace, however, was not absolute, as war never became an outright anomaly in Europe. But total war as an instrument of devastation—a merciless fight between societies—would be put off until the two world wars came and redefined human savagery.

There are those, however, who do not buy the balance-of-power argument. How safe is a world, after all, which leads to the most brutal century in the history of human conflict? For many, bipolarity, the Manichean conflict between the United States and the Soviet Union, is the true recipe for peace. The mutual balance achieved by two powers keeping each other at bay is the best way of achieving relative peace, some would argue. Again, the conflicts of Vietnam for the United States, and Afghanistan for the USSR, could have hardly been called models of "peace"; but they certainly didn't lead to world war.

Yet for others still, a hegemonic peace, one in which a single power is dominant enough to dictate terms, is the best prescription for stability. What hegemonic peace has that balance-of-power lacks, is the ability to clearly predict the outcome of a war before it even begins. We find manifestations of hegemony in the ancient Persians, the Macedonians, and the Romans. These powers not only deterred potential rivalries through their track record of military prowess, but they also utilized trade, culture, and other "soft power" tools to maintain order within their reach of influence.

Today, some contend that America is a global hegemon. In many ways it is. Its current military budget is twice that of all potential adversaries combined. It enjoys the strongest economy in the world, and its culture and commercial enterprises permeate the globe entirely. But there is a catch. The conflicts of Vietnam and Iraq have exposed cracks in the American will to play the role of "global policeman." The most important question has become not whether America truly is a global hegemon, but rather, whether it wants to be.

Toward the close of the Vietnam War, the Nixon administration sought to mitigate the impacts of super power commitments by allowing countries in the various world regions to take a more active approach in managing their own security. Nixon began courting China in earnest in the early 1970s, at a time when that country was an anti-American and anti-capitalist foe, in hopes of exploiting differences between the emerging East Asian power and the Soviet Union. More importantly, Nixon realized that a powerful China could not be averted; the only question left for Nixon was how U.S.-China relations would look like once the communist nation realized its full power potential. Nixon chose a relaxation of tensions, more often called by the French word *détente*.

As Americans observe Iran's rising power in the Middle East and look for successful policy prescriptions, they must be ready and willing to look into the near future and ask the most critical and difficult questions. What is the end goal of American policy in the region? What should be America's grand strategy, and where would Iran fit in with it? Only after successfully tackling those questions can we truly ensure that our immediate policies are not shortsighted, but grounded in strategic compass. To achieve this successfully, Iran's internal dynamics must be understood, as well as the country's role in the region—historically, and presently. What this book will attempt to do then is delve into the question of Iranian power and national character, and the strategic choices laid before the United States of America moving forward.

This book is divided into three parts, the first of which portrays a pattern toward self-determination in Iran that country specialists know all too well, but which the general public rarely has a chance to explore. This was evident in a 2002 U.S. National Intelligence Council report that spoke of Iran's slow crawl toward democracy, but which was sadly drowned out by the saturating images of Middle Eastern terror and official government policy in Iran.[2] This concept of democratization, which I refer throughout as Iran's *trajectory of independence*, comprises of roughly the last one and a half centuries of modern Iranian history. This trajectory has led Iran to violently release itself from the shackles of foreign intervention, and has put Iran closer to homegrown democracy than any nation in the neighboring Arab world. As Part II of the book shows, this promise of democracy, set in the wider scope of Iranian Shi'i jurisprudence and practice, is placed to elevate the largest segment of Iranian society—its increasingly educated and pro-American youth—to the forefront of Iranian politics. But this part also deals with the dark nature of Iran's postrevolutionary regime, and explores the legacies of Iran's past three presidents, Mahmoud Ahmadinejad, Mohammad Khatami, and Ali Akbar Hashemi Rafsanjani. These three portraits hint at the diverse and complicated nature of Iranian political culture, which will prove key to formulating a coherent and workable foreign policy. The last chapter in this section deals with Iranian power potential in the twenty-first century, Iran's continued ties to terrorist groups, along with ideas on what a U.S.-Iranian war might look like.

Part III of this book proposes a new policy for Iran, and with that it reexamines the Nixon Doctrine, which utilized a system of "regional policemen" as a useful blueprint for long-term security strategy in the Middle East. By emphasizing alliances between nation-states, not just based on immediate interests, but now also on values (in this case, democracy), Iran can and should be able to play a central leadership role in the Middle East in partnership with America. As I intend to show, a nuclear-armed Iran, while presently feared by America and its closest allies, could play a definitive role in ensuring the continued pursuit of U.S. interests in the region.

To be sure, Iranian democracy will have to occur on Iran's own terms: ones that will neither be totally secular, nor subservient and prone to external manipulation. America must not repeat the myopic mistakes of the past. A farsighted, grand-strategic approach to engagement with Iran promises to open doors to regional stability and political development. Only then can America, as global leader, reap the benefits of a new Middle East, with the Islamic Republic of Iran at the helm. Before moving forward, this chapter introduces a set of important concepts that are found throughout the book. These revolve around the formation of a grand strategy, Iranian concepts of democracy, and the role of the Muslim religion in Iran.

CRAFTING A GRAND STRATEGY

Because a country's national security policy is necessarily tied to its geographic position, it has a tendency to "show great continuity over time."[3] This geopolitical outlook on security is essential to understanding the motivation of nation-states, and can explain a variety of historic and present conflicts. Proximity—to resources, to threatening powers, and to allies—is a starting point for most security analyses. The emergence of globalization and intercontinental ballistic missiles (ICBMs) have forced nations to expand their perception of what constitutes an immediate threat. Nevertheless, geopolitical dynamics continue to play a primary role in the understanding of a country's security concerns.

Even the onslaught of international terrorism, brought home to America in earnest on the morning of September 11, 2001, cannot be entirely divorced from regional forces. The Middle East, with good reason, has been the focal point of American security following 9/11. America, with long-standing interests in that region, not the least of which relates to the vital access to oil, in essence has become a staple of Middle Eastern politics. That is, while international terrorism can move across borders, regional dimensions still play a central role in a given terrorist group's goal and strategy.

Robert A. Pape of the University of Chicago goes so far as to connect groups engaging in suicide bombings, including the all-international al-Qaeda, with regional territorial designs. For Pape, whose studies encompass every recorded instance of modern suicide terrorism, a group's territorial goals should not escape any discussion on counterterrorism or suicide bombing. He writes that "a strategy of suicide terrorism is most likely to achieve nationalist goals, such as gaining control of what the terrorists see as their national homeland territory and expelling foreign military forces from that territory."[4] As international terrorism moves seamlessly across borders, analysts must continue to keep in mind the territorial dimensions of a given organization as they are *perceived* by the organization itself. Geopolitics and terrorism do go hand in hand.

To be sure, territory also played a central role in conflicts between the super powers. During its half-century march, the Cold War played itself out largely in peripheral nations that the warring powers, the United States and the Soviet Union, attempted to bring under their respective spheres of influence. Regional questions were crucial, with the Middle East especially vital as a source of energy. And while the dark cloud of nuclear Armageddon loomed over each of the rival super powers, the principles of deterrence, and more specifically the prospects for mutually assured destruction (MAD), served to diminish the likelihood of an all-out total war between the two adversaries. Under the MAD doctrine, each side would be able to retaliate against a nuclear attack, mutually destroying the warring parties. Proxy conflicts, therefore, became a staple of Cold War politics, and the Middle East hosted its share of them.

In a pre-1979 Middle East, Iran and Saudi Arabia remained America's stalwart allies, which under the mandate of the Nixon Doctrine consisted of a "twin-pillar" policy, meant to establish leadership in the region, and do America's anti-Soviet bidding. The Nixon Doctrine itself came out of a failed Vietnam policy, in which the United States expended vast resources and political capital in attempting to change the political dimensions of a nation, and by extension, a region. Nixon recognized that America could not be at all places all the time. He sought normalization of relations with China, accepting the communist nation as a *de facto* strongman within its own region after decades of American policymakers lumping the USSR and China together, as if the two had been part of a monolithic communist enterprise. The twin-pillar policy extends from this clearer understanding of national interests, and sought to put Iran at the forefront of the arrangement, providing arms and financial support in exchange for its friendship. Having played a traditional leadership (and at times hegemonic) role in the region since pre-Islamic times, Iran as a nation fits the prescription under the Nixon Doctrine of a regionally-powerful state that could help bring stability, and thus keep America from being easily pulled into protracted, localized, military commitments.

Today, the Middle East remains crucial to American security concerns, not as a chip in the game of superpower rivalry, but rather as a source of American enmity itself. The attacks of September 11, and the subsequent war on terror, have led policymakers to focus American strategy planning squarely on the Middle East, often at the expense of long-term questions surrounding China's rise as a potential superpower, and other possible challenges to American hegemony. A military doctrine that sees terrorism as the biggest threat to American security has forced policymakers further down the road of creating a smaller, lightweight military, and away from the days in which America could commit to several war theaters at once. The Defense Department's 2006 Quadrennial Defense Review (QDR) calls for a 1–4–2–1 doctrine: the capability to simultaneously protect the homeland, deter aggression in four regions, fight in two theaters, and win decisively (including occupation) in one of them. Yet that same QDR seeks to shift the balance of forces heavily toward "irregular threats," otherwise known as terrorist groups. With forces bogged down in Iraq, it is difficult to see how seriously the U.S. government is examining long-term threats to America's global position, such as the challenge by a new superpower, and whether it is prepared to provide the necessary resources and strategy toward this aim.

When we speak of formulating a "grand strategy," we are dealing with challenges to our security by mobilizing assets toward a long-term goal. The Cold War, which saw the expansion of Soviet communism as the greatest threat to American security, undertook a grand strategy of "containment." Under this grand strategy, any perceived effort by the USSR to expand its influence—military, economic, or political—in other nations, was seen by the United States as a direct challenge to its own security. The grand strategy, which worked over a period of decades, saw each threat as a piece of a larger puzzle.

As any other state, America must first and foremost deal with its own existence. What are the prospects for American survivability in the long-term, and how is this survivability maximized? In strictly military terms, America must be able to see challenges as part of a continuum. That is, it must avoid obsessing with present dilemmas without placing them in the context of a long-term strategy. To achieve this, American policymakers must make every effort to identify what the true threats to American survivability will be in the twenty-first century, and begin to plan a grand strategy accordingly. Only then can the immediate threat of terrorism and the spread of unconventional weapons be properly tackled.

IRANIAN DEMOCRACY

Iran, prior to the revolution of 1978–1979, had served as America's premiere partner in the Middle East. The last shah, or king of Iran, Mohammad Reza Pahlavi, was mostly seen as a puppet of the United States by his discontented and oppressed population. In 1953, the United States, at the behest of Great Britain, deposed the democratically elected prime minister, Mohammad Mosaddeq, and reinstated the shah to the throne after the king's self-imposed exile in Europe. Perceived by some in the Eisenhower administration as a potential Soviet ally, Mosaddeq was responsible for nationalizing the Anglo-Iranian Oil Company (AIOC). The United States pulled the plug on a national democratic movement that, if left-of-center, would be seen by the future Iranian revolutionaries as democratic greatness nipped in the bud by an overbearing foreign power.

While "Down with USA" became the motto of postrevolutionary Iran, hatred for America is hardly a phenomenon in Iran like it is in the neighboring Arab world. In fact, opinion polls show the opposite—a trend toward significant *pro-American* sentiments in Iran. America had simply come at the end of a long line of foreign countries that sought to economically and politically influence Iran. This long line of foreign powers, at times invited by Iran and at others militarily imposing its will, had especially benefited from greedy and incompetent Iranian rulers who were too eager to seek immediate profit at the expense of the Iranian people and the development of the country's economy. In a way, open disdain for foreign intervention has been little more than a reflection of Iranians' self-chastisement, homegrown disgust at the shortcomings of the state.

But homegrown distaste for Iranian leaders, as well as the rejection of overt foreign influence, points to a dynamic inherently compatible with that of democracy. At the very least, we can speak of a trajectory of independence. This trajectory is part of an observation of patterns within Iran, which comprise of small and large political and religious revolutionary movements that span across centuries, which have pitted the Iranian people against the powers-that-be, foreign and domestic. It is this trajectory of independence that is likely to lead to an Iranian democracy that is compatible with American long-term interests in the Middle East.

While this trajectory, this path of independence, does not come down to us in a perfect, continuous line, we can at the very least surmise a vision of what could take place in Iran, given the right circumstances. Needless to say, it is unwise to seek perfect patterns in hopes of arriving at an ultimate, predictable conclusion. Such confidence might yield one to seek to "nudge" a people in a given direction, as communists, messianic extremists, and (more recently) idealist neoconservatives have sought to do. After all, if one is part of a grand design, a preset equation that will bring a desired outcome, there is no longer any value in questioning one's commitment to a specific policy approach. Yet, like radical leftists who justified terrorist actions at the turn of the twentieth century in expectation of an ultimate global state of communism, and as neoconservatives pushed America to invade and occupy Iraq in the misguided hopes of turning a dictatorship into a democracy through unprovoked violence, those who see Iran's trajectory as manageable through radical intervention will only undermine efforts of diplomacy, and likely prove counterproductive. After all, foreign intervention is exactly that which the trajectory of independence has sought to reject. Furthermore, tendencies are not guarantees of outcome, and even a democratic Iran can pose dangers to a democratic United States.

The purpose of laying out this trajectory is to provide a deeper understanding of Iranian sociopolitical realities, ones that are based, not on fearmongering or the tired slogans of Iranian anti-Semitic leaders, but rather on underlying historic and present patterns, which will prove more helpful in formulating a coherent policy. We can say with confidence that following decades of a political and economic presence by the United States in Iran, the postrevolutionary anti-American slogans that today line the streets of Tehran are a product, not of outright anti-Americanism, but of an inner shame in the Islamic Republic that has less to do with America than it does with Iran.

RELIGION IN THE ISLAMIC REPUBLIC

Iran's threatening image in the United States and around the world is perhaps most closely connected with the symbols of the theocratic state: fountains of red water signaling the "martyrs' blood," turbaned clerics ruling over matters of war and peace, and women forced to wear the veil. Even the most religious American and European observers tend to look at theocracy with unease, as it challenges the notions of church-state separation that lie at the core of most Western republics. This unease becomes magnified when speaking of theocracy in Islam, a religion that often brings to Western minds images of suicide bombings and radical fanatics calling for "death to America."

Iran is by any stretch of the imagination a conservative religious country. While many in the exile communities speak of a prerevolutionary Iran as a secular haven of miniskirts and Coco Chanel, it must be understood that much of Iran's secular façade prior to the revolution of 1978–1979 was state-imposed. Not forgotten are memories of veiled women being beaten under Reza Shah, the founder of the Pahlavi dynasty, who tried to outlaw the use of the veil in 1935. The apparent secularism under the last king, Mohammad Reza Shah Pahlavi, was far from all-encompassing—with family courts in the hands of the Islamic clerics, along with what could be characterized as conservative viewpoints espoused by even some of the most loyal within the regime.

Understanding Iranian society, then, is impossible without understanding its majority religion (and official state religion since the sixteenth century): Shi'i Islam. Nevertheless, it is important not to fall for the trap of oversimplifications by merely reciting religious doctrine as a means of understanding a society. There are political pundits in the United States who have gone so far as to claim that Iranian President Mahmoud Ahmadinejad wants a nuclear weapon so he can destroy the world and bring on Armageddon because, after all, he is a Shi'i.[5] Needless to say that any Christian who believes in the Book of Revelations also espouses a concept of Judgment Day, and while many call for messianic activism, few would go so far as to connect belligerent language by a Western head of state to underlying violent messianic impulses. The interests of a nation or even a government should not be reduced to a purely theological reading, lest we be pulled into counterproductive or even outright dangerous misconceptions.

Another shortcoming that comes with placing too much emphasis on religion, even in an overtly theocratic state like Iran, is the fact that most societies are shaped by more than one religious or historical influence. Iran has an abundantly rich pre-Islamic past—one that is remembered and embraced not only by Iranian Muslims, but by those of all faiths. *Nowrooz* is the first day of spring and the Persian New Year, a pagan celebration of renewal just as alive today in Los Angeles, as it is in Tehran and across the former Persian Empire. The poetry of Hafez, Sa'adi, and Khayam is not only Islamic but also quintessentially Persian—employing with gusto the allegory of wine, a substance banned in conservative Islamic interpretations. Modern influences should also not be discounted. Iran is a modern state that has grappled with Marxist-Leninist philosophy, theocratic reformism, and Western popular culture. Iran is no stranger to Hollywood actor Sylvester Stallone, English soccer sensation David Beckham, or American pop star Britney Spears. In fact, it is an active and connected Iranian diaspora that continuously feeds the homeland with Western music, clothing, and ideas.

The declaration of faith practiced by all Muslims is the acceptance of a single god—the God of Abraham and Jacob—as well as the recognition that Muhammad is the last of the monotheistic prophets. "There is no deity but God (Arabic: *Allah*) and Muhammad is the Prophet of God," states this declaration, which is pronounced upon acceptance of the faith. This simple procedure of conversion allowed for Islam to be easily exported to peoples around the globe, making it today a religion of over 1.5 billion adherents. The belief in this simple declaration of faith is what defines a Muslim in the way that believing in Jesus as the Son of God identifies a Christian of any branch.

At the time of his death in June 632 AD, the Prophet Muhammad had established a Muslim state that spanned across much of the Arabian Peninsula and enjoyed treaties with Persian-controlled Yemen and neighboring tribes. However, as esteemed biographer W. Montgomery Watt suggests, "he had made no arrangements for the continued administration of the affairs of the Islamic state, except that he had appointed Abu Bakr to lead prayers."[6] Abu Bakr had been Muhammad's right hand during the latter's accumulation of power, and he was elected as Muhammad's successor following the death of the Prophet.

This succession, however, was not without controversy. Ali, a son-in-law and de-facto baby brother of Muhammad (Ali was the son of Abu Talib, the Prophet's uncle who had taken the orphan Muhammad into his home early in life), also claimed that he was to succeed Muhammad. What ensued was a rift between those who favored Ali and the lineal succession he represented, and those who accepted the rule of Abu Bakr.

Ali eventually became the fourth caliph, or ruling vizier, of the Islamic community (*umma*), which by then had expanded across the Middle East and North Africa through a variety of military campaigns. Ali is recognized by Sunnis as the fourth and last of the "Rightly Guided Caliphs," whose reign is revered as just and in concurrence with true Islamic values. Those who thought Abu Bakr as unworthy of the title of first caliph, however, eventually became known as *Shi'at 'Ali*—the "Party of Ali." Shi'is followed the bloodline across the generations of the House of Ali, assigning the title of *Imam* (leader) to those who were seen as infallible religious and political rulers of their community. Sunnis themselves have never placed a burden of infallibility on their caliphs, whose power rested on varyingly corrupt tribal dynasties, and their often-violent patterns of succession.

Several sects of Shi'ism exist today. Ismailis and Zaydis each believe in original the existence of six and five Imams, respectively. Iran, however, espouses the largest Shi'i sect, which is known as Twelver Shism—a sect that recognizes twelve Imams, culminating in the last one, who disappeared in the year 874. This disappearance begins a period in Shi'ism known as the "Occultation," which continues to this day. This period will end with the return of the Imam as the *Mehdi* (Messiah). For our purposes, we will only be dealing with the Twelver Shi'i sect—Iran's majority and official state religion. Within the Twelver sect exist a plethora of schools of thought, such as the Usulis, Akhbaris, and Shaykhis, which will be explored in this book as appropriate.

Because Shiism has more often than not acted as a vehicle for opposition to the more dominant Sunnis across the Middle East, the branch is often associated with revolutionary movements that embraced the dispossessed. Non-Arabs and lower classes were often drawn to the ideas of Shi'ism, which centered in their core on turning injustice on its head. While some Imams and their followers counseled peace, many violent uprisings, especially around the time of the last Imams in the ninth century, came to define Shi'ism as an instrument of opposition to the Sunni empire.

One of the most important commemorations in the Shi'i calendar is not the anniversary of a glorious victory, but the observance of a defeat at the hands of Sunni armies. *'Ashura* commemorates the martyrdom of Imam Husayn, one of Ali's sons, during the Battle of Karbala in modern-day Iraq in the year 680. This battle is remembered throughout ten days of recitation similar to the Christian Passion play of Good Friday. Just as the lashes upon Jesus are recounted with painful agony, *'Ashura* is a retelling of a battle that decimated Shi'i forces at the hand of a ruthless Sunni caliph, Yazid.

For Shi'is around the world, the memory of their fellow faithful turning their backs on Husayn at the last minute, and leaving him and his family to be slaughtered at the hand of Yazid's army conjures up wishes to somehow rectify the past. Mourners ask Husayn for forgiveness, some beating their chests, some lashing themselves, wishing that history could repeat itself so they may be valiant enough to fight alongside their leader. Among those who turned their backs on Husayn, the dwellers of Kufa, in what is now Iraq, are among the most despised. Having promised to fight, they shut themselves at home at the last minute and refused to join Husayn's troops for their last stand at Karbala. During the Iranian Revolution, posters donned the slogan "We are not Kufis!," meaning they would not turn their backs on the revolution against the tyranny of the shah. While the revolution was an undertaking that spanned across religious and political affiliations, the quintessentially Shi'i narrative of the weak against the strong (Husayn versus Yazid) was present in the collective consciousness of the crowds. Ayatollah Ruhollah Khomeini, the eventual leader and face of the revolution, was often spoken of as the "Imam" returning from Occultation. Khomeini himself never confirmed these assertions, though he also never disputed them, leaving room for helpful ambiguity.

In terms of hierarchy, there is nothing in Islam, either Sunni or Shi'i, which resembles the rigid structures found in Catholicism. Sunnis practice a special degree of autonomy, where a mosque might contain a prayer leader, but scholars are free to associate themselves with one of four major schools of thought. Shi'is do practice a degree of hierarchy, with the acknowledgment of different levels of clerical authority. Former Iranian President Muhammad Khatami, for example, enjoys the title of *hujjat ul-Islam* ("Proof of Islam"), which shows a significant level of scholarship, but is below that of an *ayatollah* ("Sign of God"). A grand ayatollah (*ayatollah al-uzma*), the title held by Khomeini during his years as supreme leader of Iran, is also held by the influential Ali al-Sistani of Iraq. These titles are for the most part earned through the accolades of peers and students. That is, the Shi'i cream is expected to rise to the top, and often a telltale sign of hierarchy is the following that a cleric might enjoy.

Yet the recognition of superior scholarship does not automatically grant an ayatollah political power, even within the Islamic Republic of Iran. Grand Ayatollah Ali Montazeri, once heir apparent to Khomeini, broke with the supreme leader and was eventually placed under house arrest in the holy city of Qom. His house arrest lasted until 2003 and he has since been stripped in the media of his title of grand ayatollah. This latter point is part of an observed pattern within the Islamic Republic, in which the political concerns of its leaders have more often than not trumped any true religious considerations.[7]

Given that there is no strict hierarchy in Shi'i Islam, there is consequently no clear-cut blueprint for Islamic governance. While Islam from the beginning was meant as the basis for a state, and elementary questions of taxation, inheritance, family law, and punishment can be found in the codified Sunni and Shi'i traditions, the modern-day affairs of a nation can hardly be found within the pages of ninth-century writings. Yet Ayatollah Khomeini was no stranger to Greek philosophy, and the Islamic Republic of Iran can be considered a combination of Plato's philosopher-king concept, as embodied by the office of the "supreme leader" (the position that Khomeini held), and the separation of powers model of the United States and France. To the detriment of Iranians, however, the business of running an oil ministry, a modern military, and dealing with women in the workforce, are just a few of the everyday challenges posed to a leadership, whose credentials are often based purely on Islamic knowledge.

Of course, not all ayatollahs favor Islamic governance—most actually do not. The separation of religion and the state became yet another unique feature of Shi'i Islam as a minority religion throughout the centuries, and it continues to this day even in Iran and majority Shi'i Iraq. Notable figures like Sistani of Iraq have taken a mostly nonpolitical approach to their exercise of influence. Khomeini's writings, and most notably his lectures on the "Rule by the Jurisprudent" (better known in its Perso-Arabic *velayat-e faqih*), adopt a position that is alien to most modern-day Shi'i scholars. In *velayat-e faqih*, Khomeini writes that a ruler who is not an Imam can and should lead the faithful during the time of Occultation. This jurist would possess significant influence over the community, acting as a representative of the Imam on Earth. As the Islamic Republic became a reality, Khomeini went as far as to say that this jurist, or *faqih*, could even override *shari'ah* (Islamic law) itself.

But how Islamic is an Islamic state, especially when basing itself on less-than-universally religious concepts? By allowing the government to stand in contradiction to shari'ah, and by often overriding the recommendations of leading clerics, Iran underscores the difficulty of speaking of it as a modern Islamic state in the pure sense of the word. In the end, the Islamic Republic is a mere stopping point of a nation's long political development, from an ancient kingdom, to a modern republic.

PART I

CHARTING THE TRAJECTORY

Chapter 1

THE PROMISE OF PERSEPOLIS

I am a Persian. From Persia I seized Egypt, I ordered the digging of this canal from a river called Nile, which flows in Egypt, to the sea which begins in Persia. Afterwards this canal was dug just as I ordered, and ships passed through this canal from Egypt to Persia, as I wished.
— Darius the Great (on the construction of the Suez Canal, ca. 500 BC)[1]

The ruins of Persepolis, near the Iranian city of Shiraz, symbolize not only the ancient seat of a powerful empire, but also the abilities of a people to redefine their world according to a tireless vision of society, law, and religion. The columns that still stand amidst the arid landscape once housed elaborate temples and palaces, home to scribes of a new language, and priests of a rising faith.

What we now refer to collectively as the "Persian Empire" is in fact a long, historical line of ambitious states and dynasties that were culturally and politically centered in the Iranian plateau. The Persians began their journey to great power status on October 29, 539 BC, with the conquest of Babylon by an ambitious Persian king known as Cyrus the Great. As he set off on his reign, Cyrus freed Babylonian slaves and ushered in a new era of religious tolerance, ordering the Temple in Jerusalem to be rebuilt after its destruction by the Babylonian king, Nebuchadnezzar. At home, Cyrus strengthened a faith that would develop into Zoroastrianism, which stands today not only as one of the oldest living religions, but as a social system that helped shape the very core of Islamic belief and jurisprudence. Like other conquering armies would learn, the Arab Muslims that brought the Prophet Muhammad's message to Iran could not remain unaffected by the traditions and cultural pride of the ancient nation. When Iran was too weak to project its power militarily, it would do so culturally—using its unmatched abilities in soft power as a tool to shape its region's architecture, administration, literature, and faith.

During its military zenith, the territory of Iran comprised one of the largest single dominions the world had seen up to that point—stretching from Egypt to Central Asia, and down to the Arabian Peninsula. In fact, modern perceptions of Iran in the Middle East consciously borrow from past experience, with Iran often portrayed as a naturally expansive power, seeking to engulf the region through its military power, and now the exportation of its Islamic revolution. A hegemonic, all-powerful Iran remains a constant worry for many of its neighbors, given Iran's unique place as a non-Arab nation with Shi'i Islam as its state religion. Sunni Arab governments project continuous worry about Iranian aims, with King Abdullah II of Jordan recently warning of a rising "Shi'i Crescent" that stretches from Iran, through Iraq, and into Lebanon, which threatens Sunni dominance over the region.

But within the vast empires of past Iranian dynasties lie the core, inherently comfortable boundaries of modern Iran. This area is traditionally recounted as *Iranshahr* (Domain of Iran). The term "Aryan," which was strangely misappropriated by the Nazi regime to refer to blond, blue-eyed Germanic peoples, is in fact a reference to those who spoke an original dialect of the Indo-European tongue, from which modern European languages, including English, derive. It is from this term that we get the name *Iran* ("Land of the Aryans"). Modern Iranians are quick to point out differences between themselves and neighboring Arabs, who speak a Semitic language and, in typically condescending Iranian parlance, come from much more humble origins. It is not uncommon, in fact, to hear Iranians refer to their Arab neighbors as a "camel milk-drinking," and "lizard-eating" people in derogatory fashion. And despite the fact that Arabic, as the language of the Qur'an, remains an official language in the Islamic Republic, Iranians are no more inclined to learn Arabic in school today, as Polish children were to learning Russian during the Cold War. Even highly religious Iranians will express mixed feelings about the Arab-Islamic conquest of Iran, looking back with a hint of nostalgia to a pre-Islamic, seemingly decadent time.

But decadent paganism in itself is not the reason for nostalgia. Iranian pride in empires past is more closely associated with the unique character of a people. Considered by some as the oldest declaration of human rights in the world, a cuneiform cylinder commissioned by Cyrus upon his entrance into Babylon recounts his freeing of the city's slaves, his reconstruction of housing, and the restitution of the land's religion. A successor to the throne, King Darius, further solidified Iran's identity by establishing a written language in 521 BC, which forms the basis for today's Persian (also called by the local "Farsi"). Persian architectural design, as beautified by the massive pillars at Persepolis and the elaborate gardens of Cyrus' tomb in Pasargadae, inspired Greek observers to adopt the latter as the root for the word "paradise."[2]

Placing Iran first among nations of the world was its development of a postal system, a diplomatic corps, and the earliest examples of espionage. Iranian tools of statecraft are revered to this day, and remain a source of worry for officials in Washington, who quip about Persian mastery in the art of diplomatic gamesmanship and deception. But Iran's association with progressive concepts is also part of the narrative. Early Islamic writers perpetuated the image of pre-Islamic Persia as a dominion of just rulers. They write of public audiences during *Nowrooz* (the Persian New Year) in which "any subject could bring an unsatisfied complaint directly before the king, even a complaint of the king's own conduct."[3] The king would then kneel before his attorney general, swearing to accept the verdict of the court.

Arguably Persia's greatest asset was its ability to administer complex projects through the extensive use of written records, which were the domain of a highly capable class of scribes. Their administrative abilities extended to moneymaking ventures, as surviving texts from a property management company called the "Murasu Firm" attest. This company engaged in the business of issuing mortgages, as well as leasing and subletting real estate and water rights. These early capitalists conjured up sophisticated contractual terms, on which derivatives of an underlying asset (such as a canal) might be leased out to interested parties. That is, while the canal, for instance, was not itself leased, as it belonged exclusively to the king, the rights to its overflow from "the right and left sides, from the opening to the tail, wherever its waters reach," could in fact be negotiated.[4] When the Arab Muslim armies would reach Persia in 637 on a campaign of conquest and conversion, they would themselves become profoundly changed by the character and administrative abilities of the Persians.

ISLAMIC CONQUEST

Islam, the new religion of Iran, would not remain unchanged by the Persians' "institutional continuity, best revealed perhaps in the persistence of bureaucratic organization and methods from the earliest times."[5] The invading Arabs, who originated from a bedouin culture, were not only unable to completely Arabize Iran as they did most of the Middle East, which now speaks Arabic and is considered "Arab," but they were compelled to adopt uniquely Persian administrative tools—from their postal system, to the Zoroastrian concept of religiously endowed land (in Arabic called *waqf*). The influence of Zoroastrianism in fact, permeated even the Islamic faith itself, with Zoroastrian hierarchical positions adopted in Islam under Arabic names like *qadi* (Islamic judge) and *wazir* (vizier). Iranian scribes too, became the preferred administrators of the Arab-Muslim empire, and the concept of high-culture (*adab*) was passed down from Iran to the Muslim invaders, not to mention Islam's interpretation of the existence of a heaven and a hell, concepts directly and indirectly borrowed from Zoroastrianism. One of the legacies of pre-Islamic culture that largely lost ground due to the Arab-Muslim influence was the education of women, considered part and parcel of Iranian custom but later minimized or altogether abandoned. Contemporary Iran has recouped some of those past tendencies, with women making up 60 percent of university students (compared with around 50 percent in Egypt, Jordan, and Lebanon, 39 percent in Syria, and 25 percent in Saudi Arabia).[6]

While Arabs looked to Iran for its administrative traditions, many Iranians came to resent the Arab-centric character of early Islamic colonialism. Unlike today's Muslim religion, which is universal and reaches across continents, Islam during the first centuries was largely associated with the dichotomy of Arab ruling elites and disenfranchised non-Arabs. Non-Arabs would be increasingly drawn to Shi'ism as an alternative source of justice under the perceived unfairness of an Arab caliphate. A movement of revolt led by non-Arabs called the *shu'ubiya*, which originated within Persian-speaking dominions, helped significantly alter the face of Islam, and brought with it the universality of Islam that today exemplifies the diverse faith. Under pressure by the *shu'ubiya*, the Umayyid caliphate in Damascus fell in 750, and a more *shu'ubiya-*, and at times even Shi'i-friendly Abbasid caliphate would now be seated in Baghdad. Thus began the period of de-Arabization of a Muslim caliphate that would largely stay in the hands of ethnic Turks until its dissolution, which came with the fall of the Ottoman Empire after World War I.

The period between the establishment of the Abbasids and the Occultation of the last Shi'i Imam in the year 874 represented significant turmoil in the history of Islamic practice. Baghdad became embroiled in a sectarian civil war in 865, largely fueled by a crisis of succession in the caliphate. In the backdrop lay an unresolved debate, which often turned violent between Sunnis and Shi'is, but perhaps most importantly, *within* the respective sects. The battle lines were drawn between those who favored the Islamic notion of knowledge (*'ilm*), that is, a mastery of the literal reading of textual traditions, and on the other side those who preferred reason (*'aql*) as a source of jurisprudence. The latter was in line with the powerful influence that Greek philosophy had on Baghdad at the time. Yet the implication that the works of Plato could somehow influence the future practices of the new, monotheistic faith inscribed in the Qur'an, were a source of significant alarm for many Muslim traditionalists of the ninth century. Rationalist Sunni would fight traditionalist Sunni, while Shi'is engaged in a parallel debate. Uprisings in Baghdad and throughout the eastern, Iranian-inhabited regions tested the viability of the Abbasid caliphate, which itself floundered on the question of "reason" versus "knowledge," as one caliph with a certain preference would give way to a successor with an opposing view.

It was in these turbulent times that the city of Qom, near modern-day Tehran, nurtured a group of traditionalist Shi'i theologians, who produced some of the most influential writings on the interpretation of the Shi'i faith. Among these conservative writers was Muhammad ibn Yacub al-Kulayni, who counseled against expecting a speedy return of the hidden Imam, and instead sought to codify norms for Islamic law in his absence. Al-Kulayni even borrowed from Sunni antirationalist thinkers in his attacks on those within his own sect. His writings would pave an instrumental path toward brining a dominant *Usuli* (that is, roots-centered) interpretation to the Shi'i faith. Ayatollah Khomeini, who during his lifetime enjoyed wide support in Qom (now a seminary city and the heart of Shi'ism in Iran), was himself a follower of the dominant Usuli school, and like most modern Shi'i clerics, owed many of his intellectual positions to the ninth-century writings of al-Kulayni.

Ironically, it would be Usuli writers that would prove the more "rationalist" party in a later religious crossroads, a debate between the Usulis and groups known as the Akhbaris and Shaykhis. In this debate, which the Usulis had mostly won by the nineteenth century, the Akhbaris sought a literal interpretation of the Qur'an and the oral traditions of the Imams, and accepted no other source of law. This would have two important ramifications. For one, no legal framework could be constructed for making decisions based on current issues, since to Akhbaris, all necessary answers had already been provided in the texts. The secondary impact of this was a challenge to the very authority of the clergy (or *ulama*), who remained central to the interpretation of Shi'ism, at least according to Usuli practice.

The Ususlis in fact came to develop in the centuries after al-Kulayni the prerogative for using deductive rationalism to interpret law in a modern context. This was their central rationale for maintaining the influential role of the ulama. For Usulis, every Muslim was expected to follow, or "emulate," a *living* cleric. This created a double-edged sword, consisting on one side of a path toward the modernization of the religion by allowing legal decisions to be based on current times, and on the other the establishment of a monopoly of authority within the religious class. This last point was perhaps more immediately critical, as few Usuli clerics were known to go out of their way to break from established norms, let alone act as progressive reformers. The prerogative to interpret—even to legislate—would be taken to its logical extreme by Ayatollah Khomeini, who viewed the leadership and guidance of the clergy not only as critical in the realm of religious observance, but also to the practice of statecraft.

For the Akhbaris, who would lose the debate by the early nineteenth century, there was no need for a rational-legal interpretation, since by definition they would place the burden of religious practice squarely on the lap of the believer, without the need for an interpreter or arbiter. It is difficult to deduce whether a more powerful Akhbari movement would have had a liberalizing impact on the ever-transforming religion. After all, their position is not drastically different from the most radical of fundamentalist Sunni clerics, who see no need for legislation, and even less to follow the rationally deduced judgments of living clerics in tackling current legal questions. For Akhbaris, as for fundamentalist Sunnis, what isn't found within the pages of the Qur'an and oral traditions is often not worth discussing; or worse yet, it merits active opposition.

On a more esoteric end of the spectrum during the later religious debates were the Skaykhis, a Sufi-like movement within Shi'ism that was more spiritual in nature, and less legalistic than either the Usulis or Akhbaris. The consummate mavericks, Shaykhis sought an interpretation of Islam based on love for the Almighty, rather than external approaches to worship. Shaykhis would later establish the roots of the Baha'i religion, a faith that continues to inspire vehement intolerance from the ruling clergy of the Islamic Republic.

But as internal clashes of religious interpretation would have their impact on society, Persian culture continued to leave its mark across a growing Muslim empire. Once the Turkish Seljuks, and later the Mongols, took control of Persia in the eleventh and thirteenth centuries, respectively, Iranian culture made a comeback into Central Asia, touching off a rebirth there in architecture, poetry, and the arts. Shi'ism also made inroads in these largely Sunni regions and a rich new literature took hold under New Persian, a language that combined "Arabic words into Middle Persian vocabulary and grammar, and provided the vehicle to express a Perso-Islamic cultural identity."[7] In the year 1010, Ferdowsi would complete the immortal epic *Shahnameh* (*The Book of Kings*). Just as the legend of Romulus and Remus provided the Romans with a narrative of nationhood, and as *The Divine Comedy* of Dante Alighieri established Florentine as the Italian language, *Shahnameh* would tell the folkloric history of Iran and at the same time act as the conduit for the New Persian language. Today, Iranians of all walks of life can proudly recite passages from their national epic.

A SHI'I EMPIRE

The recognized beginning of Shi'ism as the official state religion of Iran is 1501, with the establishment of the Safavid Empire, under Shah Ismail. An ethnic Tajik, Ismail was not recognized as a traditional Shi'i ruler in the eyes of practicing Arabs in Lebanon and Baghdad, but he nevertheless provided an imperial counterpoint to the Sunni Ottoman Empire in the West. Tajiks, who are traditionally Persian speakers but form part of a wider ethnic Turkish umbrella that today includes Azeris, Turkomen, and Uzbeks, among others, made up the inner administrative circle of Safavid Iran. This power center was Sunni at its core, and was not unlike the Ottoman Empire in its practice and character. Yet the state moved to establish Shi'ism throughout its domains by appointing prayer leaders across the empire. It is from the sixteenth century on that Iran has remained the only truly powerful nation with a distinctly Shi'i identity.[8]

While the Safavids were concerned with the dual threats of Central Asian Uzbeks and Western Ottomans, they were forced to largely ignore the Persian Gulf. Ultimately to their own strategic peril, the Safavids left the Gulf to the administration of Arab tribes. As Columbia University historian Lawrence Potter suggests, the Iranian people along the Gulf had much more in common with their neighbors in the Arabian Peninsula than with the ruling Safavids of the higher Iranian plateau. Separated by the Zagros Mountains from the central state, the Gulf-dwelling Iranians shared with their Arab counterparts "a maritime culture based on pearling, fishing and long-distance trade, and many tribes moved freely back and forth."[9] When the British Empire would establish itself as the dominant power in the region during the seventeenth century, the Safavids' apparent lack of interest in forming a viable naval force to mirror their might on *terra firma* would haunt the Iranian people, who would have to contend with an overbearing British presence that did not officially end until 1971.

A NATION OF JUSTICE

Iran has a long history pertaining to the office of the ombudsman, which in some form or another dates back to pre-Islamic times. These ombudsmen were appointed by the king "to act on behalf of plaintiffs from the lower classes who brought accusations of oppression by the powerful or of governmental negligence or injustice."[10] This ombudsman tradition was not created merely for the good of the people. Its history is recounted as the office of a semi-independent functionary tasked with creating needed harmony among the classes—something critical for the maintenance of a sturdy economy, and for preventing dangerous unrest.

The titles associated with this ombudsman practice would change over time and at one point the office was called the "Secretary of the Powerless and Indigent." More commonly, the office was known as *vakil-e ra'aya* (Guardian of the People). It was this title that the first leader of the Zand dynasty—regarded as the zenith example of justice in Iranian government—chose to give himself. Karim Khan Zand established rule over Iran in 1757 after a series of successful military endeavors to restore order during the chaotic decline of Safavid power. Rather than put an end to the previous dynasty, he allowed its symbolic rule to continue, while refusing to grant himself the title of "king," opting instead for the more humble *"vakil."*

Karim Khan Zand is perhaps best remembered as a utilitarian, doing away with the imperial lavishness associated with the Safavid shahs, instead focusing on establishing a just system of taxation, maintaining the salaries of government officers at manageable levels, and most importantly, putting the military on a less costly, but effective defensive posture. At the same time, Karim Khan went to great lengths to lessen tribal divisions in the country, and sought the help of tribal leaders in a nonmilitary scope, and with an eye toward integration. The khan himself was of humble, tribal origins, and was not shy in reminding people of this. He was especially fond of recounting his attempt to rob a golden saddle from an Afghan officer as a young boy, which after being conscience-stricken, he promptly returned. The officer's wife, seeing that it had been brought back, prayed loudly that the person who returned the prized possession "might live to have a hundred such saddles." As the eventual ruler of Iran, Karim Khan Zand liked to think that the woman's prayers had been answered.[11]

Following the death of Karim Khan Zand, a period of renewed chaos ensued, which finally ended with the rise of the Qajar dynasty. By this time, Great Britain had become the most powerful entity in the Persian Gulf, negotiating the creation of modern nation-states like Kuwait, Oman, Saudi Arabia, and the predecessor states of the United Arab Emirates. Iran, as a gateway to Central Asia and its prized colonial possession of India, became of utmost importance to maintaining British supremacy in the region, and it would be watched with a careful eye. Actively managing the affairs of Iran, Great Britain made it clear that it would resort to staging a coup were the new Qajar rulers not to play in its favor. The Qajars would comply, setting Iran on a path of political weakness and subordination unlike anything the proud nation had ever experienced.[12]

It is not easy to surmise whether a potent navy, built under a strong Safavid Empire, would have been enough to counteract later European incursions into the region. It is unlikely that this would have been the case, given European technological supremacy. If anything, a more formidable naval capacity enjoyed by a more politically sturdy, unified Persia in the eighteenth century could have lessened the humiliating scope of the foreign intervention that was in store for Iran. And while Iran itself was never colonized by a European power, the relationship was more exploitative than it was collaborative.

The nineteenth and early twentieth centuries mark for Iran an era of unprecedented sociopolitical change, characterized by the incompetence of the Qajar dynasty, a shocking entry into the global marketplace, and a restless population longing for reform. This period of roughly 100 years would make heroes for all sides of today's struggles—the government clerics of postrevolutionary Iran, as well as the cautious reformers who wait in the wings. After the short-lived but fair dynasty of the Zands would be pushed out, a new religion would be born and almost crushed, and an unprecedented coalition of workers, socialist radicals, democrats, and clerics, would stand up to Tehran's leadership and force a monumental shift in the course of the nation.

CHAPTER 2

TRAJECTORY OF INDEPENDENCE

It is not those who inflict the most, but those who suffer the most that win their objectives.
—Terence MacSwiney, Sinn Féin Activist[1]

Upon beginning any study of Iran, contradictions will quickly surface, making clear-cut statements about the nation unhelpful, if not misleading. It is impossible to pin down an appropriate broad-brush description of Iran's national character without running into complicated dualisms. Is Iran a nation that embraces imperial grandeur, conjuring up images of pre-Islamic Persian glory, or antiestablishment grassroots movements, like those that characterize dozens of pivotal moments in Iranian history? Does Iran see itself as a natural regional hegemon, like it was during much of its history, or as the consummate underdog, a martyr fighting against all odds as Imam Husayn did at the Battle of Karbala? Is Iran a nation of blooming secular radicalism, complete with the public hangings of traditionalist clerics, as they occurred during the Constitutional Revolution of 1905–1911, or merely another bastion of anti-Western Islamist theology, like it finds itself today in the eyes of the world? The contradictions in Iranian history are plentiful, and they point to a constant internal friction in the character of the country.

Iran today is a product of historical seesawing that has pulled the nation to and from the perceived "establishment," and back and forth between individuality in religious observance (even secularism) and outright theocratic rule. Collectively, Iranians are privy to their country's past greatness, and expectations run high. This ultimate sense of nationalism, which runs deep across gender and class divides, centers on a vague, yet powerful ideal—the centrality of *justice* in society, and in the affairs of the state. Justice for Iran is a key component of its historical narrative, and the fleeting reencounters with national greatness have taken place before a backdrop that pits justice against injustice. As Zoroastrians and Manicheans saw the world as a battlefield for the forces of light and the forces of darkness, Iranians have been continuously preoccupied with the battle against injustice, as it has been perceived at any given time in history. An elusive concept, injustice has been personified in oppressive rulers, religious despots, and in the case of modern Iran, European and American interventionists. The image of the all-powerful Caliph Yazid, mercilessly sending his troops to put down the Party of Ali at Karbala, makes for a difficult relationship between the character of Iran, and the absolute power that its rulers have tried to impose on the population. No one, not shah or revolutionary cleric, can be truly immune from the label of "Yazid"—an usurping and unjust ruler.

During the pivotal nineteenth century, the battle for justice revolved around the growing pains of modernization—the fight for better labor practices, and the protection of domestic markets against foreign encroachment. While seemingly compatible with the European left, these fights were often taken up in Iran by members of the clergy, who, lining up with trade guilds and secular intellectuals, did not see social reform as necessarily antagonistic with religious duty. Women too, entered the fray and played indispensable roles in the development of Iranian political culture, at times breaking through established cultural barriers, while maintaining a religious tone, as even the most secular of Marxist reformers had learned to do.

For Iranians, concessions of their natural resources or overall economic independence, in the form of favorable tariffs, exclusive market rights agreements and even foreign stakes in Iranian resources, had served as an ultimate sign of incompetence and treason on the part of their rulers. One of the most infamous of these acts was the Reuter concession of 1872, which granted British citizen Paul Julius Baron von Reuter (founder of Reuters) the "right to farm the customs; set up a state bank; build railroads, telegraph lines, and factories; and exploit virtually all the mineral wealth of Iran."[2]

But the Qajar dynasty in the nineteenth century did not lie down quietly as Europe made its mark. Nasir al-Din Shah, who reigned through the latter half of the century, recruited an able chancellor—an Iranian Bismarck—to undertake much needed military-centered reforms. Mirza Taqi Khan, better known as Amir Kabir (Amir the Great), looked respectively to the Ottoman Empire and Europe for inspiration and assistance. The reforms centered around the restructuring of the military and the establishment of a polytechnic institute of higher learning, the first of its kind in modern Iran, which would not only provide an education to the military and bureaucracy, but also translate European works and publish the first Persian-language textbooks.

For Iran historian Nikki Keddie, many of the national headaches of "modernization from above," which was pursued by Reza Shah starting in 1925, would have been less severe had Amir Kabir's reform process been allowed to play out without interruption.[3] But this was not to be, as the secular-minded reforms of the chancellor by design stirred controversy with what was then a powerful clergy. For one, Amir Kabir gave greater rights to Christians, in no small part to attract European participation in his academy. More importantly, his efforts to diminish titles without responsibility and modernize on European terms, would prove his undoing.

A RELIGIOUS SHOCK

One of the most significant massive movements toward Iranian reform came neither from secular, European-inspired forces, nor from the Shi'i clergy, or inside the merchants' bazaar. In 1844, a religious wave brought about the conversion of thousands of Iranians and tested the traditional modes of authority within the conservative society. Still banned in Iran and considered sacrilegious to Shi'i purists, the *Baabi* movement established new trends in popular participation (including the personal freedom of women), and under persecution fomented yearnings of religious pluralism that would later be put to work for the Constitutional Revolution of 1905–1911.

The title *Baab*, meaning "the Gate," was adopted by the founder of the new, controversial religion. Sayyid Ali Mohammad, an ascetic merchant with intimate knowledge of the Qur'an and the Christian Gospel, asserted himself as a link to the understanding of God's commands in a proclamation of 1844 in the city of Shiraz. Attracted by the hope of finding the "Promised One," and drawn to the mystical aura of the Baab, pious Shaykhi Shi'is began to embrace the new religious movement, which at its core emphasized an extreme veneration of God and the Imams (through further prayer, prostration, and prolonged fasting), along with a search for mystical meaning within the holy texts. Much like Jewish Kabala, Baabis would assign numerical values to Qur'anic verses and the writings of the Baab in order to dismantle the allegory of the texts and extricate hidden meanings. Central to their quest was the return of the Imam and the consequent End-of-Days, which led to quick conversions and, in some cases, the arming and uprising of Baabis.

Among the most devoted followers, and ultimately successful leaders was Fatimeh Baraghani, a female scholar whose accomplishments before the age of thirty seem "to have qualified her as a mujtahid"[4] (a position to render legal decisions in Shi'i Islam not acquirable by a woman). Baraghani would be known as *Qurrat-ul-'ayn* (Solace of the Eye), a term of veneration usually reserved for the preferred students of religious teachers, and which was given to her by the Baab's own master, Sayyid Rashti of Karbala.

After denouncing the wishes of her paternalistic family, and leaving the husband she had been forced to marry at the age of fourteen,

Qurrat-ul-ʿayn, or "Qurratiya," as some would call her for further endearment, began to utilize her mastery of the Qur'an and oral traditions to proselytize on the revelation of the Baab, whom she had turned to, like many of her contemporaries, following the death of Sayyid Rashti. But what Baraghani represented was much more than her unique gifts as a young female religious leader, which has been the focus of many Iranian feminist writings. She was personally responsible for much of the radicalization of the religion, and the increasing perception of the Baab as the Imam himself, rather than a mere channel. Qurratiya began to preach unveiled in the holy cities of southern Shiʿi Iraq, and came to be known for her brash questioning of established norms. Openly challenging leading Usuli scholars to a debate one minute, and preaching for the abolishment of Islamic law the next, Baraghani became both a liability for the more careful followers, as well as a catapult of progress for the more radical Baabis. Ultimately, she would fall victim to Amir Kabir's anti-Baabi campaign, which enjoyed the full support of the weary clergy, who otherwise were disdainful of his threatening modernization projects. But this campaign would help Amir Kabir survive just a while longer. The clergy sentenced Baraghani to death, circumventing the prohibition of capital punishment for female prisoners. Before reaching the age of forty in September 1852, she was strangled in secret, her body dropped in a shallow well.

After the successful, nation-wide suppression of the rising Baabis, Amir Kabir would suffer the same fate as Baraghani. The ulama turned their sights on the reformer, and convinced the shah of his disloyalty. Amir Kabir was murdered in his bath just months before the secret death of Qurratiya. As the new religion later split into several branches (among them today's Baha'i), the most active saw an avenue for their cause in the ensuing protests, which promised to bring needed social reforms, and a pluralism that might undercut the conservative forces that had suppressed their once-rising religion.

THE TOBACCO PROTEST

Iran by the middle of the nineteenth century had suffered significant setbacks, both due to the inherent problems of the Qajar dynasty, and because of the country's diminished boundaries. As the modern nation of Iran became a reality, Persia's past glory as an expansive power that reached well into Central Asia dissipated into a more modest version of *Iranshahr*. For Iran's new rulers, entry into the world economy would be paramount, and as the world had became increasingly Eurocentric, this more often than not meant keeping an eye toward the economic and social trends of the European powers. Yet, while seeking foreign investment and know-how to develop the infrastructure of the country, the Qajars were unable to instill competent methods to protect their own domestic economic actors, who, while witnessing an overall increase in their exports during the course of the globalizing century, became dangerously vulnerable to world market fluctuations and the advantageous positioning of foreign competitors.

Previous to the Qajar monarchs, Iranian merchants had played a prominent role in the economic affairs of the country. British-led globalization, facilitated by British India and a British-controlled Persian Gulf, allowed Iran significant trade-fueled growth. Merchants, already considered part of a renowned class under Islamic tradition (since the Prophet Muhammad himself was of a merchant family), benefited from this growth, along with craftsmen whose guilds and bazaars "strengthened their sense of corporate life."[5] But as the 1800s wore on, Iran found itself unable to withstand British competition and encroachment. Great Britain and its powerful military, infinitely more effective in the concerted administration and promotion of its economic interests, was too big a match for lone Iranian merchants, who could barely seek protection from a defeated Iranian army following the Russo-Persian Wars of 1804–1813 and 1826–1828. The Russian-imposed Treaty of Turkmanchai of 1828, which handed over the territories of what are now the republics of Azerbaijan and Armenia, further aggravated Iran's economic woes, capping customs on Russian goods at 5 percent, while Iranian merchants were forced to pay high taxes, thus giving an unfair advantage to their Russian competitors.

By 1841, Great Britain had forged a trade deal with Iran on similar terms. Under the "Most Favored Nation" clause, the treaty ensured that the low customs that were charged of Britain had to be extended to other nations that traded with the British Empire, thus leaving Iran wide open to global exports at unfavorable terms for domestic producers.[6] The reaction to the concessions was a series of failed attempts on the part of the merchant class to force the Qajar kings on a path of protectionism.

But military weakness was not the only hurdle that opened the doors to external exploitation. Administrative duties under the Qajar monarchy were for the most part doled out, not on the basis of competence, even knowledge, but rather as purchased offices, sold by the shah to wealthy individuals who would often manage their responsibilities as profit-making ventures. Institutionalization was lacking at the core, as importance lay with the individual holding an office, rather than the office itself. This person-centric approach fomented informal channels for carrying out the business of the state. An example is late-nineteenth century minister of war, Kamran Mirza, who simultaneously served as governor of Tehran, tasked with preventing people from littering the streets.

Thus, important personalities connected with the royal family carried out tasks in a fluid manner, with their success contingent on their connections, the personal loyalty they enjoyed, as well as their financial situation. Naturally, such an informal structure and vacuum of authority gave way to challenges between office seekers, even petty squabbles over who would take over a given office or claim guardianship over a village. During one year, a village "changed hands six times" because one of the claimants was supported by the grand vizier and the other by the minister of war.[7]

Iran's export economy by the end of the nineteenth century was heavily dependent on agriculture, with cotton, opium, rice, and silk among the central exports. Land was either state-owned, privately owned, or in the hands of the clergy, in the form of religious endowments. Both non-state landowners and religious endowments had a stake in protectionism. Needless to say, this served to alienate the public from the Qajar monarchy, whose concessions were largely fueled by the need for immediate loans following the military defeats at the hand of Russia. The Tobacco Concession of 1890 granted by Nasir al-Din Shah especially struck a nerve with landowners who had profited significantly from domestic consumption of the crop. Unbelievably, the concession granted a British citizen, Major G. F. Talbot, the exclusive right to buy, sell, and manufacture "all the tobacco in the interior or exterior of the Kingdom of Iran for fifty years, in return for an annual rent of 15,000 pounds sterling," plus a quarter of net profits and 5 percent capital dividends.[8]

As expected, the merchant class vehemently protested the shah's policy, writing to the country's leaders, including the king himself, seeking the cancellation of the concession. Geopolitics, in this case, came in defense of Iran's merchants. The "Great Game" had pitted the Russian and British empires against one another in a geopolitical contest to control Central Asia. Iran, being a portal that connected Central Asia and India with the British-controlled Persian Gulf, was a key element of the Game. Naturally, Russia opposed the economic gain that the Tobacco Concession would grant Great Britain. By the terms of the Turkmanchai Treaty, Russia's agents were given significant freedom to work inside Iran, and were able to muster support against the measure. Importantly, both the Russians and Iranian merchants would seek the support of the clergy to advance their struggle against the Tobacco Concession.

The pivotal role played by the ulama in the crises should be seen from the context of the historic role of Shi'i leadership in Iran. For the Shi'i, the role of the Imams was one of providing charismatic leadership to their followers. As Hamid Dabashi states in his seminal work *Authority in Islam*, "the Shi'ite Imams were believed to possess the same mode of personal and comprehensive authority" as the Prophet Muhammad.[9] Following the Occultation of the Imam, this charismatic authority was, to a degree, passed down to the clergy. In conservative Usuli practice, followers are to attach themselves to learned ayatollahs who reach their status, not through a rigid hierarchy, but due to the acceptance of their knowledge by their students and peers. Therefore, the legitimacy of high-ranking clerics is hardly questioned, being that it does not come down from state prerogatives, but from their own prestige, as perceived by others. This allows the ulama to exercise a degree of social power that reaches far beyond questions of political legitimacy attached to the throne. And while the Qajar monarch would exult himself with titles worthy of an absolute ruler—*Shahinshah* (King of Kings) and *Zil Allah* (Shadow of God)—much of the real authority remained with the clergy, as they "were considered the true interpreters of religious law and the genuine guardians of the masses."[10] A natural, clergy-centered network therefore emerges, allowing grievances to be channeled through it. In Qajar Iran, where the state did not have the proper instruments of power to exercise complete suppression of dissent, the ulama's position within the society translated to a powerful mobilization tool.

In addition to the position of clerics, Shi'ism characteristically embraces an underdog narrative, embodied in the martyrdom of Imam Husayn and his outnumbered forces at the Battle of Karbala. This underdog narrative, emboldened by the powerful, if abstract, concept of justice, has been effectively utilized in opposition to established rule. During the Tobacco Protest, those who stood the most to lose from the concession were able to recruit the invaluable support of the clergy. A religious edict, or *fatwa*, was issued by Grand Ayatollah Mirza Hasan Shirazi calling for the boycott of tobacco throughout Iran. It is said that the ayatollah's word was so powerful that even the shah's harem refused to smoke throughout the duration of the protest. The boycott was effective, and in January of 1892, nearly two years after the agreement was signed, Nasir al-Din Shah cancelled the concession. This has come down as a victory, not only for nationalism in Iran, but for the clergy, whose influence had been effectively channeled to effect a change of policy in the country.

THE CONSTITUTIONAL REVOLUTION

On Sunday, January 22, 1905, Father Georgi Gapon stood before the Tsar's massive Winter Palace in St. Petersburg, holding a petition that sought better working conditions for the people of Russia, along with the establishment of a representative assembly and free and fair elections. This bold challenge to the Tsar's authority came after a string of demoralizing defeats of the Russian navy in the Pacific at the hand of a newly rising, non-European power: Japan. Mutiny plagued the navy, and the people of Russia began to seek an end to the humiliating Russo-Japanese war, and an improvement upon the toil of their daily lives.

The Tsar, however, never met with Father Gapon and his throng of followers. Instead, the Winter Palace guards opened fire on the crowd, igniting a revolution whose power was felt across continents. In Iran, once a victim of Tsarist Russia's wars, the message did not fall on deaf ears. The Russian military had been defeated by a non-European power, and more still, the people of Russia had courageously stood up to their incompetent rulers. And while 1905 would itself not mark the end of the Tsar's reign, the year opened a new era in Iranian history, ushering in a parliament and a blueprint for mass mobilization and revolution. By 1905, the coalition of merchants and clergy that had made the Tobacco Protest a successful endeavor would reemerge as part of a greater movement that included left-leaning intellectuals and radical secularists. The Constitutional Revolution of 1905–1911 would attempt to establish a national assembly, and ultimately a constitution in Iran.

Prominent Iran scholar Janet Afary sees the Constitutional Revolution as both a manifestation of the country's "social democratic tendencies," as well as part of a greater global climate that brought a revolution to Russia, and soon to Turkey, Mexico, and China. Iran's own revolution, which "brought several competing ideologies—nationalism, democracy, religion, and socialism—into open confrontation,"[11] represented a new movement, one that would at times manage to bring the unlikely bedfellows of secularism and Islam under one shaky roof.

Prior to 1905, Iran had witnessed a general mood of discontent, often culminating in uprisings. The Qajar dynasty had not managed to reconcile its immediate financial needs with the proper development of a country that housed strong intellectual and mercantile abilities. Between the Tobacco Protest of 1890 and the year 1905, a cat-and-mouse game had come to dominate Iranian politics, as the shah would grant yet another concession to foreign interests, and the people would initiate yet another protest. The shah would budge, but the cycle would repeat itself. To be sure, the Qajars had not been dealt a fair hand. The wars with Russia had bankrupted the state, and new global realities were as much imposed on them as they were on the rest of the Iranian people. But their out-of-control spending, which included lavish foreign trips for the king, would only force the state to negotiate further concessions at terms all-too-unfavorable to the homeland.

One of the first important developments of the constitutional period came in February of 1905, when a secret citizen council (*anjuman*) was convened by radicals and reformist clerics seeking an end to the autocratic rule of the dynasty, and the promotion of widespread political reforms. The secret council was comprised of learned individuals who were well versed in the changes taking place, not only in Russia, but also in the increasingly powerful Japan. The council bylaws opened to the anjuman not only to Muslims, but also to Zoroastrians, Jews, and Christians.

But the effect of the Russian Revolution of 1905 went beyond mere inspiration. Because Iran's economy was so closely tied to Tsarist Russia, the instability brought by the revolution there caused widespread economic problems in Iran, including rampant inflation on basic goods. This helped catapult the merchants once again into action. In March 1905, the bazaars of Tehran went on strike, and participants called for representative government. The clergy stepped in to support the action, circulating a picture of the shah's Belgian adviser, Monsieur Joseph Naus, distastefully dressed in clerical garb during a costume party—a blatant affront to their religion.

As it had during the Tobacco Protest, the clerical establishment played an indispensable role in fomenting popular support for the causes of reform. Even conservative cleric Shaykh Fazlollah Nouri (who would later become a foe of the revolutionaries) joined the strikes that called for the formation of a representative assembly and increasingly, a constitution. For liberal-minded clergy, a constitution was seen as an instrument to usher in general reforms in the country, and serve as a check on both royal *and* religious despotism. But for conservatives like Nouri, the constitution would serve as a platform to codify the central position of the clergy in Iranian society, something that early twentieth-century Iran did not provide, given the loose and informal ties between the mosque and the state. But other "Muslim" participants in the revolution were actually Baabis, possibly seeking a wider acceptance for ideas of tolerance in the midst of crackdowns and persecution. "Baabi," in fact, was an epithet often used by conservative forces to describe reformers in hopes of pegging an anti-Muslim stigma on the movement.[12]

Women too played a critical role in the Constitutional Revolution. Already in the first half of the nineteenth century, American Presbyterians had established schools for girls in the region, and the education of women had been in increasing demand. During the constitutional movement, women became organized, in large part to seek greater access to education, gain suffrage, and increase their overall rights as citizens in the conservative society. Secret women's councils were set up, one of which was even frequented by two daughters of Nasir al-Din Shah. These councils sprang up in Tehran and elsewhere, with women openly standing up to the more conservative clergy, through publications, effective political whispering, and in the case of the 1908 siege of Tabriz, by taking up arms in the struggle. W. Morgan Shuster, a legendary American financial advisor in Iran, wrote in his 1912 memoirs that the women of Iran "since 1907 had become almost at a bound the most progressive, not to say radical, in the world. That this statement upsets the ideas of centuries makes no difference. It is a fact."[13]

In the summer of 1906, a series of dramatic events pushed the king further toward constitutionalism. Sit-ins were organized, first in the Shah 'Abd al-Azim Shrine outside of Tehran, and then in the religious center of Qom. Of these events, Janet Afary writes:

The sanctuaries at the 'Abd al-'Azim Shrine and Qum became "freedom schools" where the participants learned about international events, new political ideas, the advantages of a constitutional government, and the rights of a modern nation. Calls for "constitutional government" and cheers for the "nation of Iran" were now heard loudly in the streets of Tehran.[14]

The sit-ins soon moved to a British diplomatic mission, where Secretary of Legation Evelyn Grant Duff gave the green light for the demonstrations to take place. Britain, acting on its own geopolitical instincts, knew that the protests against Russian economic interference could play in its favor. By August 1906, the king then, Muzaffar al-Din Shah, agreed to the enactment of the first Iranian parliament, or *majles*. The majles, which opened in October of 1906, "balanced the budget, decreased the salaries of the Qajar princes and the shah ... established a framework for secular legislation, judicial codes, and courts of appeals, which reduced the powers of the royal court and the religious authorities and established a free press."[15]

But this glimpse of justice would be a fleeting one. As so often in Iran's history, the advances of the Constitutional Revolution were marred by divisiveness. Irreconcilable proved to be the various factions that had once formed a coalition. As councils similar to the secret anjuman of 1905 spread throughout the country, they formed an extraparliamentary source of grassroots opposition, at times imitating the left-wing radicalism that had been fueling anarchist terrorism around the world. The religious forces too began to show their colors, with conservatives like Shaykh Fazlollah Nouri, who had originally supported the constitution, becoming one of the new order's biggest foes on the grounds that the constitution, and the freedoms it granted, was essentially anti-Islamic. Radical and conservative disputes played out both inside and outside the majles. The citizen councils were now a thorn in the side of the regime, as they represented a vehicle for organizing further protests.

A reality check for the constitutionalists came in 1907, with the Anglo-Russian Entente, which essentially divided Iran into two spheres of influence for the Great Game actors. The document grants southern Iran to Great Britain, northern Iran to Russia, and mercifully leaves the central part of the country to the Iranians. The agreement goes further, establishing a system by which tariff revenues in Iran could be used to pay back loans granted by the British and Russian banks in Iran. In a communiqué announcing the entente to the Iranian government, the British minister in Tehran employs the duplicity of a honed diplomat, stating the agreement is not to "violate the integrity and independence of Persia."[16]

These outside powers, too, worried about the citizen councils and their ability to organize resistance. Tensions mounted with a brief coup in 1908, in which the new king, Mohammad Ali Shah (with the help of the Russians) sent his forces against the parliament to open fire on the majles, and the hordes of constitutionalists sent in to protect it. As the majles was shut down, a new front of conflict opened in the city of Tabriz, in the Iranian province (not the country) of Azerbaijan. This region had given refuge to some of the most radical of constitutionalists and the uprising quickly escalated to the level of civil war, with government and proclergy forces engaging in street-to-street battles with the constitutionalists. The fighting was finally put down in 1909 with the help of the shah's trusted allies—the Russians. But the councils would not give in, and the constitutionalist movement continued, city by city, through further coalitions of disgruntled clerics, ethnic minorities, and social democrats.

In the summer of 1909, the constitutionalists would take over Tehran and publicly hang their conservative nemesis, Shaykh Nouri, and soon thereafter depose the shah. In November of that year, the majles would reconvene and less than two years later find an avenue to limit foreign power intervention: with the appointment of an American as treasurer general of Iran. W. Morgan Shuster, an accomplished U.S. diplomat with a liberal track record of support for underdog nations, was persuaded by the constitutionalists to take up the job.

Once in Iran, Shuster became a popular and respected ally of Iran's coalition of liberal and socialist representatives in the majles, who now went under the banner of the Democrat Party. Shuster immediately went to work on reforming Iran's tax code and was able to generate needed revenue and improve the overall financial management of the state. Quickly, he increased the popularity of the Democrat Party, and went so far in his support of the Iranian revolutionary cause as to "place a bounty on the shah's head."[17] Shuster's efforts were ambitious. He created a military force for the treasury (called the Treasury Gendarmerie), which was tasked with collecting tax revenues. So efficient was the force that it even seized lands from the Qajar royal family due to back taxes. With the exception of "a few European and American officers," the force was entirely Iranian.[18]

Yet Shuster's glory was to be short-lived. After an interview with *The Times* of London, in which Shuster called foul on the Anglo-Russian schemes in Iran, Russia sent a series of ultimatums seeking his removal at the threat of military action. Shortly thereafter, Shuster left for the United States. In December of 1911, Russian troops massacred hundreds of residents of Tabriz, beginning a campaign of anticonstitutionalist purges. That very month, the second majles was shut down by a cabinet that had taken over executive duties after the fall of the shah. With the end of 1911, Iran's Constitutional Revolution all but came to a close.

THE TRAJECTORY OF INDEPENDENCE

Iran's trajectory of independence would take its toll on Iranian society, ensuring that the stresses of radical modernization and staunch conservatism would always put the nation one step closer to exploding into mass civil conflict and revolution, as it dramatically did in January of 1978, following nearly a century of setbacks for the people, and particularly the ulama.

But the images of a secular-led revolution at the turn of the twentieth century, which included the public hanging of high-ranking cleric Shaykh Fazlollah Nouri, forced the 1978–1979 religious revolutionaries to act ruthlessly and push not only for their own survival, but also for an uncompromising primacy in the new Islamic Republic. The left, the secularists, and the feminists, would all be put down, at times violently and indiscriminately, in a process of consolidating power that gave rise to a more cunning but equally conservative clerical establishment.

But the legacy of the Qajar era's social movements does not end with the 1978–1979 uprising. It has become part of the Iranian conscience, permanently hungry for change, on the terms of a given perception of justice, and a staunch opposition to the established "Yazid" of any given time. Thus, the work toward women's suffrage, open and secret city councils, as well as the historic push for freedom of the press, acted not as isolated incidents, but historic points of reference—starting points toward an even greater level of freedom and more vibrant civic society.

The trajectory has thus existed on two levels: external and internal. The external level painted itself in nationalist colors, sought to rid Iran of foreign intervention, and establish the country on its own, Islamic-centered path. Today, that first level has been thoroughly established, albeit at the expense of the internal: the constant strife for personal independence from unjust rulers. And while today's Iran is politically more permissive than the shah's dictatorship, socially it has curved even the most benign channels of personal expression, and has forced a philosophically diverse people to conform to an essentially narrow interpretation of social mores and Islamic "values." Yet like throughout the nineteenth and twentieth centuries, the trajectory continues. As today's newspapers are shut down, more open in their stead; and as citizens learn to navigate the maze of "rules" set up by the clergy, their voice remains inherently powerful and diverse.

In 1912, Morgan Shuster looked back on the Constitutional Revolution. In his memoirs, he recognized the peoples' "right to develop along the particular lines of their customs, character, temperament and tendencies," despite the internal flaws in the administration and government that were replete in Iran, and that made foreign intervention all but certain. Yet by Iran's very ability to stand up to the great powers of Russia and Britain, if only for a few years, Shuster felt that one could not "fail to love the Persian people, or to sympathize with their just aspirations."[19]

CHAPTER 3

KINGS AND MEN

You are at liberty to talk with anyone you please. You are at liberty to see anything you want to see. You will not be hampered by a police guard unless you want it.
—President Harry S. Truman (speaking to the Shah about American democracy, 1949)[1]

The development of Iran's trajectory of independence has been characterized by pointed internal struggles that have reached to the heart of Iran's identity. The Constitutional Revolution pitted a broad coalition of *bazaari* merchants and clergymen, along with left-wing and democratic intellectuals, with a foreign-backed regime engaged in a cycle of dependency with outside powers. The Qajar kings' disposition to making foreign concessions cannot merely be explained by the rulers' appetite for grandiose, budget-breaking lifestyles (though such proclivities did play a major role). In fact, the Qajars were engaged in an unenviable dilemma of trying to develop their country quickly in order to truly attain independence, while seeing that the only path toward this end was mired by foreign loans, foreign development projects, and foreign "advice."

Between the tumultuous years following the 1911 fall of the second majles, and late 1925, an erosion of Qajar authority would lead to a coup by the politically savvy and ambitious army leader Reza Khan, who would ultimately establish himself as shah. Under the name Pahlavi, the dynasty of Reza Shah and his son, Mohammad Reza Shah Pahlavi, would be confronted with some of the same dilemmas that broke apart the Qajars' reign. These dilemmas centered on a thirst for quick economic development, often at the expense of nationalist voices, which cried restlessly for nonalignment and a republican form of government. These voices would ultimately prove fatal for the Pahlavi regime, whose second and last king, Mohammad Reza, would be forced to abdicate in 1979 amidst a popular revolution that put nonalignment back on the table with a vengeance.

Contrary to the memories of the postrevolutionary regime, the 1978–1979 uprising was not exclusively Islamic. While firebrand cleric

Ayatollah Ruhollah Khomeini was best positioned to lead the movement through his popularity and credibility as a high-ranking cleric and systematic opponent of the shah, the revolution took place across various elements of society and cut through religious lines. Much like the untold number of uprisings that occurred throughout much of the nineteenth and twentieth centuries, the Iranian people—Islamist and secular, white-collar bureaucrat, laborer, and intellectual alike—were engaged in loud protests for independence and republican democracy during the late 1970s, and what ensued was an Iranian Revolution that only later would be taken over, or "hijacked," by Khomeini's theocrats. Prior to the revolution, numerous opportunities arose, which if successful, would have allowed Iran to take a turn toward nonalignment and secular republican government. These opportunities were suppressed and ultimately foiled, both by the ruling monarchs bent on maintaining their grip on power, and by foreign governments, whose own analysts understood too well Iran's trajectory of independence, but whose judgment ultimately proved myopic.

This chapter deals with four protagonists in Iran's battle for nonalignment. Two are the Pahlavi shahs, whose dynasty emerged on the promise of further independence, but whose ambitions, fears, and poor judgment, set them on a path of further entanglement with foreign interests. Both monarchs would depend on overt military force to rule, and both would come to insult the very foundations of Islam, which would later set Iran up for the whiplash of the revolution.

The other two personalities highlighted here in a way represent the mirror images of Reza Shah and Mohammad Reza Shah; these figures have come down as heroes of a nationalist struggle, not only for self-sufficiency, but for the end to the massive corruption that to this day continues to rob Iran of its material wealth. These leaders were Mohammad Taqi Khan Pasyan, a colonel in the nationalist Gendarmerie, and Prime Minister Mohammad Mosaddeq, a seasoned politician who led the nationalization of Iran's oil, but who was ultimately dismissed and put under house arrest by a CIA- and British-backed coup. Both men showed a restless willingness to fight corruption and work within the system to make secular republicanism a reality in Iran.

We can place these two antagonistic camps under useful categories of "paternalists" and "nationalists." The former group, personified in the Pahlavi kings, sought "modernization from above," and European-inspired secularism, utilizing the tools of absolute power to carry out its programs. The latter group, while also secular, was more concerned with European forms of political representation, rather than patterns of dress or social behavior. To this group of nationalists, the key to reform lay in achieving political and economic development on the country's own terms. To be sure, we cannot claim that either the shahs or the nationalist thorns-in-their-sides were ultimately the bigger patriots. The Pahlavis believed their actions would benefit their nation and bring Iran economic development and greatness. The Iranian revolution of 1978–1979, however, would prove their heavy-handed approach misguided, their judgment insular, and their legacy unfortunate.

THE PAHLAVI DYNASTY

If we can accept Max Weber's definition of the state as the monopoly on the legitimate use of violence within a given territory, Iran at the turn of the twentieth century could hardly have been called one. Depending heavily on protection by Britain and Russia (later the Soviet Union), Iran was not in a position to establish authority over its own domains without the explicit support of foreign powers. During the constitutional period, the king had obtained assistance from the Russians to establish a division made up of Cossack Brigades, or Russian-style cavalry forces, to help the friendly monarchy maintain some semblance of order and protect its interests vis-à-vis the emerging constitutionalists. It was this force, led by Russian Colonel Liakhov, which had effectively staged a coup against the majles in July 1907, only to be attacked by a constitutional army two years later, resulting in a truce between Liakhov and the constitutionalists.

The pro-majles force, called the Government Gendarmerie, was tasked with providing muscle to the constitutional cause and protecting the parliament from the encroachment of the shah and his foreign supporters. This force had existed parallel to Shuster's Treasury Gendarmerie, and was able to absorb the latter's fighters after Shuster's forced ouster from Iran in 1911. During the period of instability that resulted from the Constitutional Revolution, one of the most important obstacles to national unity had been the existence of the Cossack Brigades and the Government Gendarmerie as two distinct, conflicting military forces.

The balance of influence between Russian and British forces in Tehran changed with the October Revolution of 1917 in Russia and the increasing power of the Bolsheviks. Soon enough, White Russian military officers in charge of the Iranian Cossack Brigades would lose their support at home and become stranded expatriates in Iran. Many fled to pro-Tsar, White Russian strongholds in their homeland. Many decided to stay in Iran, in an environment in which Great Britain emerged as the sole foreign power broker.

Starting in mid-1920, the idea of a coup had begun to take shape within Iranian circles, while planners of a potential attack on the Qajar monarchy recognized that "British power in Iran was too great for any coup-maker to bypass."[2] A talented and ambitious officer by the name of Reza Khan had been rising through the ranks of the Cossack Brigades, establishing himself as a popular Iranian leader and a contender for national political power. Together with Sayyid Ziaeddin Tabataba'i (known simply as

Sayyid Zia) and with the acquiescence of Great Britain, Reza Khan staged a coup in 1921 that placed Sayyid Zia as prime minister, while putting himself at the head of the armed forces and adopting the title "Head of the Army" (*Sardar-e Sepah*).[3]

Following four years of power consolidation, Reza Khan would move forward on his ambitious goal of dismantling the now-weakened Qajar monarchy. On a pilgrimage to gather clerical support in the holy city of Najaf (Iraq), he adopted the name Pahlavi, which harkens back to a pre-Islamic dynasty and language. This name was meant to foster an identity that essentially bypassed Iranian Islamic history, and it foreshadowed some of the future dynasty's overt disdain for all things religious, setting the stage for the blowback that would ultimately come with the uncompromising figure of Ayatollah Khomeini.

But before Reza Khan was able to ascend as undisputed monarch in late 1925, he would have to contend with the nationalist forces that still clung to the constitutionalist ideal. After all, having been supported by Great Britain, Reza had to walk a fine line that allowed him to maintain the support of the British Empire, while appearing to work for the greater designs of the popular constitutional nationalists. Perhaps the most testing threat to Reza's rule was encountered early on, immediately following the 1921 coup. Gendarmerie Colonel Mohammad Taqi Khan Pasyan, the governor of the massive eastern province of Khorasan, administered what would become known as an island of constitutionalism—fueled by a staunch anticorruption campaign—which was seen by the new forces in Tehran as a direct challenge to their consolidation of power.

Back in November 1915, Pasyan had established his undisputed nationalist credentials with a military expedition that led him to capture the western city of Hamedan. There, he took over a branch of the British-owned Imperial Bank of Persia to pay his troops, who had suffered systematic financial neglect at the hand of the central government. Appealing even to the patriotic sentiments of the foreign-backed Cossacks, he was able to beef up his ranks with the very forces he had beaten in battle. The British consul quickly warned of the dangers Pasyan posed, telegraphing London about the colonel's "great personal courage, undoubted intellectual ability and tact,"[4] words that despite their kind tone, hinted at the magnitude of the threat that such a figure would pose.

Like other prominent nationalists, Pasyan was fascinated with European culture. On a stay in Germany, he learned to play the piano and enjoyed reading and translating works of European literature. But his appreciation for Europe differed greatly from that of the monarchists, as Pasyan did not wish to bluntly transfer European culture to Iran, but merely learn from the positive elements of popular representation and national independence, as found in the German Weimar Republic during Europe's interwar period. But for paternalists like Reza Khan, the

European appeal manifested itself in thoroughly different ways. At times, it seemed to appear as a kind of self-pity, a disdain for things Islamic, only compounded by an unquestioning embrace of foreign advisors.

Following Hitler's rise to power in 1933, Reza Shah would adopt the paternalistic culture of Nazi Germany—forcing a kind of social engineering project on his people. And while both nationalists and monarchists ultimately wanted what they perceived as progress for their country, the latter's lack of interest in the exercise of popular will lent itself to a constant, irreconcilable dispute with the nationalists.

Through a last-ditch effort by the eroding Qajar monarchy to establish national sovereignty over all of Iran's dominions, Colonel Pasyan had been tapped to maintain a Gendarmerie force in the eastern province of Khorasan. But following months of withheld pay by the provincial authorities there, and taking advantage of the 1921 coup that put Reza Khan and his pro-British prime minister in power, Pasyan made his move, gathering his men to overthrow the provincial government. As self-appointed governor of Khorasan, Pasyan set out to collect back pay for his troops from the former governor, Qavam al-Saltaneh, and other corrupt officials by seizing their massive estates. He collected evidence against bribed officials, while his Belgian finance deputy, Monsieur Dubois, was tasked with calculating arrears for the troops of up to ten years.

During his brief tenure, the colonel made every effort to make known his unwavering patriotism, along with his disinterest in personal gain. He inaugurated two newspapers and circulated political pamphlets outlining his personal nationalist convictions. But just as Colonel Pasyan became increasingly popular with his gendarme forces and the greater population of Khorasan, his anticorruption campaign inevitably made him enemies. Boldly, Pasyan set out to financially clean up the lucrative Imam Reza Shrine of Mashhad, a holy staple of Iranian Shi'ism that houses the tomb of the eighth Shi'i Imam. High-ranking administrators and clerics associated with the shrine had profited from religiously endowed land in the region. Pasyan sent a group of one hundred volunteers from his gendarme and police force to make sweeping arrests at the accused officials' residences. Soon enough, the clergy would join in opposition to the pervasive anticorruption campaign of the popular colonel.

Unlike other nationalist personalities, Pasyan saw "that the responsibility of defeat lay, not with the foreigners, but with his own countrymen," who ultimately were accountable for the nation's weakness.[5] Pasyan had come to be known as a potential threat to the new regime of Reza, not because he adopted a combative stance against the British-backed coup that had put the khan in power, but because of the problems posed by his unwavering integrity, his effectiveness in fighting corruption, as well as his popularity—all beyond the abilities and will of Reza Khan.

The new power center in Tehran was right in its concern over Pasyan's independent approach. During the period immediately following the 1921 coup, Pasyan's brigade, which numbered between 4,000 and 5,000 fighters, was far superior to the 1,000-man Cossack unit under the leadership of Reza Khan. It was understood that had Pasyan wished to do so, he could have marched on Tehran and effectively taken over the central government.

But such an adventure was not to be. By choosing to remain in Khorasan, Colonel Pasyan's power was effectively chipped away by the increasingly assertive khan. Dismissing his first prime minister, Sayyid Zia, Reza Khan brought into that office the very man, who had been the target of Pasyan's coup in the province—Qavam al-Saltaneh. Bent on revenge for the economic costs incurred by the colonel, Qavam helped foment revolt among tribal groups, capitalizing on the economic costs of Pasyan's campaign to collect tax revenue. Further downsizing Pasyan's authority, Qavam granted the post of governor to a chief of the all-powerful Bakhtiari tribe, a true contender for military dominance inside the country. After waging a successful campaign against a tribal band in the southern part of the province, Pasyan's forces were soon outnumbered by revolting Kurdish rebels in the north. Pasyan died in the spirit of battle, against the calls for retreat by his outnumbered men. Thus met his fate a powerful leader who sought to end with the endemic corruption of his country. There is every reason to believe that his intentions were sincere and his conduct commendable. To Stephanie Cronin, who has documented the rise and fall of Pasyan, the

> movement awakened real hopes for the realization of the constitutionalist ideal ... based on legality and justice. During its brief existence the gendarme regime in Mashhad made a genuine attempt to implement reform and to eradicate corruption and abuse of power and privilege.[6]

Pasyan also encouraged the development of his province by maintaining only licensed physicians and seeking to open more hospitals, schools, and factories.

In July 1924, following the mob killing of U.S. Vice Consul Robert Imbrie in Tehran, Reza Khan declared martial law in the city and asked to be made commander-in-chief. As a form of compromise toward an increasingly powerful figure, the majles complied, essentially making him untouchable vis-à-vis the shah, since Reza Khan's new title would deny the king the right to dismiss him. On October 31, 1925, Reza Khan led the majles in deposing the Qajar monarchy, with only four members (among them Mohammad Mosaddeq) voting against the measure. Before the end of the year, a new monarchy would be established, and the ambitious fighter of the Cossack Brigades would now be known as Reza Shah.

The new king sought to fulfill a personal mission of "modernization from above," greater in depth and scope than anything attempted by the Qajar chancellor Amir Kabir more than half a century earlier. Upon coming to power, Reza Shah hit the ground running. He sought to model his nation on the European powers that had watched over Iran's affairs for decades, and he undertook this challenge on all fronts. Under Reza Shah, shari'ah was eliminated in the courts, which instead would rely on French-based civil and criminal law. A Western dress code was enforced for all males starting in 1927, with the sole exception of clerical students, who nevertheless would have to take a state exam to be recognized as such. Tribes were also tamed and increasingly brought under the control of Tehran as part of a general trend toward centralization. Tehran, as the gravitational point of this exercise, saw its population skyrocket, with a new generation of civil servants coming under the state's payroll.

Perhaps one of the most controversial aspects of Reza Shah's rule was his forced unveiling of women. Having witnessed Atatürk's Europeanization of Turkey during a visit to the neighboring country, Reza Shah kicked off a campaign to promote unveiling as a way of further "civilizing" Iran. By 1935, the shah enacted forced unveiling, along with the public desegregation of the sexes. At state functions, bureaucrats were made to bring their newly unveiled wives to parties, under threat of not receiving a paycheck or even being dismissed. Veiled women could no longer ride in carriages or receive medical treatment in public clinics, and "to add insult to injury, prostitutes were *not* allowed to unveil."[7] Failing to understand that European values centered on the freedom *not* to veil, rather than forced unveiling (European nuns, for example, wore a veil), Reza Shah had his security forces assaulted noncompliant women, whose head cover would be torn off in public. But the women, whom Reza sincerely was hoping to serve, would continue to suffer under societal pressures to remain covered. Ultimately, women were merely used as objects in the tired conflict between European and progressive-minded men who try to "liberate" them, and conservative Muslims who wish to "protect their dignity."

Reza Shah's ability to take on his ambitious modernization and social engineering projects centered on the militarization of the country, with universal male conscription established and military expenditures reaching one-third of the entire state budget (compared with only 4 percent granted for education on average). This coercive power was put to work on behalf of the shah's increasingly dictatorial rule, which, as if through an act of paranoia, saw the imprisonment and murder not only of opponents, but also of honest but somehow "suspicious" supporters. Mosaddeq, an original opponent of Reza Khan during the general's early rise to power, was lucky to be merely confined to house arrest. Censorship in this new autocratic monarchy became rampant, and "only official nationalism stressing homogeneity, anticlericalism, modernity, and strength, which were read into the pre-Islamic past, could flourish."[8]

To be sure, modernization from above was exactly that, and the gap between the secular upper crust and the religious and disenfranchised poor could not have gone unnoticed. Many of the projects that were meant to bolster Iran's independence were built through the burden of taxation on the people, often to the benefit of the elite and foreign interests. Case in point is Iran's North-South Trans Railway, which linked the Caspian Sea with the Persian Gulf. Its cost for a single track was between $150 and $200 million, and its funding "came from those least able to afford it, through regressive taxes, and a national road system could have been cheaper and more useful."[9]

The new dynasty, with its foreign backing and modernization agenda could not protect the Iranian people from the ravaging 1929 global economic depression. Iran's currency fell sharply, and Great Britain campaigned to maintain it on a free exchange. The elite, large-scale merchants, and not the more humble bazaaris, were able to reap the benefits of foreign trade, forming monopolies that would put many in the latter group out of business. But just as the British helped secure the 1921 coup, and later the ascension to the throne by Reza Shah, they would prove just as willing to sweep the rug from under the king's feet. During the 1930s, German sympathies ran high within the elitist regime of Reza Shah. In 1933, Reza Shah asked the world to refrain from calling his country "Persia," and instead opted for the local name *Iran* ("Land of the Aryans"). The Nazis, having declared Iran a pure Aryan country, became increasingly connected to it both economically and politically. Iran returned the favor, hosting German agents and pushing Nazi ideology, which suited Reza Shah's "dictatorial and nationalistic inclinations."[10]

Needless to say, the allies would have none of that. On the heels of Operation Barbarossa, Nazi Germany's invasion of the Soviet Union in June 1941, the British and the Soviets invaded Iran. By September, Reza Shah, founder of the Pahlavi regime, was forced to abdicate the throne he had so tirelessly and ruthlessly worked to attain. In the end, his love of grandeur took him on a path of friendship with the Nazi government, with which his eternal patron Great Britain was engaged in a fight to the death. In Reza Shah's stead would reign his son, a young, untested leader who would prove more obsessed with self-aggrandizement than his father, and even more prone to paranoid repression.

THE MYTH OF MOSADDEQ

Few personalities in modern Iranian history are granted the mythical status of Mohammad Mosaddeq. A hero of nationalism to some, a dangerous instigator to others, Mosaddeq is best known for carrying out the nationalization of the Anglo-Iranian Oil Company (AIOC), only to later invite an American-backed coup that brought the exiled Mohammad Reza Shah back with a vengeance and, by many accounts, set the clock in motion for the Iranian Revolution of 1978–1979.

Given the wide-ranging images that Mosaddeq conjures up, we can view him as part of a greater myth within modern Iranian history; not just for the antimonarchists who see him as the ultimate nationalist martyr, but also for the foreign powers, who, in contrast to many of their own analysts' advice, chose to see Mosaddeq as a potential puppet of the Soviet Union in the trying times of the Cold War.

Throughout Reza Shah's reign, Mohammad Mosaddeq had been widely known as a competent, noncorruptible administrator. Born to an elite Qajar family, Mosaddeq is portrayed as a tall, yet skinny and sickly individual whose political career reflected a profound appreciation for social justice, which his elite but socially conscious mother had instilled in him.[11] Mosaddeq's political career began at an early age, when his father, the financial administrator of Khorasan, died and the fourteen-year-old Mosaddeq was tasked with managing the financial affairs of that massive province. Quickly, Mosaddeq earned a reputation as a kind of political whiz kid. More importantly, he left the impression from the very beginning that he was willing to stand against corruption—something that would continue to bolster his reputation as he grew into a national political figure.

During the Constitutional Revolution, Mosaddeq was active in that movement and was elected to the first majles, though he was too young to actually serve. Following the defeat of the constitutionalists in 1911, Mosaddeq traveled to study in Europe, earning a law degree in Francophone Switzerland. It was there that the young Mosaddeq began to form his convictions around the importance of universal literacy, fair elections, decentralized government, as well as freedom of speech.[12] An important theme for Mosaddeq would be his embrace of European-like liberties for Iran, rather than European influence *over* Iran.

As Mosaddeq's reputation grew, so did his responsibilities. He served as governor of the southern province of Fars (where the ancient city of Shiraz sits) and became a national player through his work in and out of the majles. As a political figure of national importance, Mosaddeq enjoyed a relationship with the ambitious Reza Khan that was rocky at best. He had openly opposed the 1921 coup that made Reza Khan Sardar-e Sepah, and later opposed his ascension to the throne. It can be said that Mosaddeq, among a handful of other nationalists, sought to be a thorn in the side of the shah—constantly pushing for independence and democratic developments, while Reza Shah preferred to concentrate on his modernization from above without the interference of dissenting voices like that of Mosaddeq.

Perhaps one of the character traits that made Mosaddeq most endearing to the people (and made him a larger threat to the regime), was his unwillingness to be bought. Many of the problems that led to the maintenance of the status quo resulted from foreign powers' ability to create financial incentives or otherwise bribe Iranian administrators. In sharp contrast, the rising politician repeatedly declined to take even a full salary for his administrative services. For one, Mosaddeq came from a wealthy family and did not need the money. But more importantly, he viewed the collection of taxes as paramount to instituting educational and infrastructural reforms, and he preferred to put more money to work for Iran rather than into his pockets.

In the years between 1921 and the end of his reign in 1941, Reza continuously tried to rid himself of this nuisance, once resorting to imprisoning Mosaddeq, another time putting him on house arrest. More often, however, Reza sought more clever ways of outmaneuvering him, including his repeated nominations of Mosaddeq to the post of prime minister, knowing full well that once a member had served that post and was demoted, he would no longer be allowed to serve in the majles. Other times, Reza would simply send Mosaddeq away from the capital, as he did when appointing him governor of the Iranian province of Azerbaijan, where an attempt was made on Mosaddeq's life.

It was in Azerbaijan that the fervent nationalist was put to the test in maintaining his independent credentials. Because capitulation clauses of previous Russo-Iranian and Anglo-Iranian agreements had prevented foreign nationals from being tried for crimes inside Iran, the Soviet Union demanded that a Russian subject held in an Azeri prison be immediately released. Mosaddeq refused, despite a Soviet threat to send the Red Guard into the Iranian province. Interestingly, the Russian subject had been arrested for distributing slanderous materials against Reza Khan. Mosaddeq eventually won the day, and the matter was allowed to rest. The Iranian nationalist had successfully and single-handedly stood up to the Russians.

During the 1920s and 1930s, Iran's oil became one of the paramount symbols of foreign manipulation and consequently a rallying point for nationalists. Because of the importance of oil revenues for Iran's ambitious modernization projects, it was perceived even by Reza Shah that oil was too important to be left entirely in the hands of the British, although his attempts to gain better terms consistently failed, leaving outsiders to believe that Reza Shah was unwilling to commit to Iranian sovereignty. In many ways, the Iranian state's economic stability depended on payments by the AIOC, based on profit-sharing circumstances that ultimately favored Britain. The company's payments to Iran were subject to fines imposed by the British shareholders if production was in any way disrupted, and the company paid exorbitant taxes to the British Crown. Despite increases in output, Iran's oil revenues continued to decline.[13] Adding insult to national injury, Iran's oil industry was largely segregated, compounding the feelings of an invaded people. According to legend, British-frequented restaurants and other establishments would put up signs reading "no dogs or Iranians allowed."

Following a meeting of high-ranking State Department officials, U.S. ambassadors, and military attachés in the region, a top secret report was prepared that assailed the AIOC and its "colonial methods," claiming it was responsible for "the present economic problems and lowered Western prestige in [Iran], and throughout the entire Middle East." Bluntly, it was "one of the greatest political liabilities affecting United States–United Kingdom interests."[14]

MOSADDEQ'S NEGATIVE EQUILIBRIUM

The advent of World War II and the subsequent military occupation of the north and south of Iran by the Soviet Union and Great Britain, respectively, brought with it new challenges for the nationalists. Oil became an increasingly crucial factor in the Allied war effort, and yet another power, the United States, was growing in its influence and thirst for the vital resource. By the end of the war, Great Britain had not left the region, and the cycle of concessions, despite the grandiose rhetoric of the young shah's regime, did not seem to go away. In 1949, Mohammad Mosaddeq led efforts to establish a "National Front," a parliamentary coalition pushing for the nationalization of the AIOC, on the basis that Iran should maintain control over its own resources.

Because of the competitive approach of various world powers vis-à-vis Iran, Mosaddeq's commitment to nationalization was based on a principle of "negative equilibrium," in which neither world power would lose at the expense of another. While Reza Shah's ascension to the throne had overtly benefited the British at the displeasure of the Soviets, Mosaddeq sought to find a balance whereby no single power would be allowed to exercise overt influence over Iran's resources, economy, or territory. This point is important, as it goes to the heart of whether Mosaddeq indeed represented a communist threat to America, as the British later sought to convince the Eisenhower administration. To be sure, Mosaddeq's nationalization project enjoyed the support of the radical communist Tudeh party, though Mosaddeq's National Front did not espouse the ideologies of communism, and saw the Tudeh's radical, pro-Soviet stance as ultimately antithetical to its own nationalist aims. During the height of the nationalization controversy, Mosaddeq's National Front worked with the shah to quell Tudeh riots and attacks on the bazaars and other centers of traditionalism inside Tehran. In short, Mosaddeq was no communist, and analysts inside British Foreign Office and the U.S. State Department understood this.

In 1951, Mosaddeq, now prime minister, was riding a wave of significant popularity. Having acted as a tireless critic of homegrown corruption, dictatorship, and foreign intervention, he carried the banner of Iran's trajectory of independence by rejecting a 50:50 profit-sharing system, and ultimately nationalizing the AIOC. The British, afraid of the impact that such a project could have on their numerous holdings around the globe, had to be restrained by the Truman administration from invading Iran. But the nationalization of Iran's oil was not the only item on the agenda. Mosaddeq also abolished the Caspian Sea Fisheries Agreement with the Soviet Union, sending a signal that he was indeed committed to negative equilibrium.

Naturally, U.S. oil companies were not too distressed at Britain's sudden loss of its oil monopoly in Iran. A secret meeting between George C. McGhee, Assistant Secretary of State for Near Eastern, South Asian, and African Affairs, and leading U.S. oil company representatives, echoed a distressed, albeit hopeful tone regarding the entire affair. ARAMCO's representative, for one, stressed the rights of the sovereign government, and placed the ultimate burden on the AIOC's own mismanagement. McGhee too saw a "silver lining," calling Mosaddeq honest and "anti-Russian."[15]

It was not until Dwight D. Eisenhower was in the White House that Great Britain was able to convince the United States of the need to do away with Mosaddeq, not on economic grounds, but by convincing the president that Mosaddeq was prone to courting communists. In Iran, Mosaddeq sought new powers for the premiership by passing a resolution that brought the military under the control of his office. The shah, frantic to stop this, signed a royal decree dismissing Mosaddeq and placing in his stead General Fazlollah Zahedi. It was not to be. Mosaddeq simply arrested Nematollah Nassiri, the officer charged with delivering him the notice of dismissal, and the shah, in his now-infamous style, fled in panic to Baghdad, and then Europe.

Ironically, it was Mosaddeq's rise in power and popularity that precipitated his downfall. Religious activists led by Ayatollah Kashani, who had once championed his cause, began to stage a fierce opposition, as did the once-friendly communist Tudeh party. The former did so on grounds that the prime minister had overstepped his constitutional limits, while the latter thought Mosaddeq was not pro-Soviet enough. Yet the U.S. government would be convinced otherwise by Britain. With the help of the CIA and Britain's MI6, a series of anti-Mosaddeq demonstrations were staged in Tehran, and shortly after midnight on August 19, 1953, General Zahedi had the absent shah's orders naming him prime minister announced over state radio. Soon enough, armored vehicles would escort scores of pro-shah protesters to Mosaddeq's private compound for a final confrontation. Antitank missiles were fired on the gates, as mobs stormed in to ransack the residence of the prime minister, who was forced to jump the back wall of his home and seek refuge in an adjacent yard. After some resistance by Mosaddeq's guards, the premiership of the fiery nationalist was put to an abrupt end. To avoid unnecessary bloodshed, Mosaddeq had refused last-minute requests by nationalists to arm themselves against the pro-shah forces. A new era would begin in Iran.[16]

The shah was flown back from Rome, accompanied by CIA agents who observed an insecure man, afraid by the prospects of further failure, and unsure of himself to the last minute. From that moment forward, the shah would be perceived as a puppet of the United States, the country that had placed him back on the throne after he fled from his own nation. He would begin a reign of dictatorial abuses, at times justified in the name of anticommunist actions, but more likely out of a genuine recognition of his own illegitimacy. Under the shah's repression, negative equilibrium would falter, only to give way to Khomeini's infinitely more radical statement "neither East nor West," which not only opposed foreign intervention but manufactured a cult of anti-Americanism that continues to be the centerpiece of the Islamic regime.

COUNTDOWN TO THE REVOLUTION

After the coup, the oil nationalization problem was resolved, but only after the United States and Great Britain had agreed on a way forward. Iran was brought to the negotiating table ex post facto: Iran would in principle "carry out" its nationalization program, but under the banner of a new consortium called the National Iranian Oil Company (NIOC). The Iranians would be allowed 50 percent of net profits, while ownership would be divided between the United States (40 percent), the original AIOC, later renamed British Petroleum, or BP (40 percent), Royal Dutch Shell (14 percent), and Compagnie Française des Petroles (6 percent). In essence the non-Soviet victor powers "were to divide the spoils of war."[17]

The reinstatement of Mohammad Reza Shah's reign marks a departure from the status quo ante of internal political relations in Iran. Previously, power needed to be brokered between various factions, and even Reza Shah, whose taste for censorship and centralization did not make him prone to internal competition, had been forced to deal with a majles that often worked to undermine his plans. Mohammad Reza Shah too had been forced to deal with the likes of Mosaddeq prior to the 1953 coup, but things would now have to be different. In 1960, the shah allowed for elections in the majles, as well as the establishment of two political parties—"The Nationalists" (*Milliaan*) and "The People" (*Mardom*). These two entities were actually led by two closely linked politicians, both of whom were friends of the shah. Those who had been supporters of Mosaddeq, including most National Front members, were deemed ineligible for elections that would be known as a fraudulent exercise of democracy, in large part aimed at appeasing American observers.

The shah's internal control mechanisms would rest on the SAVAK (a Persian acronym for "Country's Intelligence and Security Organization"), along with his army's Counter-Intelligence Unit, which sought to purge the armed forces of infiltration by Tudeh party elements. The CIA, FBI, and Israel's Mossad provided training for the SAVAK, which eventually came to represent the brutality of the shah's rule, known for the torture and execution of thousands of Iranians. A vivid example of this is the shah's response to student protests condemning the arrest of two politically active students in 1962, which had paratroopers descend on the central campus of Tehran University. As a result the chancellor, Dr. Ahmad Farhad, resigned, stating as a reason: "I have never seen or heard so much cruelty, sadism, atrocity, and vandalism on the part of the government forces. Some of the girls in the classrooms were criminally attacked by the soldiers ... as if an army of barbarians had invaded an enemy territory."[18]

Despite the iron fist, many sought to resist. The early 1960s saw a resurgence of National Front sentiments, though this new coalition was much weaker than it had been during the heydays of Mohammad Mosaddeq. This new Front was mortally plagued with internal divisions, and though teachers and bazaaris came together to stage sit-ins and protests, the opposition movement during the 1960s lacked the broad-based white-collar sectors needed to mount an effective front. This was due in large part to the shah's increased militancy of the country, and the strong connections between the professional class and the regime. Throughout this period, the shah was able to squeeze the vices of suppression without much difficulty.

American support for the shah remained steadfast throughout his reign. The United States had positioned itself to take over the role of Persian Gulf guardian once Great Britain had completed its planned withdrawal from the region in 1971. During the Johnson administration, the United States singled out Iran as a source of stability for the region, given its inherent strength, secular outlook, and loyalty to the United States. Perhaps not lost to American planners was Iran's absence from the numerous Arab-Israeli wars. Israel and Iran maintained cordial cooperation, both economically and militarily, in stark contrast to Iran's neighbors in the Gulf, which actively assisted in the various war efforts—the aims of which ranged from gaining lost land to terminating the Jewish state.

Under President Nixon, support for Iran continued, given the new president's emphasis on finding allies to act as "regional policemen" in hotspot areas. The Nixon Doctrine borrowed heavily from the experiences of Vietnam, which had been draining U.S. resources through the over-commitment of American forces. For Nixon, it would become critical for regional security enterprises to maintain a truly regional face, thus allowing the United States the freedom from constant military embroilment.

Nixon's plan for regionalization in the Gulf was his "twin-pillar" policy, which saw to it that Saudi Arabia and Iran become dominant forces. The administration knew full well, however, the limitations of the Saudi Kingdom, given its fundamentalist streak, smaller population, and more limited room for diversified growth. Therefore, "the US was to rely primarily on Iran, since Saudi Arabia was considered too weak to enforce regional stability and security, a role which Iran could play."[19] The shah's poor record on human rights seemed to be less of a worry. After all, the Eisenhower administration had already set a powerful precedent with the deposition of Mosaddeq in 1953. Nixon did not flinch in supporting the September 11, 1972, *coup d'état* in Chile, which also deposed a democratically elected leader, and in his stead placed the right-wing General Augusto Pinochet. Pinochet justified his reign of terror to his last day, on the premise that he was saving his country from Marxist elements. For Nixon and his national security adviser Henry Kissinger, support for the shah and Pinochet was less a matter of principle, and more an issue of *Realpolitik*.

In 1963, the shah launched a project of modernization and liberalization that he labeled the "White Revolution." Through it, he sought to exert a degree of independence and achieve a level of prestige that up to that point had proved out of reach, while at the same time he sought to connect with the poor through agrarian reform, and thus undermine class tensions and potential threats of communist agitation. The reforms brought profit sharing for workers, established a Literacy Corps, and granted women the right to vote.

The agrarian centerpiece of the White Revolution revolved around decentralizing land ownership and granting land deeds to a vast number of tenants. Because of some of the more progressive elements of the proposal, which included female suffrage, the clergy stood to oppose the shah. More importantly, the ulama feared the loss of large, religiously endowed land holdings, making their opposition a matter of economic survival. The National Front, weary of larger political repression, also refused to sign on to the reforms.

Despite widespread opposition, the government claimed the referendum on the White Revolution passed with less than one percent of the registered voters in opposition. Sadly, the biggest concern the White Revolution sought to ameliorate remained: The concentration of land did not leave the hands of absentee owners, namely the royal family, and large landowning enterprises. Among those who did receive land, many would not have enough to generate needed income and would ultimately end up in the cities as laborers.

Despite the government's best expectations, 1963 marked a year of potent mobilization against the shah. The Pahlavi kings, through their modernization from above, projected a self-certainty that went beyond arrogance, since it did not establish proper channels for those left behind to have their grievances heard. Those who dared to stand up had to rely on increasingly radical tactics, given the suppression of speech, assembly, electioneering, and other forms of legitimate political participation.

Under the Pahlavi system, the rich got richer, and the poor got poorer. Compounding the problem, the latter group was squeezed socially, through a forced secularization that in Reza Shah's reign had seen the forced unveiling of women under the cloak of modernization. Callous to the effects of more than a millennium of Islamic traditions, the Pahlavis chose to identify with pre-Islamic Persian greatness, essentially bypassing the essence of Iran's contemporary social, moral, and religious basis. Economically, Iran suffered greatly from the shah's ambitions. He brought in massive deficit spending, hosting bank-busting parties for the elite and the foreign, with ordinary Iranians noticeably absent. Those who wished to invest in Iran had to provide access to the royal family, further entangling the regime in every aspect of economic life.

If a two-tiered system was established during Reza Shah's tenure, which favored elites at the expense of most Iranians, the systemic divisions under the new shah became horribly pronounced. The bazaari class suffered under the new system, as the economy was fueled by foreign trade and personal contacts, forcing many traditional, locally minded merchants into bankruptcy. This segment would later play a critical role in fomenting the 1978–1979 revolution, since "the traditional bourgeoisie (represented by the bazaar), who had seen their interests eroded by this new bourgeoisie and feared further attacks by the shah ... mobilized to challenge and ultimately remove him."[20]

The 1953 coup signaled a wrong turn at a crossroads in Iran's political development, and consequently forced a suppression of the trajectory of independence. Like a coiled spring held down under immense pressure, opposition groups became repressed and marginalized, the people nudged away from Islam. The stage was set for a massive explosion of sentiment that would accept nothing less than the immediate end to the monarchy. By the time the Iranian Revolution erupted in 1978–1979, the National Front proved too weak and divided without Mosaddeq, and could not stand up to Ayatollah Khomeini's increasing power. The Islamic power brokers of the revolution, who adopted an infinitely more radical style than the nationalists had once embraced, felt that "neither the original National Front nor its revived offshoot was sufficiently anti-American."[21]

The final analysis tells of a tragedy involving a British nation bent on protecting its revenue stream at the cost of democracy in Iran, an American government seeking regional order at any cost, and a shah afraid of his own shadow, obsessed with imposing an imagined, uncompromising identity upon his nation. But we can also speak of courageous and honest nationalists, known for their patriotism, their moderation, and their ability to inspire their compatriots into domestically inspired development. But as the kings would rule over the men and women of Iran, moderation would lose its appeal, and a new kind of opposition, armed with an obscure and radical political framework, would blindside the nation and the world entire.

Chapter 4

WHIPLASH: REVOLUTION AND THE HOSTAGE CRISIS

> Iranian society has survived over the centuries by absorbing alien concepts and mores and transmitting them into something uniquely Persian. This resiliency is once more being tested and the outcome, although unpredictable, is likely to owe more to traditional Iran than to foreign influence.
> —Secret CIA Study (1976)[1]

A feeling of utter helplessness permeated the American psyche. The images of blindfolded hostages on the grounds of the U.S. embassy in Tehran were broadcast around the globe after a months-long explosion of popular sentiment that brought down the government of Mohammad Reza Shah Pahlavi in Iran. The embassy's seizure came on November 4, 1979, and was carried out by an ad hoc group of radical Islamist and Marxist students from the University of Tehran. This gross violation of international law and practices split the diverse factions of the revolution and helped propel dissident cleric Ayatollah Ruhollah Khomeini to a level of uncontested power. It was from this point forward that the American administration would begin to truly understand the volatile and dangerous nature of Iranian revolutionary politics, which in many ways was a century in the making.

For the most radical of Iran's new power brokers, and especially Khomeini, consolidating their revolutionary power base would take top priority, and the players were unable, or unwilling, to consider the long-term consequences that their immediate actions would have on Iran's security. Establishing a hard line, a cult of anti-Americanism, would help fix their revolutionary identity in place, and establish their legitimacy as rulers. Fear of the regime's uncompromising, seemingly irrational ways would prove just as salient to Khomeini as it had for Mao Zedung during his Cultural Revolution in China. By carefully crafting an image of "us versus them," the new Iranian hard-liners would become the center of gravity, and all who appeared open to compromise with the West would

learn the unforgiving nature of a regime that came to expect total obe-
dience. The expression of political dissent would be stifled with an iron
fist as the revolution came to represent specific and orchestrated political positions, which centered on the acceptance of religious government
domestically, and outright anti-Americanism as a matter of foreign policy.

Ayatollah Khomeini had honed this cult of anti-Americanism over a
decade prior to the Iranian Revolution of 1978–1979. For Khomeini, America's unquestionable support for the shah's dictatorship had made it impossible to reconcile Iran's national interests with those of the West. In
many ways, the early days of the revolutionary regime were ideologically
driven, as resentment for America was not merely orchestrated, but, in
fact, reflected the feelings of a disenchanted population. But as the process
of consolidating power wore on, the more secular factions of the revolution, which also happened to be the most pragmatic and open to reconciliation with America, were bulldozed over by the black and white positions of Khomeini and his associates, as revolutionary rhetoric would be
converted to state policy. As most people in the world who have struggled
with belligerent leaders understand, nuances can most easily be drowned
out by a hard-line drumbeat. The arguments surrounding the formation of
the Islamic Republic and the ratification of the constitution were framed
to the public "as part of the fundamental laws of Islam which meant that
opposition to the concept itself constituted a rejection of Islam."[2]

KHOMEINI AND THE REVOLUTION

Ruhollah Musavi was born at the turn of the twentieth century in
Khomein, near Esfahan, a city referenced by the last name that Khomeini
eventually adopted as a cleric. Biographer Baqer Moin recounts the young
Ruhollah's fascination with authority, and how often, during a popular
game called "The Thief and the Vizier," Khomeini would prefer to play
the figure of power, handing down harsh verdicts to the thief.[3] As a child
of five, Khomeini had lost his father to a politically motivated murder, tied
to the elder's anticorruption stance in his province. By the time Khomeini
was in his mid-teens, both his mother and aunt had died of cholera during
an epidemic, and the young Ruhollah was taken in by his older brother,
who taught him Islamic law and reason, and set him on a lifelong path of
religious learning.

Khomeini developed his viewpoints on Islamic government over a
long period of time, and it was not until reaching his seventies that he
helped topple the shah's government in Iran. In many ways, Khomeini's
thoughts reflected the sociopolitical realities that the cleric had experienced throughout the twentieth century, especially in relation to more
moderate reform movements, which were defeated at the hand of the
government with the active support of foreign powers. A work written

by Khomeini in 1943 called *Kashf al-Asrar* (*The Revealing of Secrets*) still maintained a monarchical outlook, as it merely asked that the clergy be granted greater powers of parliamentary oversight, much as Shaykh Fazlollah Nouri had sought during the early stages of the Constitutional Revolution. *Kashf al-Asrar* was written a decade before the confrontation that brought down Mohammad Mosaddeq and the National Front, but two years after the deposition of the harshly secular Reza Shah, and the subsequent installment of his son Mohammad Reza to the throne. It was not until 1963 and the shah's White Revolution that Khomeini began to take a stronger line against the monarchy. The shah's pet project of reform, which centered on the redistribution of land and granting the vote to women, offended the more fundamentalist streams of the Shi'i clergy, who were bent not only on promoting misogyny, but stood to lose a significant amount of religiously endowed land by the reform package.

On June 3, 1963, Khomeini was arrested by the shah's forces after delivering a sermon that compared the shah to Yazid, the caliph who had martyred Imam Husayn at the Battle of Karbala. A year later, Khomeini was sent into exile for his antigovernment activities, which used as a base the seminary city of Qom. The events that led to Khomeini's ouster from Iran helped to foment increasing support for the cleric among religious Iranians. In the fall of 1964, opposition in Iran began to mount around a law that was reminiscent of the hated capitulation clauses found within the foreign-imposed treaties of Qajar Iran. The new law was to grant American personnel working inside Iran immunity from prosecution, and much like in Qajar times, this bill was tied to an American loan meant to help Iran on its road to modernization. Like the European powers had previously done, the United States was seeking a level of subservience from the Iranian government in return for cash, in a matter that could not possibly have been seen as healthy to the future of U.S.-Iranian relations. Because of his outspokenness on this issue, along with his support of the 1963 uprisings against the White Revolution, Khomeini was detained on November 4, 1964, and soon after deported. As *Los Angeles Times* journalist and Iran observer Robin Wright explains, the "date would come back to haunt Americans; exactly fifteen years later, Iranian students commemorating Khomeini's expulsion attacked the U.S. embassy in Tehran and took the staff hostage."[4]

It was also in the early 1960s that Khomeini gained the title of *Marja-ye Taqlid* (Source of Emulation), the highest position given to a Shi'i cleric, who is thereafter referred to as a "grand ayatollah." With this title, Khomeini's viewpoints and decisions carried significantly more weight for those who chose to follow him. In Shi'ism, which allows the faithful to choose a *marja* for guidance, the legal renderings of a person's chosen grand ayatollah become uncontestable. This explains the impact that the *fatwa* of Grand Ayatollah Mirza Hasan Shirazi had during the Tobacco Protest, which led to an effective, nationwide boycott of the product.

But while following an ayatollah on liturgical matters could naturally have political connotations, it was never understood that an ayatollah would be in a position to exercise uncontested political authority over a nation. In fact, the mere presence of a number of diversely minded grand ayatollahs within a given domain would make it by intuition impossible to allow the decisions of one cleric to stand above the other, equally learned and qualified ayatollahs. Yet by 1970, Khomeini was propagating a notion that sought exactly that kind of political authority for a single cleric. This concept would be known as *velayat-e faqih* ("Rule by the Jurisprudent"), which called for the establishment of an Islamic state, to be led, not by a monarch or parliamentarian, but by a nobly guided Islamic jurist. Most clerics at the time rejected this concept outright, as the Iranian clergy had long tended to espouse quietist pursuits and not revolutionary notions, let alone turning government systems upside down. Even those who had been revolutionary activists tended to be either left-leaning radical clerics, or more traditional in their aims, as Khomeini had been upon writing *Kashf al-Asrar* in 1943. But Khomeini pressed on with *velayat-e faqih*, saying:

> The need for a successor [of the Imam] is for the implementation of the laws because no law without an executor is respected. In the entire world, legislation alone is not enough and cannot secure the happiness of the people. There must be an executive authority and the absence of such an authority in any nation is a factor of deficiency and weakness. This is why Islam decided to establish an executive power to implement God's laws.[5]

It has been widely written that Khomeini borrowed the model for Islamic governance, not from the writings of the Imams, but from Plato's philosopher king concept, as found in *The Republic*. But more rarely mentioned is that the Islamic Republic, once implemented, fulfilled some of the wishes of historical Iranian revolutionaries, which were modern and Western in nature, and compatible with sturdy constitutional frameworks of elected representation. The Islamic Republic's maintenance of a contested and directly elected lower house of parliament, along with an indirectly elected Council of Guardians (half of which is chosen by the supreme leader, with the other half chosen by the majles), which acts like a veto-wielding upper house of parliament, could be paralleled with earlier versions of Western republicanism. Even the office of the supreme leader, which Khomeini held, and which granted him overwhelming power to control the armed forces and other coercive instruments of the state, is, constitutionally speaking, an office appointed and overseen by the popularly elected Council of Experts. That is, while liberal democracy is by no means practiced in Iran, the mechanisms are already in place to bring it about. In many ways, Iran has embraced Cicero's republican concept of rule by "the one, the few, and the many," with present gravity leaning toward the first. Because the Islamic Republic was to be a product of a long-running struggle toward democratic republicanism, Khomeini could not have possibly started the political process from scratch—he had to borrow from existing norms and existing currents pushing for popular will. The fact that candidates to elected office are stringently vetted by the hard-liners is yet another obstacle that reform-minded Iranians must overcome when seeking to bring the system further on a path toward truly representative government.

The start of the Iranian Revolution is normally considered to be January 1978, following a slanderous article written in a government-run publication, which accused Ayatollah Khomeini of coalescing with Marxist foreigners, serving as a spy for the British in India, writing erotic poetry under the pseudonym "Hindi" (a play on Khomeini's family connection to India), and holding homosexual tendencies. In Qom, the clergy reacted in anger, and the bazaars, infinitely tied to the religious establishment, went on strike and staged demonstrations. The shah's security forces reacted harshly, shooting at crowds and killing seventy protesters.[6] The bazaaris were not merely acting on religious piety in opposing the shah. Inflation of up to 40 percent had been plaguing Iran, and the shah had reacted in 1977 by implementing heavy-handed measures against the merchants. A force of 10,000 students was put together to crack down on the bazaaris in a campaign that resulted in the imprisonment of 8,000 sellers and the banning of over 23,000 bazaaris. Throughout 1977, the bazaar began to organize into a coherent oppositional force, as did a wide range of groups, from the militant, Islamic-Marxist Mojahedeen (known also as the *Mojahedeen-e Khalq*, or MEK), to the secular Marxist Fedayeen. In June of that year, Ali Shariati, an intellectual considered to be one of the early progenitors of the Iranian Revolution, died under mysterious circumstances in London just one month after being exiled for his lectures on Islamic and Marxist revolutionary philosophy. Shariati had enjoyed a strong following among students, and to a large degree helped influence the ideology of the Mojahedeen.

Analyst Cheryl Bernard and her husband, Ambassador Zalmay Khalilzad (largely credited with early American successes in rebuilding Afghanistan after the 2001 U.S. invasion), wrote a study on the Iranian Revolution that lays out some of the overlapping beliefs of the Marxist leaning Shariati and the fundamentalist Islamist Khomeini. They cite specifically three areas: the belief in Shi'i Islam as a strong vehicle for change, the impact of mass mobilization stemming from a singular, divine source, and a nationalist identity based on a notion of superpower oppression over the Third World.[7] The first aspect, that of Shi'ism, is especially telling when we remember the roots of the faith as a movement that stood in antithesis to a perceived injustice on the part of the ruling elite. In many ways Shi'ism and revolutionary communism hold strong similarities in their emphasis on a historical trajectory that leads to a predestined state (communism in one case, and the return of the Imam in another), along with the focus on the society's dispossessed.

Shariati's death before the age of forty-five was officially called a heart attack, as was the death of Mostafa Khomeini, the first born of the ayatollah, just a few months later. Among the Iranian population, the shah's SAVAK was widely blamed for these two deaths, and the incidents only served to stiffen opposition to the shah, from the youth and more mildly religious camps in the case of Shariati, and from the conservative clergy in the case of Khomeini's son. By the time the revolution was underway in 1978, the Muslim religion had come to play a central role in the uprisings. Khomeini had been preaching against the shah from exile in Paris, while protests would erupt to commemorate the deaths of fellow revolutionaries at the hand of government forces. Consistent with Shi'i mourning practices, every forty days such commemorations would take place, and in the context of the revolution, they would take a stinging, antiregime tone. Government forces would crack down yet again, and the cycle would repeat itself.[8]

Throughout the revolution, Khomeini was careful not to antagonize more secular elements of the revolution, always maintaining that he did not desire theocracy for his people. Masterfully, Khomeini understood the fact that Islamic fundamentalists alone, and even less, the minority of them who embraced *velayat-e faqih*, could not possibly mount an effective revolution. As a matter of practical necessity, Khomeini consistently courted Mojahedeen and National Front members, knowing that they had far-reaching organizations and could especially help in mobilizing the youth. But if Khomeini seemed to be willing to work with more secular elements of the opposition, he did not hold back in criticizing ayatollahs who had not already joined in the revolution, questioning the "relevance and validity of their quiet pursuit of jurisprudence while the Shah sells Iranian oil to Israel which in turn has endangered the very existence of Muslims."[9] For its part, the government of France, where the cleric was in exile, embraced Khomeini, understanding that militarily, the shah's Iran had been largely dependent on American firms for the procurement of new systems. France stood to gain significantly in military contracts by supporting Khomeini, and thus he was given free reign to direct *fatwas* and craft carefully worded revolutionary messages from French soil.

On September 7, 1978, the shah imposed a curfew that few people seemed to have learned about on time. The next day, a preplanned gathering went on as scheduled on Tehran's Jaleh Square, and the shah's forces opened fire on the crowds. Reports vary on casualty counts, but they range from a few dozen (as told by the shah's government), to 500 people (as claimed by the revolutionaries). Mired by popular dissatisfaction, the shah made some last-ditch attempts to appease the massive crowds, which by that fall had taken on proportions reminiscent of the French Revolution. In October, the shah had the former head of SAVAK, General Nematollah Nassiri (the loyal officer who had delivered the dismissal papers to Mosaddeq in 1953), indicted for the torture of political dissidents. Shortly thereafter, the shah released all political prisoners from custody, including the pro-Mojahedeen Ayatollah Taleqani, and pro-*velayat-e faqih* cleric Ayatollah Montazeri. (Montazeri, like other high-ranking clerics, would later have a falling out with Khomeini and become *persona non grata* in the Islamic Republic.) But the regime and the countless protesters were already set on a path of confrontation, whose outcome could then be predicted by most observers, including those in the Carter administration, who made overtures to various opposition groups but were unable to gain anything the likes of a partnership in the wake of political uncertainty and rampant anti-Americanism.[10]

Before finally leaving the country, the shah granted the revolutionaries a promise that was nearly a century in the making—that of a democratic republic. He placed Shapour Bakhtiar, a longtime National Front leader, as prime minister and gave him the plenary powers for which Mohammad Mosaddeq had ardently fought, but which had been denied to him in 1953. In fact, this last-ditch effort was also in line with the demands that the Constitutional Revolution had sought at the turn of the twentieth century. Only this time, following decades of abuse, political suppression, mimicked democracy, and foreign-power ambivalence toward the shah's human rights abuses, the opposition did anything but embrace Bakhtiar's last-minute government. Bakhtiar himself lost the backing of the National Front, as no mainstream opposition group was ready to take the shah at his word or be associated with his compromise government. And while Bakhtiar accepted the post only because he did not trust Khomeini's intentions for Iran, it was the leftist groups—the Mojahedeen along with the more secular streams—who were least willing to compromise for anything less than the abdication of the shah and the total disbandment of the military. Since these were paramilitary organizations, they saw any remaining elements of the shah's old regime, including the armed forces that were backing Bakhtiar, as an obstacle to gaining an ultimate victory.

The shah left Iran on January 16, 1979, and on February 1, Khomeini made his historic return to Tehran on an Air France flight, greeted by literally millions of jovial Iranians. A referendum calling for the establishment of an Islamic Republic was held on March 30–31, 1979, the ballot of which read: "Are you for the replacement of the monarchy with an Islamic Republic, the constitution of which will be approved—yes or no?"[11] The referendum passed with 99.3 percent of the vote. Soon thereafter, Bakhtiar was forced to flee, and high-ranking elements of the shah's military were summarily executed in a daily parade of militant determination, as the names of the dead were read over national radio to serve as a reminder of the new government's hold on power. On December 2–3, the follow-up vote to ratify the constitution was cast, and thus began the work of the new government.

But the revolution did not end with Khomeini's return to Iran. A months-long struggle would ensue between the various factions of the revolution and Khomeini's camp, who would accept nothing less than *velayat-e faqih* in Iran. Enemies of the regime would be branded enemies of Islam, and the militant Mojahedeen, along with secular leaders bent on reaching a working compromise with the United States, were purged, killed, or eventually forced into exile. The Mojahedeen eventually became a terrorist group seeking to overthrow the Islamic regime, most notorious inside Iran for its support of Saddam Hussein during the Iran-Iraq war, along with its bombings of the Iranian parliament and Khomeini's party headquarters in 1981. Masoud Rajavi, the leader of the Mojahedeen (which now also goes by the more family-friendly National Council of Resistance of Iran (NCRI)), was quoted by *The New York Times* as admitting to the killings of "1,000 government and religious officials" in 1981 alone. This paled only before Khomeini's own count of political executions, which Amnesty International put at nearly 3,000 for that same year.[12]

THE HOSTAGE CRISIS

The hostage crisis that severed diplomatic relations and kicked off a period of mutual enmity between the United States and the new revolutionary government of Iran was orchestrated by zealous, radical students bent on making a simple statement that America should not allow the shah on its shores for medical treatment. As Ali, a young, American-educated captor told his hostage, embassy public affairs officer John E. Graves, the raid of the embassy compound was not meant to last more than three days.[13] But Khomeini's official blessing of the seizure, which accompanied a call not to harm the hostages, sent the young, untested students scrambling to accommodate the Americans for an indefinite period of time. In his memoirs, Abol Hassan Bani-Sadr, the first democratically elected president of Iran, but who shortly thereafter was forced to flee the country amidst opposition from the Islamists, recounts that Khomeini wanted to make it clear through the hostage crisis that he was the one in power. To do this, he would take it upon himself to "solve the hostage problem and prevent war. If successful, he would receive all the credit."[14] The early beatings and psychological mistreatment of the hostages turned into long, agonizing months spent in separate locations throughout the vast embassy compound and around the country. It was the tiring despair of 444 days in captivity that led some brave American souls to attempt daring escapes, hunger strikes, and at times of special agony, even suicide.

As the crisis wore on, the Carter administration sought various methods to bring the hostages back safely, including secret negotiations held with more moderate, but ultimately less influential figures within the new regime. Foreign Minister Sadegh Ghotbzadeh secretly met with Hamilton Jordan, Carter's chief of staff, in Paris. But after agreeing to an offer that would set up a United Nations tribunal to publicize complaints against the shah in exchange for the safe return of the hostages, Ghotbzadeh found himself unable to persuade Khomeini to go along with the agreement. In late 1982, he was found to be plotting the overthrow of Khomeini, possibly with American help, and was summarily executed.

Once most avenues for diplomatic compromise seemed to run into impassable roadblocks, President Carter made the fateful decision to order a military rescue attempt. American tycoon H. Ross Perot had already hired former Green Berets for a successful operation that freed two of his employees from captivity in a Tehran jail. But the embassy operation was much more daring and required a higher level of sophistication. The plans called for six C-130 aircraft and eight RH-53D helicopters that would land on a secretly prepared airstrip inside Iranian territory to refuel, and then head out for the outskirts of Tehran, where unmarked cars left by CIA operatives would be driven into the capital to carry out the rescue. Helicopters would then return to pick up the hostages and special forces at the embassy compound. It was estimated that the operation would result in fifteen hostage deaths, a number that seemed suspiciously low to Secretary of State Cyrus Vance, given the risky nature of the endeavor. Following President Carter's approval of the raid on April 11, 1980, Secretary Vance secretly submitted his resignation in protest. The operation, however, was aborted after one of the helicopters experienced significant hydraulic problems. It was on the way back that one of the helicopters collided with a C-130 during refueling, causing eight fatalities. The decision was made to return on the C-130s, and the rest of the helicopters, along with secret operational plans and the bodies of the American dead, were left behind on Iranian soil.[15]

There were those in the United States who cared little for President Carter's outward empathy for the hostages. Henry Kissinger, for one, felt that the overwhelming emphasis that was placed on the hostages' safe return on the part of the administration undermined American prestige. The consummate *Realpolitik* practitioner, Kissinger felt that America could not be reduced to sentimentality on the issue. But in many ways, Carter represented the larger American polity, which came to sympathize with the professional men and women of the U.S. Foreign Service and the Marine Corps who were taken hostage by the monster of revolutionary radicalism. Carter then was in the position of having little to offer a revolutionary movement whose motto would become "Death to America," and with which every attempt to compromise only invited the hard-liners to further purge their moderate colleagues.

The fifty-two hostages who were still being held were finally released on January 20, 1981. This date did not coincide with the death of the shah, who had succumbed to cancer six months earlier, but with the swearing-in of Ronald Reagan as president, an unknown (and in many ways feared) figure, who also provided an opportunity to turn a new leaf—to back out of the crisis with honor, and not due to diplomatic pressures by President Carter. It is also true that by this time, the Iran-Iraq war was well under way, and the hostages were becoming an increasing liability for the Iranian regime, which could now use the war as a method of consolidating its rule.

As he gained power, Khomeini called for the exportation of the revolution to neighboring Gulf countries, utilizing quintessentially Islamic language (rather than sectarian Shi'i terms), all the while thumbing his nose at the United States and the Soviet Union. Iran, from thence forward, would be beholden to "neither East nor West," in the words of Khomeini. But the harsh manner in which Iran loosened the shackles of great power intervention came with a heavy price. A country that once acted as Nixon's bedrock of security in the Middle East was leaving itself wide open for disaster, politically and militarily, as one of the most devastating and bloody episodes of modern warfare would show.

AT WAR WITH THE WORLD

In the traumatic sphere of total war, internal political forces tend to co-alesce for the purpose of national survival, thus "the willingness of most individuals to bridle private or personal impulses for the sake of general social objectives."[16] This became especially true for Iran during its eight-year war with neighboring Iraq, which, as much as it drained blood and treasure from Iran, and as much as it revealed the new revolutionary government's political inadequacies, was used as an efficient rallying cry for Iranian nationalism, and helped to further neutralize internal opposition to the regime. War songs saturated Iranian radio and the conflict between Iran and Iraq would be painted as the fight between Khomeini's rightful Islamic government and the apostate Ba'ath Party of Saddam Hussein: good versus evil.

With all of his abilities at internal political maneuvering, Khomeini's view of war seemed to depart greatly from the sphere of shrewd power politics. Much to the detriment of his nation, Khomeini actually seemed to believe that there would be divine intervention assisting Iran in its deterrence and handling of an invasion. Perhaps this blind faith was a mechanism for internally justifying the needless purging of the shah's military, which occurred on several levels following the revolution. Khomeini systematically weakened his armed forces by canceling "military orders, cutting the already reduced military budget by one third, halving conscription to one year, and seeking to return to the United States [a shahtime order of] 80 F-14 aircraft together with their *Phoenix* missiles."[17]

Following months of rhetorical escalation, Iraq launched a surprise attack on Iran's oil-rich southwest, aiming for a quick, decisive victory over its unstable neighbor in order to gain the long-disputed Shatt al-Arab waterway. This gain not only would have provided Iraq increased access to the Persian Gulf, but it would have significantly upped its stake of the global oil market. For all of the rhetoric, Iran was drastically unprepared for an actual invasion, as Khomeini had felt that no one would have dared to invade the vast, uncompromising territory of *Iranshahr*. For Iraq's ten divisions that were sent into the fight, Iran could only answer with two. And, perhaps as a way of hiding the inadequacies of his military, Khomeini stressed that, due to Islamic teaching, his troops were to do "nothing to harm the cities which have no defense" inside Iraq.[18]

Needless to say, this humanitarian approach changed as the realities of war overtook the nation. Islamic law and prudence would take a backseat to the national interest, and the atrocious total war would engulf the two neighbors over much of the 1980s with little apparent regard for human life. The "war of the cities" utilized missile attacks and heavy shelling mutually aimed at populated areas. Commercial airliners, elementary schools, and other "soft targets" were fair game, while Saddam attempted, with little success, to break the front's many stalemates with the use of chemical weapons. Iran returned the favor, but the war seemed to drag on, as Iran, a country with three times the population and several times the gross domestic product of Iraq, felt that it had invested too much of itself not to seek a punishing victory. Early upsets by the newly emerging Revolutionary Guard Corps resulted in an Iraqi offer for a cease-fire in 1982. This notion was rejected outright by an Iranian regime that would accept nothing short of regime change in Baghdad. The war continued until 1988 with no changes to the political map, and with both regimes still firmly in place. The death toll for the entire conflict is estimated at nearly 1 million, with Iran taking a bulk of the casualties, as it sent unarmed children and elderly men to the minefields in the infamous "human wave" attacks that accomplished little strategically, but left a generation scarred. But if a fighter could not be given a weapon, he would be handed a plastic key before setting out to the front. The key signaled that Khomeini had granted the martyr permission to enter the gates of Paradise.

Iran's own revolutionary rhetoric, along with its unwillingness to submit its revolutionary government to the standards of international norms, led to an unprecedented consensus among Iran's Arab neighbors and the two rival superpowers, that while Iraq was the aggressor, neither side should be allowed to win decisively, and least of all Iran. The nations of the Arabian Peninsula (with the exclusion of Yemen) forged the Gulf Cooperation Council (GCC), an alliance of mutual assistance for the most part aimed at counteracting the effects of Iran's hostile intentions, Khomeini's stated wish to "export" the revolution. All actors that had a stake in the future of the Gulf sent weapons and money en masse to Baghdad. The aim was to achieve a power parity that only seemed to further bloody the endeavor, which the belligerents had painfully mismanaged from the very beginning. Military force estimates at the war's end show in numbers what Iranians must have felt in their guts: 625 tanks were left, to Iraq's 5,500; 1,050 armored personnel carriers to Iraq's 4,750; 870 artillery pieces to Iraq's 2,800; and 63 operational fighter jets to Iraq's 575. Yet, perhaps more telling was the armed forces count, as tabulated by the U.S. Defense Intelligence Agency, which put Iran's standing conventional military at 275,000, to Iraq's 1.15 million.[19]

Throughout the 1980s, Iran learned to live with the self-fulfilling prophecy of isolation. It created and nourished the Lebanese Hezbollah, which all but pioneered the concept of Muslim suicide bombing. Organizations like Hamas would later adopt the tactic and come to learn of the useful patronage that an isolated Iran can provide as the Islamic Republic seeks, no longer to break through the shackles of foreign intervention, but the bitter coldness of political seclusion. But the hardest lessons of revolutionary ideology for Iran were tied to the very forces that helped consolidate the Islamic government's power. By reaching for a most unrelenting view of Islam, Khomeini was able to separate the world into supporters and detractors, good and evil. His corevolutionaries, not bent on Islamic government, but rather the utilization of Islamic principles for the purpose of overthrowing a despotic regime, were not ready for Khomeini's shrewd political prowess, or his about-face that sidelined them into political oblivion, and often death. But as philosopher and Iran scholar Hamid Dabashi suggests, revolutionary myths open the door to revolutionary deeds:

> Participating in a revolutionary myth might send bare chests to hard bullets. It might turn a whole world of conflicting truths into a unified Satanic image. It might hold nations hostage to their dangerous imaginings. It might hang keys to the gates of heaven from the thin necks of perished youth. It might have barefoot teenagers walk on mines.[20]

When looking back at the process of Iran's trajectory of independence, it is not until the late stages of the antimonarchic movements that the dark ideologies of *velayat-e faqih* and other Islamic-centered notions come to bear fruit. In fact, Khomeini himself in the early days was a monarchist bent on securing more influence for the clergy, not outright control over the country. The moderate National Front leaders had lost the massive appeal they enjoyed during their heyday, as Mosaddeq's dream of creating a democratic republic fell apart at the hands of America and Great Britain. And while the United States, which rhetorically supported democracy throughout the Cold War, could have done more to encourage its beneficiary nations to push for political liberalization, the pressures of superpower politics would always prove the greater concern, and the strategic embrace of democracy was often relegated to the status of a slogan, and not a foreign policy.

Yet just as Khomeini had little appreciation for the Soviet Union, neither did the National Front in its heyday, and even less the constitutionalists at the turn of the twentieth century, who sought not antagonism with the West, but the same liberal rights enjoyed by the West. The longing of Iranians to control their country's own resources continued to drive opposition to the shahs; but if the Qajars drove the bazaar toward constitutionalism, the Pahlavis eventually drove it toward Khomeini and *velayat-e faqih*. Both idealistic nationalism and economic pragmatism drove the trajectory of independence, but having been suppressed by overzealous kings bent on their vision of modernization from above, and their peculiar interpretation of Western methods, the trajectory took a haunting turn toward aggression. In the end, the West proved that if compromise could not change Iran's course, Ayatollah Khomeini could. And yet the pragmatists, today comprising most of the population, are still waiting for their democracy, as both the Islamic regime and the West seem to be missing the point.

PART II

CHARACTER OF A NATION

Chapter 5

THEOCRACY IRANIAN STYLE

If thy Lord had so willed, He could have made mankind one people: but they will not cease to dispute.

—The Qur'an (11:118)

The Islamic Republic of Iran has developed using an odd recipe for government that combines an obscure religious doctrine (that of *velayat-e faqih*) with a mainstream European framework of representative government (the "Republic" part). To be sure, Iran is much more democratic in its approach to governance than many other nondemocratic "republics," such as China and Syria, in that it holds regular, contested elections for a variety of posts throughout the government. Theocracy at the same time provides for the political legitimization of religious rulings, and gives the green light to direct intervention by the ulama in the affairs of the state.

Two critical factors emerge from this direct involvement of religious figures in the government. One, perhaps more obvious by-product, is the gap in qualifications that can appear when a graduate of a religious seminary is tasked with making decisions affecting government policy. As we have seen, the Iran–Iraq war dramatically highlighted the lack of expertise shown by Ayatollah Khomeini in mounting an effective counterattack to the Iraqi invasion.

Another important, yet perhaps less spoken element of direct clerical involvement in policymaking is the sobering role that clerics are forced to play outside of their traditional roles as oppositional figures. When a cleric is not in control, he can rant and rave all he wants about his views on proper Islamic government, and indoctrinate generations on the need to overthrow the state or engage in offensive *jihad* (holy struggle). But while propaganda of this sort does saturate the Iranian curriculum and official social discourse, religious rulers, including Khomeini, quickly had to learn the worldly responsibilities of government. Soon enough, pragmatism cast a dark cloud over the "Islamic" aspect of the republic, as Khomeini himself claimed to be above shari'ah, and Khomeini's successor was chosen not on his religious qualifications (which were certainly lacking for this post), but on purely political considerations. Former president Ali Khamene'i would be made an "ayatollah" and become the supreme leader of the Islamic Republic after the death of Khomeini in 1989, thus bringing to an end the notion that a diverse and oil-rich nation the size of Iran can be governed purely on Islamic legal qualifications.

Across the Persian Gulf, in the Kingdom of Saudi Arabia, the roles of religion and the state have been inexorably tied since the consolidation of power by the House of Sa'ud and its ultraconservative Wahhabi allies. Both the Islamic Republic and the Kingdom of Saudi Arabia focus their laws upon a certain level of perceived concurrence with shari'ah. Interpretations of Islamic doctrine are thus connected to government policy through consultation with progovernment clerics. But the main difference lies in the external, oppositional role played by the Wahhabis. Their influence on the educational curriculum and their role in promoting their version of Islam beyond the borders of the Kingdom—through the funding of seminaries and mosques—allow them to maintain an ideologically rigid position in wishing for their version of an ideal Islamic state. Ultimately outsiders, the Saudi ulama have opted for "the most extreme positions open to them because they are not responsible for implementing their ideas."[1]

But how do the mechanisms for religious consultation differ in these two theocratic states? Does Iran's religious establishment favor continued revolution, or does it simply espouse a "religion of legitimization," to borrow a phrase coined by Iranian revolutionary thinker Ali Shariati? Can the religious establishment in either of these two countries move toward reform without unraveling altogether? Iran's religious institutions are intensely tied to a radical revolutionary ideology that is inherently more flexible and capable of initiating more significant reforms than the reactionary establishment of Saudi Arabia. In seeking to understand the overall character of the Middle East, especially the role of Islam in the region's political development, and its connection to global terrorism, it is important to establish the difference between these two models of theocratic rule, as adopted by the two Gulf powerhouses.

THE SAUDI KINGDOM

Saudi Arabia is the product of an alliance in 1744 between Muhammad ibn Sa'ud (of the House of Sa'ud) and Shaykh Muhammad bin 'Abd al-Wahhab of the House of al-Shaykh—a religiously conservative family that espoused a strict Qur'anic interpretation along the teachings of Ibn Taymiyya. Ibn Taymiyya, who is often referred to as the ideological father of al-Qaeda, was a fourteenth-century legal scholar of the more literalist Hanbali School of Sunni Islam. The Saudis, looking to consolidate power across the Arabian Peninsula, embraced the Hanbali puritanism of the al-Shaykh family in order to legitimize their military campaign with moral zeal, establish a defined religious affiliation, and, more importantly, benefit from the fighting prowess of the Wahhabi fighters, then known as the *Ikhwan* ("Brotherhood"). The Ikhwan perceived the world as a simple interplay between forces of righteousness and the forces of evil, and by denouncing modernity they sought to revive the lifestyle of the Arabian peninsula during the early days of Islam. This nostalgic ideology is often called "Salafi," and the terms "Wahhabi" and "Salafi" are often used interchangeably. The adherents themselves, however, are more likely to refer to themselves as "Unitarian," a title based on the name of their movement: "The Call for Oneness with God" (*al-dawa ila al-tawhid*).

To this day, government consultation with the ruling clerics forms the basis for law within the Kingdom. By issuing *fatwas*, the ruling clergy have been able to maintain a constancy of influence, even to the extent of directing Saudi modernization projects toward a compromise that seems to reach a halfway point between modernity and outright backwardness. In times of dissent between the clerics and the king, the latter has been able to overrule and push through his agenda. However, one should consider the points of contention that have arisen, which to Western eyes could seem petty in nature. A good example is the *fatwa* issued by Wahhabi ulama in 1930, which rejected the teaching of foreign languages, geography, and painting in schools. Geography, for one, because it contradicted the notion that earth was flat.[2] Such disputes have come to underscore the level of social reforms that remain controversial to this day. That most women today are still compelled not to show their faces in public, and that they are forbidden by law to drive an automobile, is a reflection of such rigid stances by the ulama.

In many ways, modernism has driven the Kingdom from the beginning of the oil concessions. Since its founding under the name Saudi Arabia in 1932, and the start of the exploitation of its petroleum by America's ARAMCO oil company, the Kingdom was pushed to keep up with a certain level of socioeconomic development. ARAMCO's establishment of infrastructure on Saudi grounds, from schools to roads and hospitals, along with the invitation of American military forces to protect the company, provided a glimpse into Western lifestyles and forced the Saudi monarchy to consider providing a higher standard of living for its own subjects.

Needless to say, this acceleration of modernity, which has hardly ceased since the early days of ARAMCO, has created a level of confrontation with the more traditionalist segments of society, specifically the clergy, who even stood in opposition to radio and the telegraph during the 1930s. As it has been seen numerous times, the royal family has been pushed to find a middle ground with the ulama. Saudi radio was confined to news and

Qur'anic readings in order to satisfy the opposing clerics and allow the technology to be used by the Kingdom.

Key to understanding the opposition to modernization by the ulama is the association of the clergy with a distinct kin and class identity. Most of the notable religious figures in Saudi Arabia stem from the al-Shaykh family, that is, they are direct descendants of Shaykh Muhammad bin 'Abd al-Wahhab. The Shaykh family has diminished in numbers, in part because members have often opted not to take multiple wives (as the royal family is known to do), and also due to the Arabian military campaign of the legendary Ottoman Egyptian governor Muhammad Ali in 1810, which forced many clerics into exile in Egypt.

Given the nature of the ulama's role in Saudi society as a specific group of nearly singular origin, modernization itself can prove to be a substantial stumbling block to their maintenance of power. After all, any significant change in the socioeconomic dynamics of Saudi Arabia could "create a new class of leaders, not religious in origin, and thus give rise to a direct threat to the ulama."[3] However, honest, ideological concerns by reactionary forces in Saudi Arabia must not be ignored in favor of a purely political explanation. There are still conservative elements, with and without formal power, that would see to it that Saudi Arabia ceases its enterprise of modernization altogether and revert to the early days of Islam.

A place where the ulama exercise significant influence is the courts. While most other Islamic countries have a dual system of law—shari'ah and "man-made"—countries other than Saudi Arabia tend to be dominated by the latter. Shari'ah, in fact, speaks to the socioreligious sensitivities associated with the basics of civil and criminal law, but in most countries does not lead to the suffocation of secular legal practice or norms, as one finds in Saudi Arabia. In fact, royal decress and positive law in the Kingdom are limited to supplements of *fiqh* (jurisprudence) in the "furtherance of public welfare, on condition that these laws offend no clear text or fundamental principle of shari'ah."[4] Religious diversity is also not tolerated in the Kingdom. As the U.S. State Department mentions in a 2005 report, the Saudi government "prohibits public, non-Muslim religious activities. Non-Muslim worshippers risk arrest, imprisonment, lashing, deportation, and sometimes torture for engaging in religious activity that attracts official attention."[5]

A REPUBLIC OF ISLAM

The arguments made by Khomeini in *Kashf al-Asrar* in 1943[6] were largely intended to counter attacks by secular intellectuals against the Iranian ulama, though the work also took pointed shots at the Wahhabi movement in Saudi Arabia. Interestingly, it is the Saudi reactionary forces, also concerned with fighting secularism, that Khomeini finds most appalling. This has been part of a larger war—of words and otherwise—between Shi'is and the Hanbali Sunnis who consider them heretics.

While stark differences of identity and historical outlook exist between the Party of Ali and the Sunnis, a critical doctrinal difference lies with the former's acceptance of *ijtihad*, or religious reasoning. Ijtihad, which in essence is the clerical authority to interpret shari'ah based on the Qur'an and the oral traditions of the Prophet (and the Imams, in the case of the Shi'is), takes the form of legislation in more modern applications. Living *mujtahids* (those who apply ijtihad) make legal decisions that are binding only upon those who choose to follow them. By the end of the ninth century, Sunni practice had closed "'the gates of reasoning' and the evolution of Islamic law was virtually arrested."[7] If one can imagine a system of common law in which the latest binding rulings are twelve hundred years old, that is what strict Sunni interpreters of shari'ah must grapple with when applying legal tenets to modern life. It is no accident that Saudi Arabia has been referred to as a nation "still living in the Middle Ages." In many ways, it is. And while some observers do contend that Wahhabis "reject the idea that the 'doors to ijtihad are closed,'"[8] it is important to note that on matters of most concern to reformists, including women's rights, custody cases, gender relations, and other aspects governing social life, revision remains stalled in the Kingdom. Issues already settled by the Qur'an, the oral traditions, and original religious commentaries are not likely to be revisited by adherents of Wahhabism anytime soon, and even efforts by the ruling family have failed to persuade the clerical class to adopt ijtihad uniformly. In Iran, ijtihad remains intact. Historian Nikki Keddie explains that although "Sunni ulama outside Iran ... made some interpretations, the latitude for Shi'i ulama to do this was greater." This is explained by "the greater socioeconomic strength and independence of the Iranian ulama."[9]

As early as 1943, Khomeini's view of an Islamic government was beginning to mold. While he accepted the proposition by Shaykh Nouri (of the Constitutional Revolution) to establish a "Guardian Council of Jurists" to take part in the work of the parliament and cement the role of the ulama in the new Iran, Khomeini went a step further and proposed a guardian council that would actively oversee the government, in many ways foreshadowing the Islamic Republic's Guardian Council that exists today. This role for Islamic jurists was backed up by nineteenth-century Mullah Ahmad Naraqi, who "argued strongly for the right of the mujtahid to act as a successor to the Imam."[10] It would be later in the century that Khomeini began to espouse the notion of *velayat-e faqih* as a source of legitimization for direct clerical rule. However, the choice to follow a mujtahid was seen from earliest times as a matter of personal will. The people, in fact, were expected to choose their source of emulation from among the most learned of the clerics, and often intermediaries were hired to connect followers with mujtahids in a kind of market of belief. Judicial authority, then, had "a certain 'populist' quality which might make it susceptible to shifts in public opinion."[11]

It is not a stretch, therefore, to understand Shi'i Islamic doctrine as espousing, if not democratic will, then a multipolar approach to decision making based on popular will. To this day, two followers of Shi'i Islam might adhere to the decisions of two different mujtahids, making the process of piousness much more diverse and individually tailored. This can explain that while the Islamic Republic continues to barbarically repress the rights of gays with imprisonment and execution, Iran legally allows for sex changes. Both seemingly contradictory realities are based on given interpretations of Islamic law, as have been considered by the judiciary, the parliament, and the Guardian Council.

An important point to note is that while Sunni tradition placed less importance on the worldly rule of the caliphs than on the doctrines established by the Qur'an and the Prophet's oral traditions, Shi'is had seen the rulings of Imams as part of a critical and accepted development of Islamic doctrine. At the same time, it became historically possible for Shi'is to accept a limited role of the clergy in the affairs of the state, since there could be a distinction between the divine rule of Imams before the Occultation, and the worldly rule of kings. To be sure, the Imams themselves were for the most part not political leaders associated with a state, but rather oppositional figures within a Sunni-dominated world. Therefore, a separation between secular and holy rule was part and parcel of Shi'i theology, and the clergy under a variety of governments remained visibly distant from politics—at times because of restrictions imposed on them, but often, and most visibly under the Islamic Republic, out of personal choice.

The individuality of religious rulings has led to multipolar dynamics of power in the post-1979 Iranian state. Members of the clergy might belong to hard-line conservative camps that place their loyalties with the supreme leader, or to the so-called "reformist" camps. Like in Saudi Arabia, there are a variety of nonclerical economic and political interests that prop up or oppose the status quo in Iran. Just as the Iranian Revolution was not waged by Muslim fundamentalists alone, but by a wide segment of society that included members of religious minorities, secular intellectuals, and everyday Iranians, post-shah Iran has benefited some interests more than others—case in point being the bourgeois bazaari class, which immediately following the revolution (but less so in the present day) benefited greatly from the emergence of a religious state, given the bazaar's historic connections to the clergy. To be sure, sources of reform have come about and will continue to originate from a variety of sources in Iranian society, not merely in the form of the clerical versus the secular.

LEGISLATION VERSUS SHARI'AH

As a rule Islamic law is seen by strict Sunni interpreters as deriving directly from the Qur'an, the orally transmitted teachings of the Prophet, and to a degree legal consensus among the clergy. It is therefore considered un-Islamic to enact legislation, at least in the parliamentary sense, according to these traditionalists. Such legislation, if binding, would be seen as an amendment to the established religious codes. It is important to note that the four Sunni schools of theocracy have by no means remained dormant in their development of religious interpretation throughout the centuries. In fact, Sunni scholarship is to this day rich in intellectual vitality and dynamism. But the main difference lies in Shi'i acceptance of the person of the mujtahid as a source of jurisprudence itself, with individuals able to choose between several *living* mujtahids as sources of emulation; once a cleric dies, one is expected to follow by a different example. And while this system has been utilized to grant greater power to living clerics, it has at the same time created opportunities for progress and modernization, as new generations of high-ranking jurists are granted reverence equal to that of their predecessors, and thus they have an ability to come to a generation-specific interpretation.

In Saudi Arabia, legislation has not been altogether abandoned. One could point to the *Majlis al-Shura al-Ahli* ("Civil Advisory Council"), which in 1925 was considered something of a legislative body. In fact, in 1926, the laws installed by the Ottoman Empire over the Hijaz—the holy cities of Mecca and Medina—were adopted by the Saudi Kingdom in order to maintain continuity. These laws were French in origin, and stood in antithesis to shari'ah. In the areas of economics and commerce, especially, the practical has superseded the liturgical. Saudi chambers of commerce "apply regulations based on the Ottoman Code of 1850, which in turn is based on the French model, which has no trace of shari'ah in it."[12] Regulations related to the ever-important oil concessions, taxation, maritime trade, vehicle regulation, foreign trade agreements, and the formation of companies, all borrow little from the Qur'an, but much more from globally accepted approaches to the regulation of capital and commerce.

In the area of criminal punishment, Saudi Arabia has been pushing to circumvent *hudud*, or Qur'anic penalties, perhaps for the sake of improving the Saudi image abroad, if not for the protection of members of the royal family. Punishment for criminal activity has increasingly moved from the strict religious interpretations that inspire beheadings and fatal stonings on "Justice Square" to the more palatable "discretionary penalties," such as imprisonment and monetary compensation ("blood money"). The punishment for drinking wine, which originally carried eighty lashes, now carries imprisonment. Sodomy now carries whipping and imprisonment, but no longer decapitation.[13]

Constitutionally, the question of legislation becomes much more complicated in the Kingdom. Iran, in contrast to Saudi Arabia, allows for the enactment of legislation by a popularly elected majles (albeit with the significant caveat of candidate vetting). In Saudi Arabia, the experiment of a new consultative, or *shura* council, has been a product of a decades-long internal debate. Finally put to work in 1993, the council's members are appointed directly by the king, whose close attention to the sensitivities of the conservative ulama places significant restrictions on the viability, efficacy, and ultimate legitimacy of the council. Different from the Council of Ministers, which was formally established in 1952[14] and included the king's cabinet, the shura council was meant to establish a step toward democratic reforms, albeit within the restraints of a nondemocratic kingdom.

Because of the way the majles is elected by the people of Iran, and because of the representation of religious minorities (Jews, Assyrians, and Chaldean Christians, Armenian Christians and Zoroastrians are afforded one seat each by law), the Iranian legislative body is bound to exercise a level of autonomy not imaginable by any council in Saudi Arabia. The right of women to vote in Iran, as well as their presence as elected deputies in the majles (14 out of 290 members, as of the 2005 election), also introduces an important perspective into the male-dominated political debate. The fact that Saudi women until very recently have been deprived of a public identity (with ID cards for women only becoming mandatory in 2006), and that they still do not have the right to vote, makes it clear that incredible road blocks keep Saudi women from pushing for reforms in their own name.

INTERNAL FORCES OF REFORM IN IRAN AND SAUDI ARABIA

With the unique role that the Saudi ulama play in crafting the educational curriculum and establishing guidelines for social conduct, the process of development and change in the Kingdom has more often than not had to originate from within the circles of power. While there are indeed a variety of interests within the royal family and outside it, there is little dispute as to the centrality of the Saudi state and the need to enact change from within, when it is to be enacted at all. But the kind of opposition that has concerned the Saudi royal family the most has been that of religious fundamentalists, unhappy about perceived deviations from the traditions of Islam, and not secular intellectuals bent on Western-style reforms or better relations with the West, as is the case in Iran.

Still regarded as one of the most significant events in modern Saudi history, the seizure of the Grand Mosque in Mecca on November 20, 1979, serves as an example of the type of opposition faced by the royal family not on the basis of its own reactionary nature, but of its perceived deviation from traditional values. At around 5:30 in the morning at the start of the Hajj (Islamic pilgrimage), Juhaiman ibn Muhammad ibn Saif al-Utaibi brandished a weapon and began firing shots in the mosque, killing a worshiper, as his associate Muhammad Ibn 'Abd Allah al-Qahtani took to the main microphone and proclaimed himself to be the Messiah. It was only three hours later, at around 8:30, that Saudi police had formed a perimeter around the Grand Mosque, and not less than *two weeks* until the perpetrators were taken out by force, tried, and executed.

The length of time it took for Saudi authorities to respond was due to the sensitive issue of engaging in armed conflict on the grounds of Islam's holiest site; a *fatwa* had to be issued that would justify the raid. What is perhaps more daunting of all is the affinity with which some of the highest-ranking ulama treated the members of the Ikhwan, a group which took its name, sensitivities, and ideals from their earlier namesakes, the fierce Wahhabi fighters who had helped bring Arabia under the House of Sa'ud. The *fatwa*'s published report showed a surprising amount of sympathy toward a fundamentalist group that had taken Muslim pilgrims hostage on Islam's holiest site. According to the carefully (and kindly) worded *fatwa* report, al-Qahtani had "exhibited enough of the expected signs for young believers to have been deceived in his case."[15]

The thirty ulama involved in the *fatwa* morally distanced themselves from their own ruling, making it clear that it had been the king who explicitly asked for permission to enter the Grand Mosque and seize the Ikhwan. Following that incident, the Kingdom of Saudi Arabia would embrace a tighter adherence to the tenets of Wahhabism in order to shield itself from further friction with the fundamentalists. The Ikhwan spoke to a large portion of society, not in claiming that they had a divine connection, but in their perceptions of "high levels of corruption in the government and the gradual disappearance of tradition in the Kingdom."[16] After all, the Ikhwan were not only related in lineage to the original power base of the Kingdom, but were a product of the Saudi institutions of learning, and their embrace of puritan Islam did not deviate too far from the state's own indoctrinating curriculum.

Iran stands in a much different position in its ability to enact reforms. In fact, it is the institutions themselves, not only as written into the constitution, but as socially codified in religious and political practice, that are more likely to act as vehicles for necessary reforms. In Iran, its "discourses of legitimacy and contest are entirely Islamic. It is also a . . . more open and diverse political field than that of most other countries in the region."[17] This discourse has in recent years come in the form of "theological debates initiated by secular jurists and women lawyers, especially in connection with family rights and women's rights."[18]

Unlike Iran's multipolar dynamism, Saudi Arabia's more centralized power structure seems less capable of absorbing the shock waves of instability. Like a skyscraper not built to roll in the event of an earthquake, Saudi politics leaves little room for maneuvering. The seizure of the mosque is perhaps the most relevant example of this, in that it showed how the government could feel the pressure to become even more conservative in its policymaking, rather than outright challenge the forces that attempted national disruption. Even as early as the 1930s, in the beginnings of the modern Kingdom, "when the King was unsuccessful in winning the ulama's approval, he preferred to use his power of persuasion rather than imposing a veto overruling the religious authorities."[19] It can be argued that the ulama wield a significant amount of power, and any sudden change in the political climate of the Kingdom causes trepidation among the ruling. And while there are indeed trends pushing for more liberal reforms within Saudi Arabia, this recent phenomenon is in itself not far-reaching or consequential enough, as it includes Shi'is—making it for many weary Saudis a nonstarter.

Another sign of the Kingdom's volatility surfaces when comparing the Saudi armed forces with those of Iran. While in Iran the Islamic Revolutionary Guard Corps (IRGC) does serve a kind of praetorian role for the ruling revolutionaries, the Guard Corps also encompasses the role of elite fighting force (as it proved to be during the Iran–Iraq war), as well as that of intelligence service and foreign policy apparatus. Saudi Arabia's national guard, on the other hand, has a more clearly defined role as a counterweight to the conventional military. At times brandishing contending tribal allegiances at top levels, the guard and military are equal in size and made to counterbalance each other. The national guard is specifically responsible for maintaining internal order in the cities and protecting the oil wells, and U.S. planners consider the army and national guard as "possibly antagonistic in case of conflict."[20] This arrangement only underscores the tight spaces for political maneuvering, as well as the volatile nature of stability in the Saudi state.

Beyond these institutional frameworks, the question of popular opinion is important. Daily life in the Kingdom is "handled by the courts and the educational system. Since the establishment of the Kingdom in 1926, both of these institutions have been highly influenced" by the clerical establishment.[21] Since the school and university curricula are strongly impacted by Wahhabi clerical doctrine, it is important to focus on the kind of effect this can have on the population itself. A 2004 poll showed significantly lower opinion ratings of the United States in Saudi Arabia in a variety of areas, including science, entertainment, policy, and values, as compared to other Arab countries.

While pro-Americanism shouldn't be equated with social progress, it is alarming when only 4 percent of the population holds a favorable view of the United States, a Western liberal democracy. Comparing these figures with Iran, when in 2002, the Iranian parliament's National Security Committee commissioned a poll, which "found that 74 percent of Iranians favored the resumption of relations with the United States and 46 percent felt that U.S. policies on Iran were 'to some extent correct,'"[22] there is significant cause for concern in the Saudi example. This Iranian poll was taken only a few months after President Bush had coined the rubbing term "axis of evil" when referring to Iran, Iraq, and North Korea.

While these numbers could reflect a position of antagonism toward the respective governments by the people (Saudi Arabia is a U.S. ally, while Iran has no formal relations with America and continues on its state-sanctioned cult of anti-Americanism), the differences are substantial enough to point to general trends that run on a deeper level. Do these numbers prove a difference in the scholarly curriculum, media coverage, or simply a matter of perception shaped by the respective societies? It is difficult to answer this unequivocally, but the extent to which anti-Western forces influence and are embraced by Saudi society has a bearing on the future, not only for America's staunch Saudi ally, but for the millions of Muslims affected by the exportation of Saudi ideology—most legendary in its past support and financing of the Taliban in Afghanistan, along with the establishment of mosques and fundamentalist religious schools around the world.

Iran and Saudi Arabia are two very different countries with different historical trajectories. However, their modern establishment as Islamic states, run by Islamic law, places them apart from numerous countries that embrace a more assorted approach to legal doctrine. Saudi Arabia is Sunni and Iran Shi'i, but similarities do exist in their espousal of traditional values in their respective societies, which include respect for Islamic economic institutions, as well as forms of criminal and civil law.

The Islamic Republic of Iran is by no means a progressive country. Laws on the books still favor a male-dominated system of divorce and child-custody, as well as an "Islamic" approach to dress, marriage, and capital punishment, but that is changing. The legal participation of women in the upper levels of the political sphere has not been seamless, but Iran has had a female vice president, which is much more than can be said of the Saudi state, where women still live an existence of absolute distinction from men.

Perhaps more important than the current state of affairs in Iran and Saudi Arabia are the legal, social, and otherwise institutional frameworks in place. Iran, with its doctrinal embrace of ijtihad as a dynamic force for issuing legally compelling, if not binding, decisions, is by definition more prone to reform than the ninth-century legal stasis of Saudi Arabia. And while the Saudi Kingdom enjoys much healthier and productive relations with the liberal West, this marriage of convenience stands on less-than-solid ground, as an overwhelming force in Saudi Arabia espouses less cooperation with America, and longs for even more staunch cultural and political detachment from the West.

But Iran too is trapped by political forces that often stand at odds with sound religious judgment. Political realities often trump the more benign representations of Islamic law—torture and death have been handed to opposition clerics for voicing even the most orthodox of Islamic views.[23] As alarming as this is, a significant change in the political trajectory, favoring even more reform, is well within the social, cultural, and constitutional boundaries of the Islamic Republic. Of Saudi Arabia, it can only be said that any and all changes it takes, but especially those that would advance tolerance in the spheres of religion, gender relations, and other aspects of everyday life, must be taken with extreme trepidation, lest the system unravel under the feet of the royal family—America's ally in the region.

Chapter 6

EAST OF IRAQ

For however swamped the laws may be by some individual's influence, however freedom herself may cower, still the time comes when they rise up, through silent judgements or in the secret elections to positions of honour. Freedom will bite back more fiercely when suspended than when she remains undisturbed.

    -—Cicero (on the need for rulers to be loved, rather than feared, 44 BC)[1]

When human beings are liberated from imposed constraints of exploitation and social enslavement, as well as from unrefined animal instincts such as violence and savagery, they will then side with truth and justice in line with their human nature . . . . (Regardless) of any school of philosophy of history we may follow, we can still share an understanding of this general and universal conception of history.

    —President Mohammad Khatami, "The need for dialogue among civilizations" (address to the United Nations General Assembly, September 21, 1998)[2]

Following the terrorist attacks of September 11, 2001, a makeshift vigil was held in the streets of Tehran to pay tribute to the victims of the worst terrorist attack ever perpetrated on U.S. soil. Among those holding candles in solidarity with America's victims were the children of the revolutionaries, those who had been taught in school to chant "Death to America" yearly to mark the takeover of the U.S. embassy, and the birth of the Islamic Republic.

Observers of Iran constantly speak of a paradox, a web of contradictions found in contemporary Iran. These contradictions are in fact part of a complicated, long-running debate between the forces of stagnation and those of change. Just as the ninth-century struggles between rationalist and traditionalist views of Shi'ism would come to a head; or as later centuries would pit the Akhbari school of Shi'ism with that of the Usulis; or as the nineteenth- and early twentieth-century social movements would include the diverse voices of traditional clerics, socialists, democrats, and even feminists, Iran today is engaged in a dialogue with itself. Some call

Iran a beacon of democratic hope, others a place of religious oppression and petrodollar corruption. In fact, Iran is all of those things at once.

Iran's current political diversity is perhaps best embodied in the persons of Ali Akbar Hashemi Rafsanjani, Mohammad Khatami, and Mahmoud Ahmadinejad, three successive presidents who represent largely different sets of interests, ideologies, and prescriptions for the future of their country. But while the three presidents disagree on a wide range of issues, from the correct approach to foreign relations, to economic policy, to freedom of speech, all three embrace the notion of an independent Iran, and have focused their work on increasing their country's influence as a truly independent nation.

Throughout the process of dialogue and conflict between the various factions in Iran, the importance of individual charisma continues to be relevant, just as it was during Khomeini's rise to power, during the Baabi movement, and naturally back during the establishment of Shi'ism as the "Party of Ali." This focus on personality, which might appear on a basic level to be incompatible with democratic principles, is also that which has fueled any strides made by reform-minded Iranians in modern times. Case in point is President Khatami, who ran on a platform of improved relations with the West, and received over 69 percent of the vote, winning in most of Iran, among "the poor as well as the rich."[3] Prominent Iran scholar David Menashri of Tel Aviv University writes:

> The massive popular participation in the elections was reminiscent of the early days of the revolution. There was a sense that the people could make a difference and that their vote might determine the course of the revolution. Of the estimated 32m eligible voters, over 29m (roughly 91 percent), cast their ballots.[4]

But just as many of Ayatollah Khomeini's ardent supporters would become disillusioned once the dust of the revolution had settled, so did the equally zealous fans of Khatami begin to question the man and the image of reform that he represented. Ultimately too heavy for his shoulders to bear amidst the hard-line attacks, the promise of a new, more liberal chapter in the revolution, complete with freedom of speech, a better economy, and improved relations with the world, would have to be put off for later. In droves, disillusioned reformists boycotted the 2005 presidential election, but Iranian politics pressed on. After the incredible upset by Mahmoud Ahmadinejad in early voting, which placed him in a runoff against "shoe-in" former president Hashemi Rafsanjani, reformers began to sweat. Had their boycott led to the possible election of a radical conservative populist, one who embodied the very institutions of hard-liner dogma that reformist Iranians had been fighting to weaken for the past eight years?

In the end, former president and 2005 candidate Rafsanjani's reputation as a corrupt element of the ruling class put the presidency squarely in Ahmadinejad's lap. As the new leader sought to consolidate power domestically and abroad, relishing in controversial statements made against America and Israel, the international news media highlighted his anti-Semitism and the renewed image of Iran, not as the initiator of a "dialogue among civilizations," the term coined by Khatami during his presidency, but as a source of threatening power and uncompromising aggression.

Since the revolution, Iran had fashioned for itself a cult of anti-Americanism that dominated its public relations machine. The diversified power structure of post-1979 Iran notwithstanding, the country's foreign policy apparatus, media, and the powerful Iraq war veterans' groups, all but monopolized the production of information—Iran's image—as it was carried by news organizations around the globe. Billboards revering martyrs of the war are read by Western eyes like Palestinian shrines to suicide bombers, and "Down with USA" placards have made perfect stock footage for twenty-four-hour cable news. The international news media, in fact, has in many ways chosen to focus the most on anti-American regime elements, rarely carrying press conferences by the moderate Khatami during his presidency, while hanging on every word of an equally weak, but infinitely more vitriolic Ahmadinejad. Most Americans are inclined to think that Iran is a bastion of anti-Americanism. And why shouldn't they? The national slogan of Iran seems to call for the destruction of America, while Iranian expatriates living in the United States dissociate themselves from their country by introducing themselves as "Persian," forcing many to believe that there is somehow a difference between Iranian and Persian culture. Many Americans love their "Persian" neighbors, but are utterly fearful of Iranians.

But is Iran as anti-American as the hard-line regime would like to portray? Opinion polls overwhelmingly contradict this notion, as do the reports of countless observers who care to make the trek to that country. But this does not point to a Middle East that is a bastion of pro-Americanism either. On the contrary, Iran is an outlier in an increasingly anti-Western part of the world. A 2006 poll shows that in Jordan, "negative U.S. ratings climbed to 90 percent from 62 percent and in Morocco ... they grew to 87 percent from 64 percent." That same poll shows that attitudes "toward American people, movies, and democracy were more negative than positive."[5] Only U.S. education was viewed more positively than negatively in the five countries polled. The Middle East is turning against America, but Iran hasn't yet.

In the end, prospects for U.S.-Iranian cooperation will have to rest on Iran's own movement toward democracy. This chapter focuses on what the road toward democracy might look like in Iran, and the progress that the three iconic, successive presidents represent in Iranian political society.

When discussing Iranian presidents, it should be noted that their powers are constitutionally quite limited. While holding the highest popularly elected office in the country, the president is not tasked with formulating foreign policy or controlling the armed forces. That is, the prerogative of the supreme leader. The president and his cabinet do have some powers to shape domestic policy, but these are often minimized by the layers of checks put before them by the supreme leadership. To pass legislation, the president must deal with a majles, whose candidates were vetted before they could even run for office. Once in parliament, even reformist lawmakers must deal with having their bills declared unconstitutional by the Guardian Council or even risk arrest by a powerful judiciary in the pocket of the hard-liners. On the streets, the president might order the police to allow peaceful reform protests, but militia elements on the ground, which are an outfit of the Revolutionary Guard and are ultimately loyal to the supreme leader, can easily challenge such an order and act independently of the president's wishes.

RAFSANJANI AND THE MERCHANTS OF POWER (1989–1997)

In contemporary Iran, few figures better than Ali Akbar Hashemi Rafsanjani personify the connection between the religious establishment and the bazaari merchant class. Former president and member of the powerful Expediency Council, Rafsanjani represents in the eyes of many Iranians the corrupt elitism and political pragmatism of a revolution gone cold. His tempered realism has seesawed between the hard-line conservative dogma of figures like Ahmadinejad, and the more reformist liberalism of Khatami. It can be said that Rafsanjani is less drawn to ideological absolutism and more to a cool and calculated stability, founded on the strength of a wealthy, religious middle class, often at the expense of the populist tendencies of the hard-liners.

Rafsanjani, whose tenure began in 1989, "sought to compensate for the absence of Khomeini's charismatic authority by developing a sustainable political structure founded on ... the commercial power of the bazaar."[6] Undertaking a period of decentralization and infrastructural development, Rafsanjani tried to normalize the revolution and bring it to a manageable level. He did this by curving vast social welfare institutions, many of which had been established to support veterans of the Iran–Iraq war. Privatization was a landmark of his administration, as free-market forces, supported by the bazaar and other sources of wealth and commerce, saw to it that Iran take a more capitalist approach. Rafsanjani's privatization of state-run enterprises would help turn "social services foundations into powerful business conglomerates."[7]

Needless to say, not everyone benefited from Rafsanjani's programs. For one, corruption increased substantially, as privatization turned into a free-for-all, with elements of the regime lining their pockets with every transaction. And while nepotism was not new to Iran, the scope of Rafsanjani's economic restructuring programs and massive construction projects brought a new level of theft to the Islamic Republic. Under Rafsanjani foreign debt and inflation skyrocketed, leaving the lower-earning groups in an increasingly vulnerable position.

A watershed moment in the Rafsanjani government was a scandal known as the "theft of the century" of 1995, in which eight well-connected figures were found to have embezzled a branch of Bank Saderat to a tune of $450 million. The public outcry was strong, and when charged, one of the men was sentenced to death. A harsh legacy of the Rafsanjani regime would be the image, in jokes and cynical parlance, of government clerics carrying suitcases full of cash into plush banks of neighboring Dubai. By the parliamentary elections of 2000, the Iranian public had lost considerable confidence in Rafsanjani, and the former two-term president had embarrassingly failed to win a seat in the majles.

Looking back on his presidency, it is difficult to imagine that a figure like Khatami could have emerged had Rafsanjani not laid the necessary groundwork for political calmness. In many ways, he provided an interregnum between the days of Khomeini and the traumatic war, and Khatami's promise of reform during the late 1990s and early 2000s. Conversely, it is also difficult to imagine Ahmadinejad's populist victory of 2005 without the legacy of Rafsanjani and the multimillion-dollar mansions built by his presidency on the backs of the Iranian poor.

KHATAMI AND THE REFORMISTS (1997–2005)

The rallies of Hojjatt-ul-Eslam Mohammad Khatami, whose clerical rank means "Proof of Islam," served as cathartic reformist pageants, frequented by an increasingly restless generation—the youth that had grown up only knowing a revolutionary Iran, but which nevertheless was painfully connected to the outside world through satellite television, phone calls from relatives in Europe and America, and an occasional barhopping stint in neighboring Turkey. Realizing what they were missing in Iran, the youth rallied to Khatami, who promised them further liberties, freedom from religious harassment, an end to "male supremacy," and importantly, improved relations with the West.[8] Just as scores of Ayatollah Khomeini's followers would yearn to touch the "Imam" when near his presence, so did the believers of reform behave toward Khatami, becoming enthralled by his charisma and promise of liberal freedoms. Women would cry, and some would even faint from excitement during his campaign speeches, reminding us of the euphoria of Elvis Presley and Beatlemania.

Khatami's call for better relations with the outside world spoke volumes of fatigue with revolutionary slogans in the Islamic Republic. Iran observers Ali Gheissari and Vali Nasr explain that the generation that voted for Khatami in 1997 was a "principle constituency of pragmatism. Its cultural outlook and political expectations diverged from the rigid conservatism of the country's leaders and it demanded jobs and economic prosperity."[9] In America, policymakers watched carefully for signs of development and potential openings to establish rapprochement.

But Khatami's landslide victory, which brought him nearly 70 percent of the vote, and which was garnered across all sectors of society and throughout the provinces of Iran, could not guarantee a true "second revolution," as it was originally dubbed. While Khatami was able to make monumental strides in relaxing social restrictions associated with dress, as well as strangleholds on the media and the arts through his oversight of the Ministry of Culture, the hard-liners still maintained control over the coercive elements of the regime, making a significant change in foreign policy all but impossible. Reformist newspapers would open under Khatami, but many would be shut down by the conservatives, who had the judiciary in their pockets and the militia boots on the ground to enforce their decrees. Protests would be put down brutally, and Khatami in return could do little more than protest himself. Khatami eventually came to be known for his powerlessness on the most important cultural issues, while his social agenda lacked economic teeth, something a nation with official unemployment rates consistently hovering above 10 percent (and unofficial ones reaching much higher) could not accept for too long.

Ultimately, conservatives were also able to capitalize on the lack of progress made on the U.S.-relations front. After all, Khatami's conciliatory language toward the West had bought him alarmingly few allies within the U.S. government. Containment sanctions remained in place, as American policymakers considered Khatami too weak to negotiate a truce with him, given his position within the Islamic Republic hierarchy. Hard-liners were also able to capitalize on America's knee-jerk backlash against Iran following the attacks of September 11. In typically myopic style, the U.S. Congress acted hastily to restrict visas to Iranian students—one of the few streams of communication between the two societies post-1979. This while students from Saudi Arabia, the nation to which fifteen of the nineteen hijackers belonged, would still be allowed to come to America. The last nail in the coffin of mutual mistrust came with President Bush's 2002 State of the Union address, in which he labeled Iran as part of an "axis of evil," alongside Saddam Hussein's Iraq (which had fought an eight-year war with Iran), and North Korea.

The Iranian religious right utilized the "axis of evil" phrase as a source of vindication for their years of calling America the "Great Satan." To them, Khatami had failed on the foreign policy front not because of domestic constraints, but because America was itself unwilling to make peace with Iran. In large part, they were right. With America's sights on Iraq as a target of invasion, it would only be a matter of time, many thought, until the other pillars of the "axis" would be targeted.

The invasion of Iraq helped empower Iranian hard-liners and their attitudes toward the United States on several levels. This became obvious on the heels of the Iraq invasion, with the United States glowing in overconfidence after an effective application of *Blitzkrieg*, which utilized the tactics of mobility over brute force, and was able to take down a powerful ruler in a matter of weeks, and with relatively few troops on the ground. Iran, fearing that "it would be next," sent a secret "letter to the White House, offering to talk about everything from its controversial nuclear program to support for Hizbullah and Hamas. . . . But the Bush team dismissed the offer, and even scolded the Swiss ambassador in Tehran at the time for passing the message on."[10] It is not a stretch to believe that American planners thought Iran was the next logical target of their project of democratization through force. After a meeting with President Bush in the summer of 2003, Jay Garner, the first American Viceroy in Iraq, recalls being asked by the commander-in-chief if he wanted to "do Iran" next.[11]

The United States, seeing its position advanced by the unprecedented success of the invasion, found itself unwilling to negotiate with another member of the "axis." Perhaps it expected Iranian leaders to crawl on their knees and ask to be pardoned for years of verbal abuse. Perhaps Iran actually was "next," and nothing could have been done to stop the administration from moving forward on regime change. But President Bush's foreign policy team must have known the obvious, that Iran had never signed a peace treaty with Iraq following their eight-year war; it had simply observed a cease-fire. Iran had consequently maintained its own long-term policy of regime change vis-à-vis Saddam Hussein. As former Iranian Ambassador to the United Nations Javad Zarif said, at "a time when every country, including the United States, was supporting Saddam Hussein, we were supporting the opposition. And it is this opposition that now sits in the halls of power in Baghdad."[12]

Iran, with its considerable network of operatives and now enjoying a more porous border with Iraq, could tighten the screws on its once arch enemy. If America didn't want Iran's help, as it had requested in a limited way for Afghanistan, Iran would help itself. It would have been foolish to think that Iran, having attempted wide-ranging concessions toward America and having been unequivocally turned down, would simply sit by and wait for the United States to turn its project of military democratization on Tehran. The only way out of this scenario would then be for Iraq to fail, at least so long as American troops were in the country. Soon enough, Iran was engaged in a deadly balancing act of making life difficult for America, through its support of anti-American militias such as

Muqtada al-Sadr's Mehdi Army, while still supporting more mainstream, and pro-American Shi'i elements in the country—those that would ultimately have to be in charge of the country. Iran was helped by the fact that even its own enemies looked for a failed U.S. presence: old secular Ba'athists of Saddam's former regime as well as Sunni al-Qaeda, who were flocking to the Sunni al-Anbar province to wreak havoc on America's ambitious social project.

The election of conservative populist Mahmoud Ahmadinejad in 2005 was in many ways an answer to America's unwillingness to engage Iran. America's long-running distrust of Iran is natural. It is based on countless images of Iranian hostage-takers, anti-American slogans, and flag-waving "Hezbollahis" in Lebanon. Even a reformist like Khatami could not contend with the distrust that permeated, first the Clinton administration, which maintained a sanctions-system of dual containment vis-à-vis Iran and Iraq, and later the Bush administration, whose plans would take it on an even greater path of confrontation.

Even after leaving office, Khatami, a turban-wielding cleric, could not shake the image in America of belonging to a savage, America-hating country. In a November 2006 blog entry written for *Newsweek* and *The Washington Post*, Khatami expressed his support for diversity of opinion over fundamentalism. He writes that any "proprietary claim to the full possession of the absolute truth ... remains as groundless as the categorical rejection of truth in principle."[13] Perhaps having difficulties understanding the former president, or more than likely out of a need to vent residual anti-Iranian anger, respondents were overwhelmingly negative. "Fine words, indeed. Unmatched by Fine Deeds," read one comment. Another asked not to be lectured on "'sacredness' by a man who ruled a country that denies women's rights and executes homosexuals." Lost on that blogger was Khatami's strides in relaxing dress codes for women, and his legacy of appointing the first female vice president of Iran. Some even questioned Khatami's words, assuming they were a front for truly despicable positions, which somehow lay hidden beneath a veneer of tolerance. To be perfectly clear, women's dress codes and the executions of gay Iranians have been the work of a hard-line judiciary and conservative militias that had very little patience for Khatami or his throngs of liberal-minded supporters.

On the foreign policy arena, the end of Khatami would come to symbolize a self-fulfilling prophecy of enmity between America and Iran. And while mostly domestic forces are to explain the election of Ahmadinejad, the establishment's eventual willingness to allow such a polarizing figure free reign points to a vindication of the hard-liners' belligerent attitude toward America. The politics of open reconciliation, as espoused by Khatami, had proven an utter failure, just as had been the case for the pragmatism of establishment politicians like Rafsanjani. For Amir Mohebian, editor of the conservative paper *Resalat*, the move toward an aggressive posture vis-à-vis the United States came as a result of America's own seemingly uncompromising actions: "As a counterpoint to George Bush and his irrational behavior, the right choice was not Mr. Khatami; the right choice was Mr. Ahmadinejad.... If the US can calculate our behavior ... the US could attack us."[14] Ahmadinejad's unpredictable behavior, in fact, is not so unpredictable at all. It is grounded on a masterful art of diversion and power consolidation.

AHMADINEJAD AND THE "TRUE BELIEVERS"

President Ahmadinejad is often talked about as part and parcel of the "war generation," a true believer of the revolution who fought in the struggle with Iraq and came to expect a vindication of the Islamic system. This "generation," whose members fit into a wide range of ages, from thirteen to fifty, was disserved by Rafsanjani's emphasis on material wealth and economic liberalism, and perhaps more importantly, by Khatami's social reformist movement, which came to offend many conservative war veterans and the families of "martyrs." Left uncared for by mismanaged and corrupt veteran funding organizations, the world seemed to be leaving behind many disaffected believers, and moving on. Counted as members of this generation-only-in-name are even the youngest members of the *Basij* ("Mobilization") militia, many of whom were actually born after the war. These volunteers take it upon themselves to enforce Islamic codes in the streets through intimidation and violence. The generation relies on "war values to attack political opponents and perceived cultural foes."[15]

For Ahmadinejad, support for the "dispossessed"—a common revolutionary theme—was part and parcel of his agenda coming into office. During the campaign, he went out of his way to avoid the scathing rhetoric that has earned him infamy in the world community since coming to power. Shockingly, soon after taking office, he quoted Khomeini's wish that Israel be "wiped off the map" (literally, "vanished from the pages of time"), and went on to host what many have called a Holocaust denier conference—a gathering of several anti-Semitic authors and personalities to present new "evidence" on one of the world's most heinous crimes. This would be the new president of Iran.

Manouchehr Mottaki, Ahmadinejad's hard-line foreign minister, said of the Holocaust denial conference, which was held in Tehran on December 11–12, 2006: "If the holocaust is questioned officially, then the existence of the Zionist regime will also be questioned."[16] Mottaki goes on: "Even if the holocaust is proven to be a historical fact, why should the inhabitants of Palestine pay the penalty for the Nazi crimes?" This one-two punch to counter Jewish victimization is typical of arguments seeking to delegitimize Israel as a state. Adolf Hitler himself has become an important symbol of anti-Israeli sentiment within segments of the neighboring Arab world, as he has come to represent for many a powerful symbol of anti-Jewish hatred. And while the term "anti-Semitism" is often misdirected at people with even the most honest of disagreements with Israeli policy, it is no secret that anti-Semitism has existed in the Middle East and has played an important role in Muslim perceptions of Zionism, the movement that supports the establishment of a Jewish homeland, and which culminated in the founding of the state of Israel in 1948.

Many in the Middle East take exception with the idea that anti-Semitism thrived prior to the massive European immigration of Jews into Palestine. Some correctly point to the rights that various Muslim empires extended to Jews and Christians (the "Peoples of the Book," a Qur'anic reference to believers of the Old and New Testaments, which are also embraced as holy scripture by Muslims). But like all other nostalgic visions of a perfect past, Islam's embrace of Judaism is only part of the story. Anti-Semitism to one degree or another existed in the Muslim world, with Jews at best asked to pay a religious tax, and at worst being the target of unfair accusations and violence. At the turn of the twentieth century, Palestinian Jews would be called *awlad al-maut* ("children of death") by many local Arabs. Jews in Muslim tradition, as in Catholicism, were often depicted as deniers of the faith, despite (or rather because of) the fact that these religions actually stem from Judaism.

Following the massive Christian violence perpetrated upon Jews during the European pogroms, and later the Holocaust, waves of Jews migrated to Palestine with the purpose of ultimately establishing a state in the ancient land of Israel. While many Palestinians were complicit in selling lands to the newcomers at a high price, many more were dispossessed by the immigration, and this just as Arab nationalism was beginning to take hold following the downfall of the Turkish Ottoman Empire. What resulted was an Arab-Israeli conflict that would continue beyond Israel's War of Independence of 1948, which formally established a Jewish state in Palestine. Israel continued to fight wars with confederations of Arab states throughout the century. With the exception of the Yom Kippur War of 1973 (which regained Egypt a considerable amount of pride due its early military successes and masterful deception tactics), these conflicts generated a profound sense of impotence on the part of the Arab populations, which had seen their armies beaten, even decimated at the hand of Israel.

In Iran, the issue is somewhat more complicated. Iran never fought a war with Israel and the shah was one of the Jewish state's fiercest supporters. Following the revolution, hundreds of thousands of Jews left Iran—mainly bound for Israel and the United States—but sentiments of Iranian nationalism still linger with many, who may even "root for Iran during the World Cup."[17] Back in the Islamic Republic, Iranians point to the official recognition of Judaism as one of the accepted religions in the postrevolutionary constitution, and remind observers of the parliamentary seat given to a member of the Jewish community by law.

In the Arab street, sentiments of loss have only helped to fan the flames of hatred toward Israel and helped maintain anti-Semitic positions. From the beginning of his presidency, Mahmoud Ahmadinejad was able to capitalize on such sentiments, just as Iran's nuclear program became an increasing concern for pro-American Arab governments in the region. By quoting Khomeini's wish to have Israel "wiped off the map," along with holding the Holocaust denial conference in Tehran, Ahmadinejad has perhaps done more to safeguard Iran's nuclear program vis-à-vis opposition from Arab regimes (whose populations increasingly support Ahmadinejad) than most any diplomatic initiative could have accomplished. Just as importantly, through these harshly clever tactics, Ahmadinejad was able to secure early support from his domestic power base: the low-income and radical conservative activists inside Iran that had served as foot soldiers during his election campaign.

Through Iran's continued support of the Sunni Hamas and the Palestinian Islamic Jihad (PIJ), as well as the ideologically compatible Lebanese Hezbollah, Iran has been able to maintain a high degree of credibility in the Middle East as a nation willing to stand up to Israel, and perhaps provide a glimmer of hope to those still longing for Israel's ultimate demise as a state. Putting Arab regimes on notice during the July 2006 war between Israel and Hezbollah, ultra-conservative ayatollah and Chair of the Guardian Council Ahmad Jannati, went on state media to claim: "We expect Muslim nations to support Hezbollah in a variety of ways, through arms, medicine or food supplies."[18] By later calling for a cease-fire, Ahmadinejad masterfully showed that Iran could not only play the part of agitator, but also peacemaker—a necessary component of great power behavior. That is not to say that Hezbollah is a mere proxy of Iran. As Major Richard Wrona, a Hezbollah expert with West Point's Combating Terrorism Center, is quick to point out, Iran did not likely orchestrate the kidnappings that led to the war, nor is Iran "calling the shots on Hezbollah . . . which is starting to increase its own stature in that relationship."[19] But Iran did make the most of the war, seeking to upstage "moderate" Arab leaders, as their governments were forced to walk a more careful line as U.S. allies with an increasingly potent grassroots Islamist movement. The 2006 poll previously mentioned shows that negative attitudes of Arab citizens toward the United States is at least in some part related to America's "challenge of Iran's nuclear program."[20] In other words, Ahmadinejad's efforts have paid off.

On the home front, Ahmadinejad has proven capable of garnering support among key constituencies, not only in relation to the nuclear program, but through populist measures aimed at alleviating burdens on the working class. These expansive social service programs have continued to drain Iran's treasury, while providing a leader that is less than universally loved inside Iran with a useful power base. One parking lot attendant interviewed by *The Christian Science Monitor* put it thus: "These representatives don't do anything for the people. . . . They are all the same, except for Ahmadinejad. He's helped most of the people, and solves their problems."[21]

PROSPECTS FOR DEMOCRACY

Looking at the end of the Cold War, thinkers like Francis Fukuyama, author of *The End of History*, have spoken of a world in which liberal democracy has triumphed, due to the nature of man and the general trajectory of history. But looking at the Middle East one may surmise the opposite—not that liberal democracy has triumphed, but rather, that it has been largely discredited in the minds of millions of Muslims who associate democracy with America and the West, and consequently with heavy-handed intervention in their domestic affairs.

But contemplating Iran and its own trajectory of independence, a different picture emerges, one of a country that has successfully used radical Islamism as a means to achieve that which millions of Arab Muslims have only dreamed about: loosened ties from the West and a historical development on their own terms. In fact, Iranians during the peak of Russia's and Britain's Great Game could hardly have imagined a day when an Iranian ayatollah would stand up to the global powers and proclaim Iran to be "neither East nor West."

Iranian independence has come at a cost, but it has been a product of the country's own design and a source of power that reaches beyond quantifiable military strength or economic activity. But independence from outside powers has also been closely tied with independence of thought and democratic civil society. While the rest of the Muslim Middle East has moved steadily toward uncompromising, Saudi-style Islamism, Iran has continued to hold on to its rationalist tendencies. Reformist newspapers are closed, only to reopen later under different names. Iranian blogs, many of which courageously deal with sensitive topics like freedom of speech and feminism despite constant attempts by the regime to take them offline, have granted the next generation of Iranians a new, increasingly potent voice. Between 2000 and 2006, Internet usage in Iran grew by 2,900 percent, giving Iran 34 percent of the Middle East's total web traffic, a figure that includes Israel and Turkey.

Yet, speaking of *eventual* democracy is not the same as speaking of a *process* of democracy. The early proponents of the Iraq war had a cathartic invasion in mind, one that would allow U.S. military power to bring freedom to millions in one fell swoop. Supporters saw the invasion of Iraq as a process that would help spread democracy across the Middle East, and at the same time undermine anti-American Islamist extremism. Some who qualify their distaste for the war by pointing to the execution of the invasion, and not the inherent idea behind it, in essence support the principle of democratization through force. They cite the fall of Germany in World War II, for example. Yet there are other processes to model, such as the end of communism in Eastern Europe. The chain of events that led to the fall of the Berlin Wall and the liberalization of Europe paint a picture that might prove relevant in Iran, albeit in a less dramatic fashion than anything conjured up by neoconservative idealists or extremist opposition groups in exile.

Gerardo L. Munck and Carol Skalnik Leff have looked at democratization in both Eastern Europe and Latin America as having been comprised of diverse processes. Among ones that have not involved revolutionary change, they cite three models, which they call "reform through rapture," "reform through extrication," and "reform through transaction." The first, which they assign to democratization in Czechoslovakia following the fall of the Berlin Wall in 1989, and Argentina at the close of its military dictatorship following the Falklands War with Great Britain in 1982, took place as a swift and relatively painless transition to democracy. The old elite, who clung to little power, were merely pushed aside as a new democratic government took hold. For the second ("reform through extrication"), the authors point to Hungary as an example of what they call a "negotiated revolution," that is, a transition that was brokered between reform-minded communists and moderate opposition groups.[22]

The third, and by their analyses least confrontational, is "reform through transaction" as was practiced in Poland and Brazil. By far, this is the slowest type of reform. The authors explain: "As in Brazil ... the Polish transition began when incumbent elites allowed a marginal opening that undermined the *ancien régime*, while retaining sufficient control over the transition process to force anti-incumbent elites to negotiate."[23] In Poland, the leading opposition group *Solidarność* (Solidarity) was founded in 1980, but the downfall of communism did not come until 1989. In Brazil, the change from military dictatorship to democracy began in 1974, but not until 1990 did "Brazil's transition come to an end."[24] To be sure, the authors of the study see a variety of drawbacks with this form of drawn-out reform, including the continued incumbency of old regime elements and the chipping away at reform movements by the old system. So long as the old regime can have a stake in the process of democratization, it can do its best to continuously undermine its political enemies.

In Iran, we can hardly imagine a process much different from Munck's and Skalnik Leff's "reform through transaction." Though the forces of change are now in the air in Iran, change will more than likely come through a drawn-out evolution and not a swift jolt of change. Because of this, current, mostly ageing leaders, will likely cling on to power until death, always keeping a finger on the trigger of repression and an eye toward their own personal safety. Having themselves ordered mass executions following the revolution, the current elite are all too familiar with the dark face of instant regime change. Another important reason to expect transaction reform is the already diverse field of opposition. Political affiliations in Iran come in every shape and size. Like Poland following the reform movement, Iranian reformists are no monolithic movement, and barring another charismatic figure like Mosaddeq or a more powerful Khatami, Iran cannot be expected to lead a coherent charge for dramatic, overnight regime change.

As in Poland, Iranian democratization will have to come in baby steps, at times to the displeasure of Washington and the vast numbers of diaspora Iranians longing to return to their homeland under different political circumstances. But small steps will allow Iran to capitalize on its republican system of government, which includes popularly elected officials at high levels of government, and a youth that comprises most of the country and is eager to rejoin the global community.

CHAPTER 7

THE IRANIAN CRESCENT

The Athenians perceiving all this preparation to be made upon an opinion of their weakness, and desirous to let them see they were deceived ... manned out a hundred galleys, and ... made a show of their strength.
—Thucydides, *History of the Peloponnesian War*[1]

For nation-states, their ability to carry out their designs unimpeded rests on their power capabilities. For Iran, these capabilities are currently significant, but likely to increase, given the country's sheer power potential. Iran's population is young, increasingly educated, and growing. Iran's economy has been mismanaged, but given significant shifts in policy, it could attain impressive magnitudes. Its physical size has played a critical role in its ability to deter potential invasions throughout history, and it will likely continue to do so.

When analyzing how Iran projects its power abroad, we find the Islamic Republic pursuing a grand strategy of regional dominance, or hegemony, and not a blind, religious mission to destroy Israel or simply cause massive death. Terrorist connections are more a symptom of Iran's calculating *Realpolitik* than a wish to merely carry out some Islamist goal. In many ways, Iran's revolutionary idealism has been fading fast since the death of Khomeini in 1989, and save for the slogans, it is now almost nonexistent from the vantage point of the regime. To highlight this, we can compare Iran's support for Sunni terror groups like Hamas in the Palestinian territories, with the apparent shyness it has about supporting anti-Russian Muslim rebels in Chennya. After all, Russia is one of the main suppliers of advanced weapons systems and nuclear know-how to the Islamic Republic. It would be unwise to side with Islamic idealism against such a powerful friend, and Iran understands this.

When speaking of power potential, we can look at various manifestations of it in order to arrive at a clearer picture of a nation's capabilities. Economic and military power, in terms of quantifiable elements such as gross domestic product and armaments are one thing; quite more elusive are concepts such as nationalism, national unity, physical size, and regional political clout, all of which we find in the case of Iran. We can generally speak of Iranian "soft power" as growing in scope and sophistication. No longer can Arab states easily collude against Iran, as most did during the Iran-Iraq war, without any noticeable repercussions. The ability to maintain infrastructural projects in neighboring states like Afghanistan and Iraq, and provide key support for Hezbollah and other terror networks, along with its willingness to unabashedly stand up to the United States and Israel, are all sources of Iranian "soft power" in the neighboring Arab world.

In 2004, King Abdullah II of Jordan warned of a "Shi'i crescent" forming from Iran through Iraq and into Lebanon, essentially undermining the order of the Sunni-dominated governments. It becomes increasingly difficult, from a perspective of power politics, to observe the various Shi'i movements—be they the rise of Hezbollah, the political power of Iranian-backed Shi'is in Iraq, or the agitation by Saudi Arabia's Shi'i minorities—without seeing an Iranian component in the works. Shi'i power, after all, complements Iranian power quite seamlessly. We should speak, therefore, not of a Shi'i crescent, but of an Iranian one.

ECONOMIC POWER

Iran's economic capabilities are far from being fully realized. With the compounding effects of state mismanagement, the impact of U.S. sanctions, and the general global perception of Iran as a politically unstable country, it has been difficult for Iranian homegrown industries to benefit from needed technologies and foreign direct investment. Heavy business regulations, which make hiring difficult, have also contributed to Iran's high unemployment.

Iran has had difficulty tapping its own oil reserves, even as oil constitutes 85 percent of its exports and up to 65 percent of total government income. Its "daily oil output of about 4.2 million barrels is almost one-third below its 1970s-era peak."[2] Yet once pumped, the oil is refined and sold to the people at heavily subsidized prices, leaving a mere 40 percent of its tapped crude for exports, and making Iran a net importer of gasoline. Recent attempts by the oil ministry to develop the southwestern field of Azadegan with Japan fell through. While the Asian country imports 14 percent of its oil from Iran, some believe that U.S. pressures, along with Iran's precarious international position, forced the deal to fall through. This has proven to be just a single instance in a long list of economic blunders by Iran, whose oil production does not yet meet the ceiling set by the Organization of Petroleum Exporting Countries (OPEC). In fact, Iran has sought to lower the OPEC ceiling on oil exports because it can hardly keep up with faulty equipment and leaks that cost the industry upwards of $10 billion per year.

In many ways, however, Iran has sought to make do with what it has by generating its own industrial base, along with increasingly sophisticated military research and development facilities. When needed, Iran has found black-market solutions to anything from arms, to aircraft spare parts. When U.S.-held technologies have been out of reach due to sanctions, Iran has been able to find European equivalents, and just as often, stimulate its own industry and ingenuity to make do with Iranian technology. Iran's GDP (by purchasing power parity) of $570 billion, which is the second highest in the Middle East after Turkey, will continue to be utilized toward furthering Iran's security, given continued instability in the region, and Iran's own strategy of attaining greater influence. Iran's Shahab-3 missile is already capable of reaching Israel; and its Shahab-4 and Shahab-5 models, which are still in development, will be capable of reaching beyond Great Britain, and represent Iran's aspirations to push the envelope of its military capabilities. To be sure, so long as the world community maintains an appetite for oil and petrochemicals, Iran's two largest export segments, the Islamic Republic will be able to quench its own thirst for military grandeur.

In a "cold war" scenario, in which bullets are likely to remain in the chamber, homegrown industrial capacity affects a country's ability to maintain and grow its deterrent capabilities. An educated population that is put to work is one of the most important assets to a nation's security. In fact, Iran's nuclear energy program, slow in the making and far from exemplary, is only the tip of an industrial iceberg that supports Iran's power and regional aims.

WAR-FIGHTING CAPABILITIES

The Iran-Iraq war of 1980–1988 had a lasting impact on Iran's political and economic position. For one, it had a deteriorating effect on the economy, and directly following the war, Iran was forced to dramatically reduce its bloated military expenditures. But the war also allowed Iran the ability to consolidate power internally, and in essence solidified the newly formed revolutionary government's grip on power. While Saddam Hussein aptly calculated that Iran's immediate, postrevolutionary instability would provide one of the only opportunities to overtake the disputed Shatt al-Arab region, his invasion also allowed the Iranian religious leadership (and its trusted Revolutionary Guard) a solid grip on power, effectively cementing the new Iranian republic in place, impeding "political development inside Iran by nearly a decade."[3] Reform and dissent was scrapped in the name of national unity, and as Saddam's scud missiles fell on Tehran, it became increasingly difficult to question the authority of Iran's religious leadership.

Another lasting impact of the war was the clarity of the consequences of Iran's revolutionary rhetoric, and Ayatollah Khomeini's plans to "export the revolution." Arab nations and the United States, once the shah's consummate partner, lined up to help Saddam Hussein in what would otherwise have been a manageable endeavor for Iran, given that it boasted a significantly higher GDP than Iraq, and a population three times that of its Arab adversary. Sanctions made Iran's U.S.-purchased air force dangerously ineffective, as the lack of simple airplane parts grounded squadrons of jet aircraft.

Today, Iran's military inventory reflects both a limitation of its current capabilities as well as its ambitious aims for deterring future attacks. For one, Iran has observed America's war with Saddam's Iraq and learned important lessons about how to defend itself from the sole superpower's forces. The United States, now one of the only nations with the capability and possible interest of carrying out a war with Iran, has found it difficult to war game victorious scenarios that come to terms with the impacts of Iran's missile arsenal as well the Islamic Republic's feared asymmetric warfare capabilities. Concern for Israel's safety, the integrity of Gulf shipping lanes (especially in the narrow Strait of Hormuz), and the possibility of Iranian mobilization of suicide attackers, both in the United States and around the globe, would make any potential war between America and Iran a risky endeavor, at best.

The Islamic Republic's force strength can be divided into conventional military, Revolutionary Guard, and paramilitary forces. The Islamic Revolutionary Guard Corps (IRGC) is largely credited with being the boldest, most capable Iranian force during the Iran-Iraq war, in large part due to its ideological commitment as well as its ability to mobilize large numbers of volunteers. The IRGC was formed as a kind of praetorian guard to prop up the regime against conventional domestic threats, including ethnic separatists.[4] The Iran-Iraq war mobilized it to function as a professional, more elite military that works parallel to the conventional, largely conscripted armed forces. The IRGC maintains a unit called "Qods" ("Jerusalem"), which trains for foreign intelligence and unconventional (and terrorist) warfare. Qods forces are divided regionally into directorates: one for Iraq; another for Lebanon, Israel/Palestine, and Jordan; one for Afghanistan, Pakistan, and India; one for Turkey and the Arabian Peninsula; one for the republics of the former Soviet Union; one for North Africa; and finally, one for Europe and North America.[5]

In terms of Iranian conventional war-fighting capabilities, figures point to an underattended, yet formidable military. Iran has a considerable ground force that is complemented by organized militia elements, many of whom double as enforcers of "Islamic codes" at home. Iran's conventional army comprises over half a million troops, nearly 60 percent of whom are full-time military, and supported by an army reserve of about

350,000. Put into context, we can compare this to Israel's 167,000 active forces and 358,000 reserves, and Saudi Arabia's 124,000 active troops and 20,000 reserves. Iran also maintains over 1,500 battle tanks, 300 combat aircraft, and 600 helicopters. Its conventional and IRGC navies include "3 submarines, 2 corvettes, 3 frigates (armed with anti-ship missiles), 10 missile patrol craft, 7 mine warfare ships, 44 coastal and inshore patrol craft, and 9 amphibious ships,"[6] forty Revolutionary Guard patrol boats, nine landing craft, twenty-three support ships, three mine warfare helicopters, and six RF-4E reconnaissance aircraft, among other elements. Saudi Arabia's air and naval forces are comparable in size to Iran's (currently minus the submarines), but are significantly better kept, with the Kingdom not only free of sanction restrictions like those imposed on Iran by the United States, but also able to outspend Iran year by year more than a dozen times over. But there are limitations to the numbers game. Of the problems with attempting to quantify power, Anthony H. Cordesman of the Center for Strategic and International Studies writes:

> Aside from the many uncertainties inevitable in trying to quantify what every government in the region does its best to conceal, no one can predict what element of a given nation's forces will be used in a given scenario or conflict. Quantitative balances do not apply to many aspects of the asymmetric wars in the region, or . . . the capabilities of extremist, guerrilla, or terrorist groups.[7]

The size of a country's population can play an important role in defining power relationships, but this metric also has limitations, and does not automatically point to a given nation's ability to effectively or quickly mobilize a competent fighting force. A case in point is Israel, a country that has been able to cope with numerous wars against coalitions of Arab countries, each with a population several times that of its own. David C. Rapoport of UCLA writes of Israel as a nation-at-arms, which, like the neutral but surprisingly powerful Switzerland, has "on occasion mobilized one-eight of [its] inhabitants in forty-eight hours."[8] The effect of this mass mobilization is compounded by the central role played by the military in the nation-at-arms' social and educational framework. Militancy becomes a part of life, and like the ancient city-states of Sparta and Athens, a small nation-at-arms is designed to fight to the last person, thus compensating for any population disparity.

However, population cannot be entirely dismissed when speaking of a protracted conflict. There is a question as to the viability of Israel's conventional forces in the event of a prolonged war, and Israel's foes have understood this. When speaking of the strategic value of the War of Attrition (1968–1970) between Egypt and Israel, Egyptian journalist Muhammad Heikal wrote: "If the enemy succeeds in inflicting on us 50,000 casualties in this campaign, we can go on fighting nevertheless, because we have manpower reserves. If we succeed in inflicting 10,000 casualties, he will unavoidably find himself compelled to stop fighting, because he has no manpower reserves."[9] It is worth noting that Iran has such manpower reserves as it is projected to have, by 2025, one of the highest populations in the Middle East, second only to Egypt.

Importantly, Iran's nationalistic unity, which cuts through much of its ethnic and religious diversity, was eagerly exploited by revolutionary leaders during the Iran-Iraq war. Vast numbers were sent to the front without proper arms or training, and some were expected to pick up rifles from dead soldiers, and even detonate land mines for the company behind them. Although misused, the eagerness with which volunteers came to the Iraqi front cannot be overestimated, and that same population under siege, given proper resources and training, could be expected to mount a significant defense force.

ASYMMETRIC WARFARE

Asymmetric warfare is the art of turning a negative power disparity into one's advantage. During the Vietnam War, the Viet Cong was able to inflict significant American casualties by engaging in hit-and-run tactics, and thus avoid engaging U.S. forces directly. And while the North Vietnamese were in fact capable of fighting in conventional warfare, it was the dragged-out fight that eventually forced the economically and militarily superior United States to withdraw. In many ways, the essence of asymmetric warfare is the psychological impact it can bear on the militarily superior enemy, who, more often than not, has much more to lose from the endeavor.

The American War of Independence also used asymmetric war to the colonies' advantage. Hit-and-run tactics, sabotage, and terror campaigns by the Sons of Liberty helped weaken British and Loyalist morale, eventually contributing to America's independence. For our purposes, the word "terrorist," while a loaded, emotionally laden term, can be described as a nonstate actor inflicting civilian casualties for a strategic political aim. While other definitions exist, such as those referring to "state terrorism," it becomes more difficult to utilize the word in such contexts, and can quickly turn into a game of subjectivity. Terrorism, for our aims, is used to define nonstate groups such as Hamas, the Palestinian Islamic Jihad (PIJ), and the Lebanese Hezbollah, all of which receive material and technical assistance from the Islamic Republic of Iran. While these groups employ a clear religious identity, their goals can be associated with specific political disputes within a given territory. This puts them in a different category from al-Qaeda, a terrorist group whose aims are much more difficult to define, given their global scope and overtly Salafi aims. To many, al-Qaeda resembles nothing more than a mass-murder enterprise.[10]

Without a doubt, terrorist actors have been effectively employed by post-1979 Iran. Given the relative isolation that the Islamic Republic has created for itself through its stark nonalignment policy, nonstate actors have proven to be a useful tool. These groups provide Iran with a negotiating card, a vehicle to gain legitimacy in the Arab street, as well as a practical extension of its military might. In critical negotiations, Iran can use its beneficiary groups to gain concessions, or otherwise hint that, given the right set of circumstances, Iran can altogether cease to support terrorism. The former example is perhaps best exemplified during the Iran-Contra affair, where members of the Reagan administration secretly sold weapons to Iran during its war with Iraq, in return for Iran's help in releasing Hezbollah-held hostages in Lebanon. While none of the groups mentioned here take direct orders from Tehran—they are independently managed, self-interested groups—Iran's material, logistical, and technical support does grant the Islamic Republic some degree of influence. In the example of Hezbollah, it is not uncommon for Lebanese militia fighters to venerate the likes of Ayatollah Khomeini, as a political leader and as an important Shi'i mujtahid. As for the "carrot" that Iran can use by promising to cease all support of terrorism, this very thing has been proposed by the Iranian government, only to be turned down by the United States on the basis that the president who proposed it, Mohammad Khatami, wasn't powerful enough to carry out his promise.

As previously mentioned, Iran's support for nonstate groups also aids that country's aim to garner support in the Arab street. Given the disparity between hatred for Israel by the "moderate" Arab populations, and the actions of their leaders—which can include dialogue and mutual assistance with Israel—Iran surfaces as a kind of uncompromising figure, not only unwilling to recognize Israel as a state, but also actively fighting it. The July 2006 war between the Lebanese Hezbollah and Israel garnered significant public support in the Arab streets, as did President Ahmadinejad, who bluntly embraced the kind of anti-Israeli language that Arab heads of state had abandoned long ago. All this happened while concerned Arab leaders were looking for constructive ways to limit Iran's nuclear program, without seeming like they were selling out to Israel and the United States.

A third application of terrorist actors by Iran is the mere extension of its military infrastructure. This is especially the case with Hezbollah, which was founded by Iran during the Lebanese civil war as a Shi'i fundamentalist fighting unit. Arguably, it was Hezbollah that brought suicide terrorism to the Middle East and first employed it as an effective political tool. The 1983 bombing of the U.S. Marines headquarters in Lebanon, which killed 241 service members and forced President Reagan to withdraw peacekeeping troops, underscored the veracity with which terrorism could impact the realities of the war theater. The July war, in which Hezbollah employed a vast array of rockets and Iranian-provided anti-tank missiles, only serves to remind policy planners in Israel and abroad of the idea that elements trained and supplied by the Iranian military are much closer to home than Iran's western border.

Some have placed Iranian assistance of Hezbollah "between $10 million to $20 million a month."[11] Professor Ahmad Bakhshaiesh of Tehran's Azadi University puts it thus: "Iran sees itself as more than just the moral father of Hezbollah. Iran seeks to become a major force across the region as a counterbalance to America and Israel."[12] Of the scope of Iran's support for Hezbollah, Richard Russell of the National Defense University writes:

> Syria acts as a conduit for Iranian supplies to Hezbollah. Tehran in 1982 deployed a 1,500-man contingent of the Iranian Revolutionary Guard Corps to Baalbak, Lebanon that organized, trained, supplied and supported Hezbollah and although Iran in the 1990s reduced its IRGC presence in Lebanon to about 150 fighters, Iranian-Hezbollah ties remain strong.[13]

Domestically, Iran also employs militia elements to maintain political order. These militias are radical and loyal to the regime, and they help enforce dress codes and other protocols related to religious conduct. They are mostly staffed by young men of impoverished families, left behind by Iran's systemic unemployment, and often disdainful of the more well-off and liberal elements of the Iranian educated class. The most notable militias are the *Basij* ("Mobilization") and *Ansar-e Hezbollah* ("Helpers of the Party of God"), a force that assumed for itself "the responsibility of 'cleansing' the cities from moral and political corruption, in the name of war veterans" of the Iran-Iraq conflict.[14]

THE "IRANIAN CRESCENT"

Given the proportionally higher Shi'i populations in the countries termed by King Abdullah II as part of a "Shi'i Crescent," along with U.S.-backed movements toward democratic "one person, one vote" representation, Shi'ism in recent years has become a central concern for the Sunni-dominated Middle East, if only out of fears that greater representation of the minority faith will benefit Iran politically. After all, Iran is the only country with such an overwhelming Shi'i majority (89 percent), and to a degree it is seen as a de facto figurehead of the faith. In hopes of slowing Iran's rise and mitigating its effects on local Shi'i communities, the Saudis have even initiated talks with the Lebanese Hezbollah.

From a perspective of international relations, however, we find limitations in trying to look at Shi'ism itself—a religion—as the main focus in examining the rising power of Iran. We can more specifically speak of an "Iranian Crescent"—a manifestation of Iranian grand strategy that seeks to put Tehran in a position of regional leadership, even regional hegemony. State power, after all, has been and will continue to be a critical component in analyzing the Middle East. While fundamentalist Sunni Islam and fundamentalist Shi'ism have sprung up in different countries, utilizing different aims, it is often through the work of specific governments that such fundamentalist streaks play out in neighboring countries. That is, while we can hope to imagine random, uncoordinated manifestations of Shi'i identity, we cannot discount the care that Iran has taken in seeking to export its revolution following Khomeini's consolidation of power. Needless to say, this exportation is less connected to piety and doctrinal issues, and more to the real political isolation of Iran, and the need to find ways of bypassing political encirclement by its Sunni neighbors.

Saudi Arabia too, has sought to export its own Sunni Wahhabi approach through the funding of fundamentalist schools in places like Pakistan, the publication of its Salafi Qur'anic translations across the globe, and most infamously, its political support of the Taliban regime of Afghanistan during the 1990s. And while not all roads of fundamentalist Sunni Islam lead to Saudi Arabia, the concerted effort with which the Saudi government and religious establishment have sought to export their version of Islam cannot be discounted. Just as we can remember that the Crusades were tied to very real political goals on the part of both the European kingdoms and the Muslims who fought against them, we can allow ourselves to be cynical in our interpretation of present activities, and see religious manipulation for what it is. In the end, we must remember that while sectarian and political differences make natural friends and enemies, and doctrinal associations might be paramount in an individual's world view, state interests cannot be ruled out of any equation when crafting foreign policy.

The funding of opposition groups, both religious and secular, can also be observed in the general trend of foreign policies adopted by the countries of the region. Neighbors have continuously engaged in the financial, logistical, and political support of opposition groups in adjacent countries. Landmark examples are Syria's support for Kurdish guerrillas in neighboring Turkey, and Saddam's support for the Iranian Mojahedeen. Conversely, Iran continued to support Shi'i opposition to Saddam Hussein until the dictator's fall. This support for Iraqi Shi'is has only increased with their rise to power in Baghdad following the U.S. invasion of 2003, with instances of Shi'i militias receiving arms from Iran, and training in Hezbollah-held parts of Lebanon.[15]

We can also point to Shi'i uprisings in Bahrain not only supported by the Islamic Republic, but with roots based on Iranian irredentist claims that date back well before 1979. With a Shi'i population of over 70 percent, Bahrain has been the center of a hush competition between Saudi Arabia and Iran, with the former providing significant economic support to the island state in the hope of essentially buying off its political ties and having it turn its back on Tehran. A U.S. Department of Energy report explains that Saudi Arabia

> produces oil jointly with Bahrain, from the Abu Saafa offshore oilfield. As a way of supporting their neighbor's economy, since 1996 the field's Saudi administrators had donated all of the income from its 150,000 bbl/d [barrels per day] of production to Bahrain. However, in late 2004, with output from Abu Saafa doubling to 300,000 bbl/d, the Saudis apparently reduced this share to 50 percent. In addition, Bahrain traditionally has received around 50,000 bbl/d of Saudi oil from other fields, apparently at a significant discount.[16]

But if Iran has its sights on Bahrain, it certainly has an interest in the political development of neighboring Afghanistan. In September 1996, following the Taliban's capture of Afghanistan's capital, Kabul, the fundamentalist Sunni militia seized and executed a group of Iranian diplomats, prompting Iran to amass its troops along the Afghan border, in what could have escalated into all-out war. Following the U.S. overthrow of the Taliban, Iran has seized the opportunity to bring stability to its neighbor, seeking to keep the Taliban permanently out, and lessen its own burden of Afghan refuges domestically. Consequently, today's Sunni Afghan government is a recipient of critical aid by the Islamic Republic, which has paved roads, built schools, and provided infrastructure, all while working on relatively constructive terms with the United States in that country. In essence, Iran has been "employing American cold-war tactics to increase its soft power in the region,"[17] and perhaps most effectively in neighboring Afghanistan than anywhere else.

One of the more elusive, but nevertheless critical sources of Iranian influence in the region has been its ability to act entirely independently of superpower interests following the 1978–1979 revolution. If we can speak of independence, and indeed, legitimacy, as a source of power in itself, Iran has fought for this power during centuries of struggles to free itself from foreign intervention. Few countries in the region can be said to act entirely independently of others. The countries of the Gulf Cooperation Council (GCC), though maintaining sophisticated militaries, largely depend on America's security umbrella to deter potential external threats, especially following Iraq's invasion of Kuwait in 1990 and America's consequent strengthening of its military presence in the Gulf. In fact, the GCC is more capable as an instrument to deter revolutionary activity within its member states, than an alliance poised to fight a concerted military effort.

Turkey, as a member of NATO (and which also seeks European Union membership), played a critical role during the Cold War as part of the Western front against the Soviet Union. In essence, its foreign policy was directed by Euro-American aims. Israel too, largely dependant on U.S. and European aid for its military and economic well-being, could not afford to sever ties with its benefactors. Perhaps Iran, as a nation that in the words of Ayatollah Khomeini is "neither East nor West," is best poised to maintain a leadership role among strong and growing anti-Western elements in the Middle East. While its Shi'i identity is a source of concern and even fear among the largely Sunni region, Iran's capacity for free agency in foreign policy has put it in a unique position to express its interests from a position of authority.

"WAR IS HELL"

One can only imagine what war might look like between Iran and other actors in the region. As Saudis have made it clear to the U.S. administration, an American withdrawal from Iraq could force Saudi Arabia into that country, if only to protect the Sunni minority. This could potentially bring about a direct confrontation between Iranian-backed Shi'is and Saudi-backed Sunnis. Given such a scenario, total, direct war between Saudi Arabia and Iran would become a frightening possibility. Such a war in many ways would be the most destructive of any scenario, as oilfields would likely become the immediate target on both sides, touching off an unprecedented global energy crisis. This would not only mean higher gasoline prices, but noticeable shortages, keeping goods and people stranded en masse, as cars, freight trucks, and airplanes would be grounded. Millions would be left without food or electricity, potentially creating a long-lasting global recession, as oil futures contracts would remain painfully high years after the end of the conflict.

To prevent this, other actors, including the United States, would have to either completely align themselves with the Saudis in the effort, or step up diplomacy to bring about an immediate end to the conflict. Significant promises would have to be made to both countries, since militarily punishing Iran beyond the pale would still leave the world's second largest oil reserve (after Saudi Arabia) untapped for a significant period of time. If the two sides were left alone to fight it out (a most unlikely scenario), Iran would likely win the conflict, given its greater naval and naval air power capabilities.

As for a war between Israel and Iran, this endeavor would make use of strategic targeting, using aircraft and missiles as the weapons of choice. Ground forces could not easily meet each other on the battlefield, and any and all forces approaching Israel would have to pass through Iraq, which could, for some time, continue to house American troops. Syria could be quickly pulled into the battle on the side of Iran, as it could use this as the only opportunity to regain the disputed Golan Heights by force, and would be generally seen as a combatant by Israel as soon as Syria were to allow Iranian aircraft to use its airspace to reach Israel. Of course, Israel would hold two important cards: the United States, and its nuclear arsenal. Should the former enter the fray, Israel would gain an invaluable tactical advantage, with a barrage of sea-launched missiles and aircraft sent by the United States against the Iranian defense infrastructure.

In the event of gross escalation, the question naturally arises of whether Israel's nuclear arsenal would remain on the table. A short answer is that it is unlikely that Israel would use such a weapon lightly, even if it were involved in a challenging conflict. The 1973 Yom Kippur War is a historic example of Israel's (and its enemies') care in handling the prospects of an Israeli nuclear strike. Neither Egypt nor Syria aimed to destroy Israel in this conflict; rather, they were seeking to redeem lands lost during the 1967 Six-Day War, along with their prestige. Israel understood this and refrained from using the ultimate weapon. (Yet the presence of Soviet troops inside Arab territory during that conflict makes it impossible to know whether deterrence played a bigger role than self-restraint.)[18]

To be sure, Israel would lose significantly from the use of such an arsenal. Victory on those terms (which might include the destruction of Tehran, and with it, the dissolution of the Iranian state as we know it) would open up a never-ending international movement seeking total Israeli disarmament on the basis of genocide—a charge that would sadly be justified in this case. The use of tactical nuclear weapons against forces advancing through Iraq or Syria would also be incredible, if anything, because of potential problems with radioactive fallout. Any conventional attack against Iranian infrastructure, however, would likely invite American involvement at least similar in scope to the July 2006 war with Lebanon, in which the United States became part of Israel's weapons supply line, and provided needed logistical support. But, as Gary G. Sick of Columbia University points out, sending "the U.S. to war with Iran against its will is not something many Israeli leaders would be willing to do."[19]

In a war involving Iran and the United States as the main combatants, it is not simple to imagine an easily manageable outcome for America. For one, Iran would quickly pull regional actors into the fray, using its missiles to target Israeli cities or Saudi oilfields. It could also blockade oil-shipping lanes in the Strait of Hormuz, a two-mile wide stretch through which about 40 percent of the world's oil supply passes. Iran could call on its international operatives to hit targets in the United States and elsewhere, generating homegrown casualties, and possibly economic problems, while escalating an already tense relationship between Muslim Americans and the greater U.S. population. Iran's nationalism too would limit the feasibility of any U.S. ground operation, as citizens' brigades would fight any invasion in a manner reminiscent of the human wave attacks of the Iran-Iraq war.

In many ways foreshadowing the circumstances presented by Iran's support of militant activity in Iraq today, a 1980 CIA memo laid out what the agency saw as the Iranian regime's reasoning for providing support for anti-Soviet insurgents in Afghanistan following the 1979 invasion by the communist superpower. The Iranian revolutionary government, the memo explained, calculated that the Soviets would not retaliate against its country, since "invading Soviet forces would face heavy casualties from Iran's numerous paramilitary groups and massive civil unrest from a population versed in the tactics of mass protest."[20]

The upside of such an attempt by the United States today, if any can be imagined, is that if and when the United States were to ultimately prove successful in reaching the capital before quitting the costly operation, "winning the peace" might prove much easier in Iran than it did in Iraq. After all, the same national unity that would make any invasion perilous would also help the country get back on its feet more quickly after defeat. The kind of sectarian violence that brought Iraq into a civil war would not be a concern in Iran, whose national identity cannot be diminished to simple sectarian, ethnic, or even tribal lines. Postbellum conflict would take the form of political factions, with secular Mojahedeen, Marxists, and Islamists fighting each other, but this would hardly be a genocidal enterprise. Political reconciliation would always remain on the table.

In the end, however, such a conflict would only do away with the relative and welcome pro-Americanism that exists in Iran today. An invasion would reset the clock on Iran's trajectory of independence, and the anti-Western sentiments that were fomented for over a century of foreign power intervention would come back with a vengeance. As is predicted by most experts, and has been shown during Israel's conflict in Lebanon, air strikes would not bring about the regime change that many hawks in the United States desire. Iranian citizens, as they have before, would rally around their country and flag, and any form of civil disobedience would be crushed with the ruthlessness of wartime powers. In the case of a war, the development of Iranian democracy would only be further delayed. A young, highly educated Iranian said it most clearly: "I hate the regime more than anything, and I love the United States. But if the United States drops bombs on us, I will join hands with the regime. This is exactly what my government wants and it's what America should avoid."[21]

The question remains as to whether a stronger Iran—something that in large part is unavoidable—is necessarily antithetical to U.S. interests. It is no secret that state power and despotism can limit the ability of illegitimate, nonstate activities like terrorism. Saddam's Iraq was no playground for terrorists, though it has become exactly that following the U.S. invasion and the consequent collapse of the Iraqi state. A strong Iran, willing to exercise a heavy-handed foreign policy, could potentially benefit the United States in its war on terrorist extremists. Just as a Hezbollah-led terrorist response is feared as a potential retaliatory measure by Iran in case of a U.S. attack on suspected nuclear sites, by that same logic, Iran could help limit the maneuverability, funding, and overall effectiveness of organizations it has helped to establish and train. To be sure, Iran's support for terrorist movements will continue so long as Iran remains internationally isolated. And while this isolation is of Iran's own making, the warming of relations between Iran and the West would mark a turning point in the so-far failed democratization process in the region, as it would represent homegrown progress in a Middle Eastern state, one void of allegations of U.S. or European puppetry, and capable of providing its own security, and on its own terms.

So long as Iran continues on its current course, nations like Russia and China, which will seek to curb uncontested American power, will continue to do business with Iran, not only because Iran has oil, but more importantly, in order to prevent the United States from having its way.[22] Because Iran will play an increasingly powerful role in this critical region it can make itself out to be either helpful or harmful to the world's sole superpower, and any of its global rivals in the making.

PART III

A NEW POLICY

CHAPTER 8

DEVISING A GRAND STRATEGY: LESSONS FROM THE NIXON DOCTRINE

The best servants of the people, like the best valets, must whisper unpleasant truths in the master's ear. It is the court fool, not the foolish courtier, whom the king can least afford to lose.

—Walter Lippmann

Détente, the French word meaning "relaxation," refers really only to that process by which tensions between states are eased. Détente, in and of itself, is not tantamount to peace anymore that a cease-fire is an alliance treaty. If anything, détente acts as a go-between, separating a mere absence of war in the face of possible hostilities, from actual, lasting peace.

We saw détente play out in the Cold War, not only in connection to U.S.-Russian relations, but more effectively in dealings between China and the United States. Today, America and China are still in an era of détente, long after the dust of the Cold War has settled. That is, the United States and China are still perceived as natural competitors, engaging in what some see as a temporary truce, facilitated by a mutually lucrative trade relationship, while little has been done to quell political hostility—in the form of State Department allegations of human rights abuses, and China's frequent military exercises in the Taiwan straights.

It is perhaps only the populist, protectionist movements in America that explicitly cite the serious concerns that any realist would have over China's increased power potential. While the cries against outsourcing and growing trade deficits with China have come largely from marginal groups in American society, the prospects of reaching a point in which American supremacy is directly challenged by China become less distant as the Asian country grows in strength and ambition. This very dilemma underscores the limitations of détente.

Some say that the Soviet invasion of Afghanistan, and America's subsequent support of anti-Soviet Afghan forces, reigned in the end of détente between the United States and the USSR. But détente, as a mechanism for relaxing tensions, can only be defined in the narrowest of ways. The absence of direct war was the most the superpowers could hope for in the heydays of the Cold War. After all, mutually assured destruction was seen as a possible alternative outcome in a war between the United States and the Soviet Union. A mere relaxation of tensions, not outright peace, was the best possible option, given the choices present.

In today's unipolar world—one that has not yet been directly challenged by rival powers such as China or the European Union—America is allowed the comfort of not fearing its total destruction. No scenario, even the most pessimistic, such as a group of nuclear-armed terrorists attacking the American homeland, could result in the total destruction of the American state. Presently, of highest concern to this superpower is not the Armageddon-style conflict between two titanic rivals, but the continuing erosion of American power over the long term, forcing the United States to retreat—militarily, economically, or otherwise—from parts of the world previously under its support and influence. This casual chipping away at supremacy could allow rival powers to step up their efforts and gain a wider reach in the world. Not only China, but also the European Union and other "benign" powers could play the role of America's geostrategic rival, given a large enough vacuum of influence or political presence left by today's superpower in the twenty-first century. Historically, such systemic changes in the world have been associated with chaos and carnage. Most recently, such a power struggle was played out in World War II between the rising powers of Japan, Germany, the United States, and the Soviet Union, amidst the backdrop of Britain's and France's declining global reach.

In today's unipolar world, the United States must revisit the notion of how it commits itself to military and diplomatic hot zones. Overreaching could be disastrous, as it would invite the kind of bold rivalry associated with a global power vacuum. If the war in Iraq does not itself prove the damage that can be done by trying to overemphasize the effectiveness of purely military means, one need only imagine another war front opening tomorrow. Could America sustain another protracted, troop-intensive military endeavor, given the fact that it must operate under real economic and political constraints? How many more troops can America commit to conflicts that are not essential to its survival? If the United States needs to maintain an active presence in the world and keep other potential rivals from rising to the occasion of a power vacuum, then it must be poised to better manage world conflicts within its budget of current resources and political capital. The United States must be resourceful in order remain strong.

Détente, the mere absence of war, is not enough for America to maintain its position in the world. A significant degree of peace must exist between key international players and the United States. While diminishing the likelihood that a state will too aggressively pursue a challenge of dominance against this country, the effect of this peace with key states can go far beyond that. If America is to revisit the tenets of the Nixon Doctrine, which allows for "regional policemen" to exercise leadership in specific areas, this might serve as the recipe for continued American supremacy. In fact, it is difficult to conceive another approach that would allow the United States not to be charged with "policing" the entire world at all times, and also help define the boundaries with which states could enjoy influence, and within which they could grow in power. In a perfect Nixon Doctrine world, those allied with America as regional leaders would not seek to overstep their boundaries or reach beyond their natural spheres of influence.

From a strategic vantage point, the Nixon Doctrine is the essential outsourcing of America's commitments around the world. One of the least venerable legacies of this doctrine was the passivity with which it forced the United States to treat human rights violations on the part of its allies. Under this doctrine, America turned a blind eye to the actions of corrupt political actors (notably the shah's Iran), all in the name of anticommunist policy.

Some observers have suggested that the Nixon Doctrine itself led to America's current difficulties in the Gulf by overemphasizing America's role in the region and inviting retaliatory action, in the form of the Iranian Revolution and eventually terrorism. But the shortcomings of the Nixon Doctrine, in the framework of the Cold War's *Realpolitik*, do not point to what are necessarily inherent flaws of the regional security apparatus. Instead, they point to a Cold War that was often waged with a myopic mindset, all too often blinded by an exaggerated and simplistic understanding of the Soviet threat as monolithic and omnipresent. Yet today, given the limited resources of the American military (relative to the heydays of the Cold War), the establishment of close, mutually beneficial relationships with leader states should be reconsidered. This could be an especially attractive approach if the regional states at hand meet certain critical benchmarks for allegiance.

Given the current problem of fulfilling American leadership gaps in the globe, these benchmarks should logically revolve around the notion of limited appetite for expansion. That is, any country too focused on what could be construed as destructive regional ambitions, cannot be given the support—political or material—that would allow it to engage in wars of conquest. Saddam's Iraq, for that very reason, would not have fit this bill. Neither would most other countries in the Middle East, mired by incessant domestic struggles and the Arab-Israeli wars of the twentieth century, which not only sought to mobilize coalitions of armies against a single nation, but openly sought to annihilate it.

In the case of Iran, concern for any sort of military expansionism would be unfounded. Iran's capacity for growth cannot be expected to be in the exponential and gargantuan levels of a China, and it would gain little in attempting the occupation of culturally and linguistically distinct Arab populations. As the United States, Ottoman Turkey, and European colonial powers have seen, occupying or otherwise coercing Middle Eastern populations into submission is no easy task. To its credit, Iran has not invaded a neighbor at any time in its modern history.

Another important precondition for close alignment with a regional power under a new Nixon Doctrine would be a certain level of sociopolitical compatibility. One of the most tarnishing legacies of the Cold War victory was the trail of graves left by dictators once supported by American endeavors throughout the world. It is important to note that waging *Realpolitik* in a post-September 11 world must essentially mean winning a war for the hearts and minds of people around the globe, especially those of Muslims. Because the post-September 11 struggle is not against a state or other entity with finite military or economic resources, it is crucial that more enemies are not created in the process of attempting to win the conflict. As neoconservatives have rightly suggested, democracy does matter in these times, and any state closely aligning itself with the United States should be expected to meet certain criteria of political development toward democracy.

Iran can and most likely will meet these criteria. As we have seen, it is likely that Iran will not only grow in military power, but also continue on a path of further democratization—a trajectory of independence at its own pace, and on its own terms. Should trends continue, the effectively pro-American youth that is to inherit the country's political leadership can also be expected to employ the republican establishments put in place by the victors of the revolution of 1978–1979 in the spirit of popular participation. As more power is taken away from the supreme leader and put in the hands of elected officials, a culture of popular democracy is not only a possibility, but a likelihood.

GRAND STRATEGIES AMUCK

The attacks of September 11 reignited a debate among policymakers and the public regarding the level to which the promotion of democracy should play a role in U.S. foreign policy. The terror attacks undercut much of the progress made during Bill Clinton's presidency toward a neoliberal philosophy of globalization. "Liberalism," as an international relations theory (not necessarily related to the "liberalism" of U.S. Democrats) promotes economic interdependence among nations as a strategy for peace. By fostering economic ties, liberal theory suggests, nations are forced to work together, if only in the name of profound economic interests.

We can point to President Clinton's China trade policy as a means for the United States to establish greater security under a liberal framework, while developing its competitive role in a new, market-driven global environment. The 1990s brought America significant growth and post–Cold War cooperation with former adversaries, most notably Russia. America's GDP grew by $2.76 trillion (adjusted for inflation) between 1994 and 2000.[1] During the Clinton era, global security concerns would amount to localized ethnic conflict, such as the Bosnia and Kosovo crises and the Rwanda genocide—tragic chapters in human history, but undeniably lacking a global context. The world, in fact, seemed to be moving from the imperial tendencies of alliance and intervention that characterized the Cold War, toward independence and fractionized endeavors. Yugoslavia broke apart, and many of the former Soviet republics, countries such as Kazakhstan, Georgia, Azerbaijan, and even the Ukraine, set out on a path away from Russia and into the arms of the global marketplace, with America at the helm.

But not everyone was singing the praises of globalization as it stood, and less so under the banner of peace through interdependence and liberalism. "Realists," those ascribing to a different theoretical framework, saw the increasing power of countries like China as a source of concern. For realists, a zero-sum game always lurks—that which one side gains the other invariably loses. For a true realist, China's economic boom as a result of its acceptance into the World Trade Organization, and its consequent ability to increase military spending and play a greater role in the Western hemisphere, would at the very least raise flags of concern.

Neoconservatives, who espoused a blend of hawkish conservatism, liberal thought, and an added emphasis on cultural dynamics, were also hardly silent during the 1990s. For them, the liberal part of the recipe was not merely about peace through economic interdependency, but rather peace through democracy. Taken beyond the liberal mindset of forming a "natural alliance" of democratic nations, which holds that in essence democracies do not go to war with each other, the neoconservatives saw democracy as a reality that could be imposed on a nation, even through violence, as became evident with the pre- and post-September 11 public relations campaign to wage war on Iraq.[2] In international relations theory jargon, neoconservatives are closer to the theory of "constructivism." Though many progressive constructivist thinkers would balk at this, neoconservatives share their concern with looking *inside* nations—cultural tendencies, social problems, and even religion—rather than merely focusing on relations *between* countries.

To Lisa Anderson, former dean of Columbia University's School of International and Public Affairs, then-U.S. National Security Adviser Condoleezza Rice seemed to have changed her theoretical stance from that of a realist, to one of a constructivist following the attacks of September 11.[3] But this shouldn't come as a surprise. The Bush administration saw the entrance of leading neoconservative thinkers to the forefront of U.S. policymaking. The vindication they seemed to receive after 9/11 in relation to their emphasis on culture, religion, and other internal dynamics only gave them more power within the White House. Militant Islam, after all, had been behind these attacks, whose apparent motivation seemed to fly in the face of conventional wisdom about power relationships and reasons of state. If a group of terrorists could penetrate American territory to inflict mass casualties on innocent people, could the economic interdependence of liberal policy, or even the deterrence-based strategies of realism, still be seen as adequate? Or would the twenty-first century see a "clash of civilizations," in the words of prominent political scientist Samuel Huntington, who put religious and cultural identity at the forefront of a new global conflict?[4]

In March 2003, the Iraq war, a conflict that was envisioned and promoted well before September 11 by key neoconservative thinkers, was set in motion. The impetus for the war rested on the concept of a reverse domino effect. Just like the "Domino Theory," espoused by President Eisenhower, envisioned nations as a series of dominos that would fall under Soviet influence, as communism in one land spread to another, the neoconservatives who fashioned the Iraq war could foresee a democratic movement, initiated by an American invasion, that would show the populations of the Middle East the possibilities of democracy. Dictators would fall, and Israel and America could relish in their newfound security.

But we can borrow further from Cold War jargon. During much of the Cold War, U.S. policymakers systematically spoke of a "Sino-Soviet bloc," an alliance between China and the Soviet Union that existed mostly in the imaginations of State Department bureaucrats and White House staffers. This monolithic view of communism also led to the perception that Ho Chi Minh's movement in Vietnam was a piece of the greater communist puzzle. Yet the Vietnam War, now largely understood as an extension of Ho Chi Minh's war of independence with France and not a product of Soviet communist expansion, has once again come to the forefront of America's policy discussions, as the war in Iraq rages on. This war in Iraq, like the misperceptions of communism during the Cold War, was predicated on an imagined connection between Saddam Hussein and al-Qaeda.

Leading up to the Iraq war, Vice President Dick Cheney continuously spoke of a link between the Iraqi regime and the terrorist organization that masterminded the attacks of September 11. The vice president, indeed the entire public relations machine of the Bush administration, sought to make the distinction between the Iraqi government and al-Qaeda nebulous, even nonexistent. While some have suggested this was part of a larger plan of deception upon the American people, we should also keep in mind that many of the neoconservatives themselves saw an uninterrupted continuum of anti-American Muslim political actors in the Middle East and around the world.[5] How could one expect the White House to publicly explain the major differences between countries, religious sects, and interests, let alone the intricacies of political philosophical differences, if most high-level officials themselves were seemingly oblivious to them? A crude reality for a country that prides itself in its sensitivities toward ethnic diversity, America seemed to perceive all Muslims in the wake of the September 11 as a uniform mass of anti-Americanism.

The main public rationale for the war centered on Iraq's alleged pursuit (and possession) of "weapons of mass destruction" (WMD). This too was an argument based on a general misunderstanding of unconventional weapons. Most persuasive was the doomsday scenario of Saddam Hussein lending a nuclear weapon to terrorists. Again, there was a genuine feeling that since Saddam was an anti-American Arab ruler, his obvious next step after proliferation would be to share his new arsenal with other anti-American Arabs. Not only a racist proposition, this is a logically flawed assumption, one that hardly should have made the grade as a driver for U.S. national security policy. Did reasons of state no longer matter? Would a police state under the watchful thumb of Saddam Hussein give up that which it would have fought so hard to gain—the ultimate WMD; handing it over to terrorists who would have no inclination to avoid the destruction of Iraq through a nuclear reprisal by the United States? For reasons that defy logic, the architects of the Iraq war seemed to think exactly that.

As for dealing with the generally murky perception of America's new threat in this new war on terror, the neoconservatives made a policy prescription based on a hardly new proposition: that the promotion of democracy should be the grand strategy. This promotion of democracy could come in many forms: diplomatic, economic, and even military. In Iraq, a central test case of the neoconservative grand strategy, democracy was expected to grow out of the barrel of a gun.

Many have referred to Iraq as a "preventive" or even "pre-emptive" military effort. A pre-emptive war, one that hardly fits the Iraq case, is that of a strike carried out before the enemy can carry out its own. An example of this is the Six-Day War of 1967, fought between Israel on one side, and Egypt, Jordan, Syria, and Iraq on the other. Arab powers had been amassing their forces along the Israeli border while their rhetoric was intensifying in hostility and war was all but certain. Israel attacked first, in preemptive fashion. As Richard Betts of Columbia University's Institute of War and Peace Studies says, a pre-emptive war is like two cowboys are facing each other at high noon, and one draws before the other and shoots. A *preventive* war, on the other hand, would amount to walking up to a cowboy in a saloon while he's playing cards and shooting him point blank in the head. In other words, preventive war seeks the early elimination of a potential future adversary.[6]

Yet the Iraq war as a purely preventive endeavor is also problematic, if only because of the nature of neoconservative grand strategy. While much was assumed about Iraqi intent and future weapons capabilities (as well as the future intent to share those capabilities with terrorists), the Iraq war contained a more complicated dimension, that of *conversion*. In all practicality, the Iraq war was part of a campaign to *convert* the people of Iraq into democrats. An ideology, rather than merely a perceived future strategic threat, was at issue. Democracy building, after all, was the grand strategy of the war on terror. Like a war of religious conversion, the assumption was that once a nation is converted to one's ideology, the attacked could be counted on to join in alliance. The neoconservative aim at creating democracy is rooted in decades of American policy and experience, embodied in President Wilson's post–World War I commitment to a League of Nations, one that would embrace democracy and self-determination at the expense of dictatorship and colonialism. Wilsonianism carried over to Cold War theorizing. Journalist Walter Lippmann counseled against the doctrine of containment, focusing instead on building an alliance of like-minded nations—those that shared America's values. Liberal thinkers, and by adoption, neoconservatives, have focused on the perception that democracies don't tend to go to war with each other. This idea, which harkens back to the writings of Immanuel Kant, has, in spite of some exceptions, proven to be right.[7]

But if neoconservatives were correct in their embrace of democracy promotion as a means of security building, they were treading in difficult waters as to the concept of means. Could democracy be brought about by force, in a kind of war of conversion? In making the case for Iraq, neoconservatives such as Defense Secretary Donald Rumsfeld would point to postwar Germany and Japan as a source of inspiration. With the fall of fascist regimes at the close of World War II, America had occupied former adversaries, turned their political institutions and economies around, and in the process created for itself prosperous, unabashed allies of democracy. But there was a problem in this logic. Both Germany and Japan were relatively homogenous nations—that is, ethnic diversity had been historically minimal. And while Germany was only unified in 1871, the concept of *Germania* as a land of Germans had existed for millennia. Nazi Germany would become the poster child of brutal dictatorships in 1933, but one should also remember that Hitler's party came to power through all-too-democratic parliamentary maneuvers during the Weimar Republic. Germany's Social Democrats, the country's first political party, founded in the nineteenth century, exists to this day as a major political force, and during Hitler's regime, it was one of the only tried-and-true underground movements in opposition to the Nazis.

Japan too had seen ethnic uniformity and state unity. During the Meiji Restoration of 1866–1869, a burgeoning and assertive landowning class developed, allowing for a new level of individual agency. But there was no such national unity or democratic movement in earnest in Iraq prior to 2003. The institutions simply were not there. A country held together by foreign powers, both European and Middle Eastern, Iraq often found itself prone to manipulation—with Ottomans granting special status to minority Sunnis, and Shi'is fomenting civil war and opposition to Sunni statehood. Iraq often found itself a battleground for neighboring Persia's wars with empires to its west. Even while the Islamic caliphate sat in Baghdad for much of the Abbasid caliphate (750–1258), Iraq as a nation-state might have been more of an abstraction, an immediate extension of a great city-state.

Needless to say, the March 2003 campaign in Iraq would prove misconceived for the United States. Much to the discredit of neoconservatives in the White House, the Iraq war created a power vacuum that triggered a civil war between (and among) religious sects. What we found was not the institutions of democracy, but the overt lack of state power. The government of the new Iraq could not exercise its influence or even live up to Max Weber's classic definition of a state: an entity with "a monopoly over the legitimate use of violence."[8]

Iran today is closer than Iraq to democracy, if merely because Iraq's future hangs in the balance. Civil war does not bring a country closer to reconciliation, a requisite for democracy. After all, if votes can be challenged with bullets, what good are the votes to begin with? Yet the failures in Iraq altogether should not topple the core of the neoconservative argument—that the growth of democracy itself is a useful source of potential allies. And while democracy should not be sought by force, an alliance with democratic-leaning countries is essential if the mistakes of the Cold War are to be avoided. A new, more coherent grand strategy must be formed, one of a "natural alliance" of democracies, as Cold War journalist Walter Lippmann suggested, utilizing democracy not as an end in itself, but rather as a means.

AN ALTERNATIVE DOCTRINE

Much like debates surrounding the current conflict in Iraq, the Vietnam War was associated not only with mounting human losses, but with the budgetary considerations of fighting a seemingly endless war. Having emerged out of the myth of a Sino–Soviet bloc, and into the perception of the very real Sino–Soviet split, the Nixon administration began to see

China, not as an ally, but as a nation whose regional presence could help quell concerns of an American vacuum left by the defeat in Vietnam. In fact, U.S.-China rapprochement could "contribute to the creation of the stable regional conditions which would permit the orderly devolution of American power (politico-military retrenchment)."[9]

In America, not everyone agreed with Nixon's change of strategy. Critics of Nixon and then-National Security Adviser Henry Kissinger did not envision a need to fill a gap of credibility left behind by an American retreat from Vietnam. To these critics, the retreat would simply embody the correction of a mistaken policy—the war itself.[10] But Nixon and Kissinger, who understood the geopolitical realities of the Cold War, knew that leaving Vietnam without initiating a concurrent overture toward China might prove against America's long-term interests.

If we may draw parallels to the war in Iraq, we find that an American redeployment is *more* likely than Vietnam to create a significant power vacuum. After all, the Vietnam War was essentially fought between two factions—one stronger than the other. When America pulled its support from the South Vietnamese government and Saigon fell, there was hardly a question as to which side would win and take over the country. In Iraq, the vacuum of power has resulted in a civil war. This civil war has no easy end in sight, and no single faction appears to be strong enough to mount an overwhelming, decisive victory. If anything, the situation in Iraq presently resembles Lebanon's sectarian conflict of 1975–1990 and Afghanistan's civil war of 1989–1996, conflicts that permitted the rise of Hezbollah and the Taliban, respectively.

To be sure, Iran has benefited strategically from the U.S. invasion of Iraq. Two of the most powerful factions in Iraq, the Supreme Council for the Islamic Revolution in Iraq and the radical Shi'i Mehdi Army, have counted on leadership that has at some point either lived in Iran or enjoyed continued Iranian support. A report from the Royal Institute of International Affairs in Great Britain flatly claims that Iran has been the "chief beneficiary of the war on terror in the Middle East."[11] This suggests all the more a need to consider the potential repercussions that an American pullout from Iraq will have on Iran's already-growing power. And if China, a communist country and strategic foe of the United States during the Cold War, could be brought to the table by Nixon in order to retreat from American overcommitments in Southeast Asia, we must at the very least entertain the notion that Iran could play a central role in the Middle East after an American pullout from Iraq, and that this could ultimately lead America to embrace Iran's regained status as a regional powerhouse.

The Nixon Doctrine, when applied to the Middle East, had followed a period of strict balance-of-power policy, as favored by both Great Britain and the United States under presidents Truman and Eisenhower, and to a lesser extent Kennedy and Johnson. But for Nixon, the concurrent pullout of Great Britain from the Persian Gulf, coupled with the mounting losses in Vietnam, made gambling on balance-of-power quickly lose its appeal. The "twin pillar" policy was thus introduced to place Iran and Saudi Arabia at the helm in the region. And while the two nations were all but politically incompatible, with Saudi Arabia a Salafi nation and Iran at the time on a road to rapid industrial and cultural modernization, their ability to work together was perceived as critical, given the rise of pan-Arabism and other Soviet-friendly threats.

With the end of the shah's Imperial Iran, the rise of U.S.-Iranian hostilities, and the increasing aggression of Saddam's Iraq, the United States began pursuing a policy of "dual containment." Political scientist Jalil Roshandel calls this policy a "balance-of–weakness" approach. Through it, both Persian Gulf neighbors were prevented from posing a serious threat to the region. From this policy, a cycle of political and (to an extent) economic alienation came to define Iran's relations with the West. Yet with the fall of the Iraqi pillar of "dual containment," a new policy must be considered to cope with the rapidly changing dynamics of power in the region.

Because of Iran's unique place as a nation-state that is ardently anti-American as a matter of state policy, while at the same time actively supporting terrorist organizations, its rogue state status has placed it in a post-September 11 world squarely in the forefront of the war on terror. In arguing the challenges of fighting this greater war on terror, scholars such as Stephen Biddle of the U.S. Army War College have laid out sobering assessments of the prospects for success. Biddle has suggested a choice in grand strategy that would involve either continuing with an all-out offensive in Iraq and other "vague" campaigns for democracy building, or retreat to less offensive stance of containment, which by definition would only limit the threat of terror, without altogether eradicating it. Robert A. Pape, one of the preeminent authorities on the causes of suicide terrorism, has suggested a renewed "offshore balancing" approach, whereby American military personnel do not take the position of occupiers, but rather maintain a safe distance from hot zones, ready to engage when necessary.[12] But as Biddle suggests, there is a lack of clarity as to the true nature of the war. Like a "war on poverty," or a "war on drugs," the current offensive leaves much to the imagination as to its endgame. After all, terrorism is itself a tactic, not a people (like the Carthaginians) or even an ideology (like communism).

Fortunately, responding to concerns over the vagueness of the war, some Bush administration officials, including the president himself, eventually began referring to the greater struggle as a "war against militant Islam," or even a "war against Islamic fascism." While this helps to clarify the status of al-Qaeda as a tried-and-true target of the war on terror, where does this leave the Islamic Republic of Iran? Is Iran a target of the war on terror because it supports Hezbollah (which itself is a terrorist actor), or simply because it is led by a circle of radical conservative Muslims? Were Iran to cease support for Hezbollah, would it no longer be a front-and-center strategic threat? More importantly, but seldom asked is whether Hezbollah would continue to pose any real threat to the United States once U.S.-Iranian relations restarted. Iran sponsors terrorist groups, but these target Israel and not America. At the same time, one of Iran's greatest foes in Iraq is al-Qaeda, America's number one enemy.

These points might seem like pulling hairs, but such specificity is essential in formulating a coherent strategy, and indeed a long-term grand strategy for the region. If Iran itself is a threat, what kind of threat is it? A point that must be discussed (despite its potential controversy) is whether Iran is a foe at all. It is not politically convenient, in this era of sound-bite journalism, to speak of the nation whose motto is "Death to America" as a potential ally. After all, what kind of ally is a country with which the United States has no diplomatic relations? The key, however, does not lie in the immediate state of relations, but in Iran's trajectory of independence. As we have seen, Iran is one of the few states in its region, which has maintained coherent natural boundaries that had little to do with colonial impositions, and everything to do with the natural development of the nation. Iran, with a population that is relatively pro-American and growing in representation, will increasingly fit in with the notion of democracy as a natural factor for an alliance.

If realism provides any indication of how the world operates, China will soon emerge as a challenger to American primacy. China's GDP per capita has grown by an average of 8.4 percent annually between 1990 and 2004, with some predictions forecasting a continued annual growth of 8 percent through 2010. With a population of 1.3 billion, China is expected to also grow in its aspirations in the coming decades. While at times expressing concerns over a China with a booming economy and a growing military budget to go along with it, the United States continues on a path of liberal engagement, in which the economic ties that bind the two nations are perceived as a buffer for future conflict. Yet for legendary realist Kenneth Waltz, the thought that America would "remain the dominant power without rivals, [is] a position without precedent in modern history."[13]

Dynamics of power should not be ignored. If Iran's power potential places it both on a trajectory of independence, and in a position to exert regional strength, China's trajectory leads it to the role of a superpower. The Middle East, with all of its problems, is not presently on a path toward challenging America's position (let alone its existence) in the world. China is. Military strategist Colin S. Gray explains it thus:

> [It] is one thing to show that the First Punic War did not have to begin in 264 B.C. or the First World War in 1914; it is quite another to assert that Carthage

and Rome could have avoided an armed struggle for supremacy or that the European balance-of-power system could have maintained order for long after 1914 without a general war.[14]

In the context of a new Cold War, one that would potentially pit the United States and its closest allies against China or a China-led alliance, America would not only require the stability of the Middle East, but it would benefit from not being embroiled in open-ended military campaigns in the region. The sobering state of America's overcommitment can be found within the pages of an otherwise optimistic Department of Defense Quadrennial Defense Review of 2006, which boasts spending in the magnitude of $1.3 billion for initiatives to defeat improvised explosive devices, or IEDs. These low-cost explosives, which Iraqi insurgents have planted on roads to detonate as U.S. patrols pass, have generated a large bulk of the U.S. casualties in that conflict. But the larger question should be whether American military personnel should be patrolling the streets of Baghdad to begin with. The overcommitment of America's military is significant and should be treated as a disheartening limitation of the United States' ability to effectively project its power and deter future conflicts.

The involvement of American troops in Iraq years after the fall of Saddam Hussein's regime has forced American military planners to deal with a black hole that severely limits the United States' ability to deal with other rising threats. Over a decade before the Iraq conflict, and at a time of Cold War-era military spending, Paul Kennedy described in his epic *The Rise and Fall of the Great Powers* an inescapable dilemma that had haunted previous nations. Even in the late 1980s, the United States ran the risk of "imperial overstretch." Put simply, it was the "fact that the sum total of the United States' global interests and obligations is nowadays far larger than the country's power to defend them all simultaneously."[15]

Because of the problematic way in which Middle Eastern borders were drawn by colonial powers, the region will likely continue to remain a source of conflict, which, lacking a new approach, will continue to invite direct American involvement. Ethnic, tribal, and religious tensions are likely to continue, with militant Islam playing a central role in the political struggles for representation and governance. Iraq itself could remain a battlefield of ideologies and affiliations well into the future, as it has often tragically served throughout its history. But a nuclear-armed Iran, under the framework of a new and revised Nixon Doctrine, could allow the United States to militarily disengage from the region without compromising its continued interest in Middle Eastern political and economic stability. Unlike the often morally depraved approach to alliances during the Nixon administration, a new Nixon Doctrine would place democracy as a litmus test for support.

To be sure, the Nixon administration embraced brutal dictators like the shah of Iran and indicted human rights violator Augusto Pinochet of Chile. In 1971, in relation to the democratic rise to power of socialist president Salvador Allende in Chile, Nixon is quoted as saying that "[no] impression should be permitted in Latin America that they can get away with this, that it's safe to go this way."[16] On September 11, 1973, a coup overthrew Allende, putting in place a military junta headed by General Pinochet. Pinochet would become synonymous with Latin American fascism, resorting to torture and mass disappearances. Both the shah and Pinochet have stood as merely two examples of America's all-too-nearsighted commitment to fighting communism at the expense of moral distinction, and the benefits of "natural alliance," as eagerly sought by thinkers like Lippmann, who were opposed to hard-nosed tactics during the Cold War. Democracy under the new framework must exist on Lippmann's "natural" terms—it cannot be imposed on a nation by design, and it cannot be hurried up through military intervention. The Iranian Revolution shows how easily heavy-handed management and superficial alliances can be derailed by a populace hard-set on political independence.

For American policymakers, the notion of a powerful, self-reliant, and relatively pro-American Islamic Republic must be explored in the context of a new Nixon Doctrine. That two-thirds of Iranians are under thirty, and that this pro-American demographic will one day take the reins of power in the country, should not escape U.S. leaders. The United States must avoid looking for shortsighted fixes for its current dilemmas, since shortsightedness risks the loss of a future ally, whose power potential will not be neutralized by any air strike campaign or sanctions package.

In formulating policy for the twenty-first century, American officials, and indeed the American public, should be concerned with the failed effects of past strategic approaches. The neoconservative view, which properly foresaw the nature of the nonstate Islamic militant threat, depended too heavily on simple answers to a complicated, multifaceted problem. Perhaps the biggest misconception of all involved not differentiating a nonstate actor like al-Qaeda from a nation-state like Iraq. While the former is not constrained by the logic of deterrence, the latter can only operate globally in the realm of international relations. The government of Iraq could not hide in an Afghani cave, in a friendly London neighborhood, or in the mountains of Northwestern Pakistan. Its targets were visible from space, in the form of buildings, roads, bridges, and radar stations. Its armies could not move in silence, and most of its airspace was controlled by the United States and Great Britain, two enemy powers, under the no-fly zones program. Saddam Hussein did eventually go into hiding, crawling into a spider hole near his home town of Tikrit, but only after American and British misdirection had essentially dissolved the nation-state of Iraq and plunged the future of the region into an abyss of doubt.

Iran, as Iraq once was, is a coherent nation-state with defendable boundaries. While led by anti-American Islamic conservatives, Iran is not immune to the requirement that nation-states act in what they perceive to be their own self-interest. Iran's targets too, are visible and prone to attack. Dealing with the Islamic Republic of Iran necessitates a logical and pragmatic foreign-policy approach. For that to be possible, an end-game result has to be conceived. While many focus on the pressing matters of the minute, we should also be concerned with the long term. What international structure would be most favorable to the United States in the long run? Where would Iran, should it continue on its trajectory of independence, fit in?

In a world in which the destruction of the American state is not the immediate threat, but rather the devaluation of America's power is at risk, much more political capital must be invested in assuring a certain level of ideological congruence with other countries. In the case of Iran, a powerful, nuclear-armed nation would be a perfect candidate for this position, but only after it had become further democratized. After all, it is difficult to envision why a purely democratic Iran would not see America as a natural strategic partner, given the inherent pro-Americanism already present in the country. Sadly, this affinity for the United States could not be expected from any democratic Arab country, should one eventually emerge, as countless opinion polls have shown.

But as it is difficult to envisage a freer Iran turning away from America, it is equally unlikely that an alliance between Iran and the United States could be forged any time soon. Détente is possible with the current regime, but one must keep in mind that in the end, the mere cooling of tensions is not what America should be after. It should be after peace and alignment on terms that respect Iran's independent nature, and America's need for global stability and continued leadership.

As Iran moves toward acquiring nuclear power, a certain degree of nonmilitary confrontation should be expected. In fact, this confrontation itself—this war of words—is the only thing likely to push the Iranian hard-line down a path of self-destruction, given that America plays its cards right. If the United States does not acquiesce to hard-line demands for escalation, and refuses to grant the Islamic regime the kind of impetus for power consolidation it experienced during the Iran-Iraq war, America will have gained in further disempowering its enemies within Iran.

In today's Iran, not only is the nation's sovereignty prized by all, but Iran's right to nuclear power is contested by very few, regardless of their position along the vast political spectrum. And while most analysts agree that an attack on nuclear facilities would only put off the inevitable for a few years, the harm done by the violation of Iran's sovereignty would come in the form of a Middle East that is further embattled, with no regional actor able to rise above the ashes of a failed balance-of-power doctrine, and tackle regional challenges on its own.

But we must not fear the inevitable. Nuclear deterrence works. There is no reason to believe that Iran would have an interest in incurring any form of military retaliation, invited by the sale or use of nuclear weapons or technology. If we accept the premise that Iran and the United States will enjoy a stable, secure, and mutually beneficial partnership in the long run, and that the United States might resort to once again employing Iran as a key player in ensuring Middle Eastern security, the prospects of a nuclear-armed Iran become less distasteful, or at least easier to swallow.

An alliance with Iran will not be about finding the right diplomatic tone, or providing a definitive economic aid package. Such peace between the United States and Iran can only come directly from the streets of Tehran, in the form of an unexpected succession in the religious leadership, an election that empowers a new generation, or in the slow erosion of power among the current political elite. A political transformation continues in Iran today, which, if unimpeded, will challenge our views of that country's abilities to tackle regional challenges—not in opposition to, but in conjunction with the United States. This transformation can only happen if it is an Iranian transformation. It cannot be inspired by the airwaves of the American-funded *Radio Farda*, or *Voice of America*, and it will not follow an American threat or air-strike campaign. In fact, peace between the United States and Iran will have little to do with America, and everything to do with Iran.

CHAPTER 9

NUCLEAR THRESHOLDS

You must have the soul of Abraham in order with light to see the mansions
of Paradise in the fire.

—Rumi

In the early 1960s, while the People's Republic of China (PRC) was moving fast toward its first test of an atomic bomb, President Kennedy considered military action as a means of delaying the communist nation's entrance into the nuclear club. Recently declassified documents show how the Kennedy administration struggled with the notion of allowing yet another communist rival to maintain a nuclear deterrent, making effective coercive diplomacy all the more difficult. Nevertheless, these documents also provide a glimpse into the levelheaded nature of Kennedy's White House. Just as they would handle the Cuban Missile Crisis of 1962, with strength, but with the courage to maintain faith in the role of nuclear deterrence, the administration finally learned to come to terms with a nuclear-armed PRC.[1]

China's first nuclear test came on October 16, 1964, and while President Johnson was now in office, Kennedy had set the groundwork for accepting as inevitable and manageable the prospects of a nuclear-armed China. Nearly ten years later, President Nixon walked on the Great Wall, and a new era of slow, carefully applied détente paved the way for one of history's most mutually lucrative trading partnerships.

Today, America finds itself at a crossroads not too different from the one faced by the Kennedy administration. Communism, as the chief security concern for the United States, has been replaced by an equally murky and dynamic enemy: terrorism, or radical Islam. In the face of this threat, should the essentially Islamist state of Iran, an avowed enemy of the United States, be allowed to develop a nuclear capability? Or should America risk the potentially destructive escalation of a military endeavor, when Iran might turn out to be yet another China? These questions are not easier to tackle today than they were forty years ago. But perhaps the legacy of China, and our leaders' purposeful passivity then, lends clues to the approaches of our last two administrations and the prospects of waking up to a nuclear-armed Iran.

"WEAPONS OF MASS DESTRUCTION"

As the United States continues to move toward confrontation on the issue of Iran's nuclear program by attempting to link potential cooperation on Iraq and Afghanistan with the immediate cessation of nuclear enrichment, the irony is that America has thus systematically forced Iran into a corner, from which it is only likely to emerge armed with a nuclear warhead—turning what is considered by many a nightmare scenario into a reality.

In the *Art of Warfare*, Sun-Tzu advises: "In surrounding the enemy, leave him a way out; do not press an enemy that is cornered."[2] While arguably not the most advisable approach to waging total war, Sun-Tzu's phrase does echo the ultimate negotiation technique—paint yourself into a corner and thus you have no option but to win. Legend contends that in his campaign of Mexico, conquistador Hernán Cortés burned his ships upon reaching the shore, forcing his troops to forget the thought of ever returning home and thus remain fiercely loyal to their commander to the bitter end. It worked, as Cortés' badly outnumbered forces (with the help of local peoples) defeated the Aztec Empire and solidified Spanish rule over the new colony.

In negotiating issues of war and peace in the nuclear age, the Cold War provides various instances of the Hernán Cortés doctrine. The United States, for one, provided an unwavering security guarantee to Western Europe, stationing high-ranking military officers in West Germany in order to convince the Soviets that should they attack, America's response would be up to the general on the ground, and not diplomatically minded Washington. Soviet premier Nikita Khrushchev also knew how to play along, and always maintained that in the case of an American attack, Soviet rockets would fly "automatically." This approach to deterrence borrows heavily from the deadly game of "chicken," in which two cars drive directly toward each other, with the first driver to veer off losing the game and earning the label of a coward. Eventually, it was figured out that the first driver to toss the steering wheel out the window would invariably win, since the choice to steer away would now rest with the other driver, who would have to move out of the way to avoid certain catastrophe. Nobel Prize-winning economist Thomas Schelling refers to this as the doctrine of the "last clear chance":

> The one that had the "last clear chance" to avert collision is held responsible ... Xenophon understood the principle when, threatened by an attack he had not sought, he placed his Greeks with their backs against an impassable

ravine. "I should like the enemy to think it is easy-going in every direction for *him* to retreat."[3]

Today, as Iran pushes deeper into nuclear territory, both the Islamic Republic and its declared arch nemesis, the United States, seem to have taken from the playbook of no return, essentially burning the ships behind them. Leaving no room for ambiguity, President Bush has declared before the American people and the international community that Iran "shall not have the means, the knowledge to develop a nuclear weapon."[4] At the same time, Iraq fatigue has affected the president's ability to maintain this position. At the end of 2006, only 40 percent of Americans believed that Iran could be stopped from getting nuclear weapons.[5] In stark contrast, the nuclear issue inside Iran is nothing short of a call to patriotism—bridging gaps of political affiliation, age, and gender. Nuclear energy is a matter of national pride, making its abandonment a tricky issue for even the most accommodating of Iranian politicians. Needless to say, having two adversaries painting themselves into a corner makes diplomacy all the more tricky, and minimizes the likelihood of forging a peaceful settlement.

Officially, the debate in Iran carefully remains in the realm of nuclear energy for "peaceful purposes." Because of Iran's overwhelming domestic energy subsidies, it only exports around 40 percent of its oil. Domestic consumption is anything but frugal, as the cost of a liter of gasoline hovers around nine U.S. cents (or thirty-four U.S. cents per gallon).[6] It is not a stretch to consider peaceful nuclear energy as a realistic goal of nuclear development, and the Iranian regime is quick to point to the hard numbers in justifying its program. But Iran's troubled neighborhood has led many to believe that a parallel and equally compelling need for going nuclear is the attainment of weapons. After all, having a nuclear-armed Pakistan to the East, American troops present in neighboring Afghanistan and Iraq and based along the Persian Gulf, facing the strategic rivalry of the GCC, and being within reach of a nuclear Israel, are all apparent incentives to go nuclear.[7]

Perhaps one of the most poignant and unintended lessons of the Iraq war for the international community has been that it is better to *really* have nuclear weapons, lest the United States attack. In Iran, it is considered a given that "the US invaded Iraq because it was weak, but sought a diplomatic solution to North Korea's blatant proliferation because Pyongyang stood its ground."[8] While many suggested that Iraq did, in fact, possess unconventional weapons, mostly in the form of chemical stockpiles, and that the American military was preparing for the contingency of being attacked with such an arsenal, it was universally accepted that Iraq was nowhere near the development of a nuclear warhead—a true "weapon of mass destruction" (WMD). (Many argue that chemical weapons do not truly qualify as "mass destruction" weapons, as they are generally used for their psychological impact during wars of attrition—such as World War I and the Iran-Iraq war. As a general rule, conventional bombs are more cost-effective than chemical weapons in causing death. So much for the WMD argument for the Iraq war.[9]) North Korea, which could already have an arsenal of over a dozen nuclear weapons to complement its already sturdy ground forces in the Korean Peninsula, has reaped the benefits of deterrence, making any U.S. military endeavor highly unlikely. For Iran, the lessons of Iraq and North Korea—its supposed partners in the "axis of evil"—have not gone unnoticed.

But Iran knows that there are limitations to reversing the side effects of obtaining such doomsday armaments. As North Korea has proven, nuclear weapons can provide generous negotiating cards, but just as easily they can drag a country further into isolation and crippling sanctions. Some analysts suggest that Iran has a different strategy. Gary Sick, formerly with the National Security Council and now Executive Director of the Gulf/2000 Project, puts it thus:

> Iran is going to enrich uranium and have an infrastructure that will put it within reach—which could be several years—of having a nuclear weapon. This doesn't mean having a nuclear weapon already built, but may be enough from a negotiating perspective.[10]

This could allow Iran to avoid going back on its continuous public word not to arm itself with a weapon, and it is a step that would necessitate merely not acting on its capabilities, rather than retreating for them in order to strike a deal with the international community—a face-losing proposition. This view echoes the shah's own reasoning for starting Iran's nuclear program in the 1960s with the help of both the United States and the Soviet Union. The shah claimed he "didn't want the bomb yet, but if anyone in the neighborhood has it, we must be ready to have it."[11]

If proliferation is to continue at its current rate, however, it is critical to understand the true threat that a nuclear-armed Iran might pose. From the outset, important misconceptions must be abandoned. These revolve around the true application of nuclear weapons in the military theater, as well as the emphasis placed on recent virulent anti-Israeli and anti-Western remarks by Iran's president, Mahmoud Ahmadinejad. The latter is more easily addressed by simply reminding ourselves that the Iranian president has no control over the military, foreign affairs, or other coercive elements of his country. Had that been the case, former reformist President Mohammad Khatami might have been more successful in carrying through with his call for a "dialogue among civilizations," a slogan picked up by the United Nations in 2001, but which nevertheless fell on deaf ears among the Iranian ruling elite. The military, as well as Iran's nuclear program, is under the ultimate control of the supreme leader, the post once held by Khomeini, and now by Ali Khamene'i, and not the president of the republic.

As for the actual use of nuclear weapons, the following questions are critical: Are these weapons practical? What function do they actually serve? And, are they inherently defensive or offensive in nature? To explore these questions, we should revisit a classic debate in international relations studies—one that pits the very notion of proliferation against the mainstream advocacy of nonproliferation. This is the debate between Kenneth N. Waltz and Scott D. Sagan. Their discussions, which formed the basis of their book *Nuclear Weapons: A Debate Renewed*, are mandatory reading for college students delving into international relations and arms-control policy. The positions of Waltz and Sagan are straightforward, and they underscore how seemingly easy it is to disagree on something most of us might consider to be second nature: that nuclear proliferation is essentially undesirable. Most of us have grown up thinking that the spread of nuclear weapons is necessarily a bad thing, but to Waltz and Sagan, this is just the beginning of the debate.

Sagan mostly takes a mainstream position: one that states that horizontal proliferation should be avoided. By horizontal, he means the spread of nuclear weapons across countries. Vertical proliferation is what the Soviet Union and the United States engaged in during the Cold War—an amassing of stockpiles that reached into the tens of thousands. Sagan's argument is based on the idea that human organizations, and particularly military ones, are inherently fallible. Sagan considers it possible that a country possessing a nuclear weapon could unintentionally use that weapon because of a breakdown in the chain of command, or overall organizational structure.

Waltz, on the other hand, takes a quintessentially realist position, one that perceives states as calculating entities, which act on the behest of their own, rational self-interest. By rational, it is meant that states calculate on a cost-benefit (as opposed to ideologically blind) basis, not necessarily that they always come to the right conclusions. The realist view is taken to its logical extreme with Waltz' arguments, essentially favoring continued horizontal nuclear proliferation. Waltz takes the position that nuclear proliferation is actually a good thing, since as countries acquire nuclear arsenals, they are forced to become much more responsible in their handling of foreign policy. This is because, according to Waltz, if a country new to the nuclear arena is seen as a direct threat to other nuclear powers, that threat all of a sudden becomes magnified manifold, to the point of possibly inviting tremendously punitive military action. Waltz tells us that "nuclear states do not want to fight long and hard over important interests—indeed, they do not want to fight at all."[12] Just as arguments exist, which claim that democracies don't tend to go to war with each other, given the logic of deterrence we can say with certainty that nuclear powers do not go to war with one another.

Waltz' argument is not only purely realist, but characteristically counterintuitive. Americans, and in fact most citizens of this world, tend to see nuclear proliferation as an inherently dangerous proposition. Similar to saying that the outsourcing of jobs can be a good thing for America, or that raising taxes in some instances might help the economy, arguing for proliferation is a sure-fire way to be branded a lunatic anywhere outside of defined academic circles. For our purposes, we should at least approach the Waltz argument with an open mind. With Iran looking to acquire a nuclear arsenal, as China did more than forty years ago, it is important to ask oneself what the true (not imagined) consequences of a nuclear-armed Iran might be.

A constant fear associated with Iranian proliferation is the case of A. Q. Khan, Pakistan's top nuclear scientist, who was accused by his own government of acting as a renegade actor in selling nuclear technology to Libya, Iran, and North Korea. During the mid-1990s, it is widely believed that Dr. Khan sold centrifuge designs to Iran. Centrifuges are fast-spinning machines used to compress ("enrich") uranium 235, the element needed to produce nuclear fuel for energy or weapons.

Scott Sagan has recently taken a strong position against Iranian proliferation, warning that dealing with Iran would be much like dealing with a nuclear-armed Pakistan and the likes of A. Q. Khan. The problem with Sagan's argument, however, lies in his perception of the IRGC—the outfit tasked with guarding much of Iran's nuclear infrastructure—as a ragtag army of brainwashed "true believers," possibly willing to sell secrets to terrorist cells. And while certain offshoots of the IRGC, particularly those tasked with enforcing Islamic codes in the streets of Tehran, might fit this characterization, it is hardly a proper description of Iran's most formidable fighting force, which coordinates various sophisticated research and development projects inside the country, and commands the most sophisticated naval air force in the Gulf.

Sagan does not, however, support a military strike against Iran. As a model, he instead finds the 1994 Agreed Framework between the United States and North Korea helpful. The parts of the agreement that ultimately failed centered on suspicions surrounding North Korea's circumvention of the terms, as well as America's unwillingness to go through with its promise to build light-water nuclear reactors and stabilize its relations with the communist nation. Yet the positive, for Sagan, is worth repeating. Such an agreement, then, would be structured "in a series of steps, each offering a package of economic benefits ... in exchange for constraints placed on Iran's future nuclear development."[13] Yet it is difficult to know whether President Clinton's agreement, which was backed by the threat of military strikes, was destined to ever work. Normalization of relations and a security guarantee might have ultimately worked (and some contend, could still work in making North Korea abandon its current stockpile of weapons), but for Iran, it would be an entirely different story. Iranian hard-liners enjoy nothing close to the monopoly of information and dictatorial control that North Korea's Kim Jong Il maintains. The Iranian conservatives would lose significant influence inside their own, much more moderate and factionalized country, if and when they were to give in to the very country, whose antagonism they have embraced as a matter of political identity. Policymakers in the United States should be cautious about their immediate expectations of a diplomatic breakthrough on Iran's nuclear program.

To be sure, an Iran with a nuclear arsenal, given current political hostilities, would only be emboldened to continue on its current intransigent path. It is difficult to push around a country that cannot be conceivably affected by implicit military threats. Just as the United States can only hope to persuade Russia and China to see things its way through the use of economic and political incentives, Iran could never be expected to give up its political positions out of fear of military coercion, especially if its own interests lie in antithesis to the immediate needs of the United States. This was not the case with Iraq when it did not have a nuclear deterrent in March of 2003. Iraq's eleventh-hour agreement to allow unconditional inspections of its suspected weapons facilities came too late for Saddam Hussein's government. Such a request would have never been granted by a state powerful enough to either defend itself with a nuclear weapon, or at the very least cause significant damage to the invading military or its allies.

But just as a nuclear Iran would be able to dissuade outside actors from intervening too closely in its affairs, other nuclear powers, most notably Israel, would continue to enjoy a deterrent capability vis-à-vis Iran. As Waltz states, many warheads are not needed to effectively deter an enemy's actions, since most states maintain most of their populations and industrial capacity within small geographic areas. This is especially true in Iran, whose capital Tehran houses around 20 percent of its population, along with much of its industrial capacity. In the case of Iran, it is irresponsible to paint its road to nuclear power as a direct threat to the existence of Israel, simply because President Mahmoud Ahmadinejad has quoted Khomeini's wish that Israel be "wiped off the map." Anti-Semitic as this rhetoric may be, we should hope that policymakers would not suffer from cloudy judgment and throw the foundations of deterrence, on which the relative peace of the Cold War relied, out the window.

There has been significant chatter in the American news media regarding the weight carried by Ahmadinejad's words. Naturally, parallels are drawn with Adolf Hitler and the lessons of appeasement. Following the 1938 Munich Agreement that acquiesced to Germany's annexation of Czechoslovakia's Sudetenland region, British Prime Minister Neville Chamberlain declared to have accomplished "peace for our time." Not six months later, Nazi Germany proceeded to occupy the entire country of Czechoslovakia, setting the wheels in motion for World War II. This point in history, which portrays Chamberlain as tragically naïve about the true intentions of Hitler, serves as a constant reminder to those who wish to never again appease a hostile nation. Naturally, the twentieth-century calls of Muslim leaders in the Middle East to "push Israel into the sea," which were often backed up by military campaigns, have led some observers of the Holocaust to see the threat of Muslim countries toward Israel as nothing short of a campaign of annihilation—an unappeasable movement. And though Iran has never fought a war with Israel, President Ahmadinejad's anti-Semitic diatribes, replayed ad infinitum in the global media, only serve to further the confrontational resolve within Israel and America.

Making a reference to Hitler's extermination camps, a conservative Israeli newspaper writes that to "Ahmadinejad and some leading Ayatollahs the 'final solution' is clear."[14] Michael Ledeen, a resident scholar in the "Freedom Chair" of the neoconservative think tank, The American Enterprise Institute (AEI), in an op-ed titled "Active Appeasement" warns against "talks with the mullahs," lest they lead to "normalization" of relations.[15] It is difficult to imagine why neoconservatives would be so disinclined to support a normalization of relations between the United States and Iran, or any country for that matter. Yet if some are led to believe that Ahmadinejad is actually a Hitler, we should remember that the comparison has not been reserved for Ahmadinejad alone. Referring to the leader of the secular Palestinian Liberation Organization (PLO), former Israeli Prime Minister Menachim Begin claimed, "Hitler is a pussycat compared to what Arafat will bring upon us."[16] Leaders of Hamas—the archenemies of the PLO—have also been compared to the Nazis, as have been Saddam Hussein and former Egyptian leader Gamel Abdel Nasser. Conversely, Palestinians have compared Israeli figures such as Benjamin Netanyahu and Ariel Sharon to Hitler.

Needless to say, such analogies are seldom helpful. As if it were necessary to state this, Iran is a different country, with a different agenda than Nazi Germany, despite even Ahmadinejad's language. Important, but rarely mentioned, is the central role of hyperbole in Iranian culture. An Iranian walking through the bazaar might be told by a vendor to simply "take the coat. It's not worthy of you!" But actually taking the vendor up on the offer without paying would land the customer in jail. Phrases like "step on my eye" (*qadam-etaan roo cheshm*) and "I will sacrifice myself for you" (*qorban-e shoma*), are all-too-common pleasantries (*taaruf*) of Iranian daily life. Merely getting directions from a stranger in the subway in Iran might prompt a long-winded, seemingly exaggerated expression of gratitude: "May your hand not have hurt (in helping me), thank you, I will sacrifice myself for you, thank you, goodbye." This can explain what is otherwise unexplainable: a country populated by moderate Muslims adopting the phrase "Death to America" as a national slogan. Yet anyone with experience in Germany will be quick to point out that any talk of stepping on one's eye or being sacrificed should prompt a quick exit and a call to the authorities. In other words, the lessons of appeasement should not preclude Americans from examining present circumstances in their proper context.

NUCLEAR WEAPONS AND TERRORISM

In assessing the costs and benefits of a more powerful Iran, U.S. policymakers must keep in mind that Israel's and America's nuclear deterrent is strong enough to repel any hostile military endeavor by the country. The question, really, is not whether Iran would seek to obliterate Israel—that could never happen—but whether America feels comfortable not having the ability to compel Iran to specific action. The discussion surrounding Iran's future possession of nuclear weapons should center on the assumption that such weapons are of a defensive nature, not a tool for conquest or senseless obliteration. Unfortunately, the television news media often fails to portray this topic in a mature manner, usually reaching for the lowest common denominator—Iran as an irrational nation-state, ready to blow up anything that comes in its way.[17]

Given Iranian ties to terrorism, some have suggested that Iran could potentially provide nuclear weapons to terrorist groups, or even help them develop their own. This is a difficult notion to accept, not only from a strictly realist perspective, but also from a basic understanding of Iran's political structure. Judith S. Yaphe and Colonel Charles D. Lutes of the National Defense University explain how most "experts agree that the Iranian government is unlikely to share its new nuclear weapons technology with terrorist groups, including the Lebanese Hezbollah." They cite the level of operational sophistication in the IRGC, which is at the head of such programs.[18]

Arguments that seek to break down concepts of nuclear deterrence are based on one or more of the following key concepts: the delegation of authority, the preemptive use of weapons as a "decapitation" tool, and the emotional impulses of war. The first is the A. Q. Khan example, which points to the suspected inability of certain countries to keep control over their nuclear capabilities. But Pakistan is dramatically different from Iran, especially in the area of national unity. For one, Pakistan does not enjoy the natural, long-standing borders that Iran does. And while Pakistan was partitioned from India for religious reasons, Iran as a nation existed well before the advent of Islam. Today, Pakistan enjoys significant collusion with a variety of external actors, not the least of which are Sunni Wahhabi fundamentalists, who have opened *madrasas* (or religious seminaries) and continue to spread their Saudi brand of Islam in the country. The Taliban continue to mount operations in Afghanistan, using Pakistan as their headquarters. A. Q. Khan himself has been associated with Taliban sympathizers. In Iran, however, nationalism is of utmost importance, even to the most religious individuals. A nuclear warhead there would be an "Iranian weapon," not a "Muslim" one.

The concept of using nuclear weapons preemptively to decapitate an enemy; that is, to be used in the war theater before anyone can retaliate, ignores the very notion of collective security. Should Israel be provided with a more unambiguous security guarantee by the United States, no country could merely seek to "decapitate" its command and control systems without expecting an American nuclear reprisal. Even without the guarantee, however, America's two most important assets in the region, Israel and Saudi Arabia, enjoy the benefits of sitting on Islam's holiest grounds (Mecca, Medina, and Jerusalem are the three most sacred cities in the faith)—hardly attractive targets of nuclear annihilation for any potential rogue fundamentalist.

The last element—the emotional one—is much more difficult to deal with, in that it relies on images of the enemy as a barbaric, irrational being that is consumed with hatred and is willing to engage in national suicide only to inflict loss of life on another country. This argument becomes problematic if we remember Iran's long, national narrative. Iran's institutional memory reaches far beyond the advent of Islam, and this is not lost to even the most radical of Islamists. Supranational movements, embodied in the fight of *Dar al-Islam* (the "House of Islam") versus *Dar al-Harb* (the "House of War") are at the very least mere academic exercises in the history of Islamic theology, and at most, part of a fascination among al-Qaeda sympathizers and not the work of nation-states.

Those who have pointed to Iran's "exportation of its revolution," have correctly referred to geopolitical exercises to extend Iran's influence beyond its borders, and not the manifestation of a religiously pure or selfless missionary endeavor. Suicide bombing is a concept by which organizations utilize individuals as weapons. Suicide attackers (including World War II Kamikaze pilots) have not historically been part of any one particular religion, as the most authoritative studies on the concept suggest.[19] Needless to say, suicide operations carried out by individuals on behalf of an organization do not point to a suicidal organization. Hamas, the PIJ, and Hezbollah are not organizations bent on self-sacrifice. Quite the opposite, they are bent on furthering their influence and power by employing low-level recruits to carry out suicide bombings. States too, seek their own survival, and when the opportunity presents itself, they can seek to acquire more power as an aim to maximize their survivability. And while

Iran has by extension (through its support of terrorist groups) backed numerous suicide operations, Iran as a nation-state is far from suicidal. At the end of the day, nuclear deterrence works when dealing with nation-states. There have been plenty of chances for nations to engage in massive suicide campaigns, and none have been taken, even by the most verbally outlandish of Islamic regimes: Iran.

THE ARMS RACE SCENARIO

One of the more troubling prospects that could arise from Iran's nuclear program would be an arms race in arguably the most volatile region in the world. While Middle Eastern nations have previously called for a Middle East Nuclear Weapons Free Zone (NWFZ), Iran's continued push for weapons have prompted alarm by weary neighbors. These red flags have come in the form of press releases and leaked reports. In December of 2006, the GCC announced it was considering a nuclear program of its own for "peaceful purposes." Not a month later, a report was leaked to *The Sunday Times* of London, disclosing alleged plans by the Israeli government to attack Iran's web of suspected nuclear sites using "bunker busting" bombs—low-yield tactical nuclear weapons that are better equipped than conventional munitions to destroy underground facilities. But both Israel and the Saudi-led GCC are in the unenviable position of seeing America bogged down in Iraq with limited political capital, while seeing their own position vis-à-vis Iran eroding with every claim of uranium enrichment. There is a real sense that these countries are trying to get the United States to notice their security concerns once again.

However, when it comes to an arms race, Barry R. Posen, a global security expert with the Massachusetts Institute of Technology (MIT), explains that an arms race would not be an automatic effect of Iranian proliferation, since the domestic scientific, engineering, and industrial base necessary to build a self-sustaining nuclear program would take Saudi Arabia, for one, several years. In the interim, the Saudis would need nuclear security guarantees from the United States or Europe, which would in turn apply intense pressure on Riyadh not to develop its own arms.[20] Given technological constraints and the impact of sanctions, it is believed that Iran would be capable of producing enough fissile material for a nuclear bomb in 2015, a time period that is long enough to make diplomacy work, but also too short to alleviate the concerns of Iran's rivals. It is also possible that Iran could accelerate the process of enrichment, achieving a weapon much sooner.

Despite problems associated with America's presence in Iraq, the United States has continuously sought to strategically up the ante with Iran, while in many ways pushing for diplomacy to work. January 2007 was an especially busy month, with American troops raiding an Iranian outpost in the Iraqi city of Irbil on suspected links to Iraqi terrorism, just as President Bush had announced a surge of American troops in that country, along with an additional aircraft carrier group in the Gulf—this last move seen as a way of putting Tehran on notice.

For U.S. policymakers, often internally conflicted with the type of threat that Iran represents, and faced with the variety and often contradictory political signs emanating from the Islamic Republic, their ability to send the correct signal to Iran and keep good on America's promises to its allies, while not escalating the conflict into a full out war, will be a daunting task. And while some observers have been quick to accuse the Bush administration of seeking a war with Iran, the U.S. government has been hampered by the Iraq conflict to the point of making war a gamble that even the most hawkish in Washington are cautious about. Some neoconservatives have been quick to distinguish between the need for an aerial assault on suspected nuclear sites, which many support, and the kind of ground war that many critics of the Bush administration have been warning about. Yet opting for air power alone will not guarantee any lasting damage to Iran's nuclear infrastructure, which experts agree is dispersed throughout the country, with much of it hidden from plain view or the grasp of foreign intelligence services.

For Israel, the prospect of a nuclear-armed neighbor is considered a grave and unacceptable threat, and the Jewish state has proven that it is willing to go to great lengths to stop any such development in its tracks. In June of 1979, the bombing of a French factory carrying $23 million worth of internationally approved parts for an Iraqi light-water reactor was attributed to Israeli agents, as was the murder of Dr. Yahya al-Meshad, the chief engineer of the Iraqi nuclear project. On June 7, 1981, the Israeli air force put an end to Iraq's hopes of becoming a nuclear power when it bombed the Osirak reactor south of Baghdad, making it known to the world that nuclear energy in a neighboring country would not be tolerated by Israel. Iran has learned a lesson from these events, and its declared enrichment site in Natanz is considered by many observers to be merely a front, with Iran's real capabilities likely hidden underground and dispersed throughout the country.[21]

Israel's leaked "bunker buster" plan can only be taken to be a bluff, a signal sent to the American government that Israel is willing to escalate matters significantly if Washington is to merely stand by and allow Iran to continue forward with its nuclear program. Today, Israel benefits greatly from its policy of nuclear ambiguity, which has thus far allowed it to ignore calls to create a NWFZ, while still pushing for the nonproliferation of its rivals. Bunker-busting bombs would end this ambiguity and not guarantee that Iran could not rebuild its program, and with greater help from a disdainful international community. But there are fears that should Iran become a nuclear power, Israel might be tempted to make its own arsenal public, and thus send the region further into horizontal and possibly vertical, nuclear proliferation.

In gauging the interests of the United States in the short term, the nuclear proliferation of Iran seems to be a clear nonstarter. With Iran still maintaining a policy of outright anti-Americanism, openly taunting America's ally Israel and forcing other regional actors to potentially contemplate proliferation on their own, the United States must be prepared to deal with the current challenge with poise. But looking at the long term, and given Iran's trajectory of independence and likely future role as a natural American ally, any and all approaches to the current nuclear issue must maintain a balanced view between present conditions and grand strategy. This is indeed a dilemma that America faces: allowing Iran to proliferate will make the president's position seem impotent in the eyes of U.S. allies. Japan, which for long had embraced its post-World War II, U.S.-drafted constitution that calls for a defense-only military, has begun to revisit America's commitment to its protection and has even started considering the development of a homegrown nuclear arsenal. North Korea's 2006 underground test of a nuclear weapon, coupled with numerous hair-raising spectacles of military showmanship by the communist nation, which included the launching of missiles over Japan, naturally are of concern to the small and populous island nation. But Iran's development of a bomb could point to a hands-off policy by the United States toward nuclear proliferation, rather than merely an aberration in the North Korean example. As Japan considers its own entrance into the nuclear club, one must ask whether the security umbrella of America, which provided comfort to its allies during the long and bitter Cold War, can be trusted to maintain security in a post-Cold War security environment.

At the same time that America must care about its erosion of credibility, it must look ahead to a time in which a nuclear-armed Iran might be best poised to provide the necessary stability sought by the United States in the Middle East. By pushing too hard on Iran, and most certainly by launching air strikes against a country that is significantly more pro-American and democratic than most other allies in the region (with the notable exception of Israel), America would be losing its most important hand if it is to adopt a new grand strategy. This grand strategy, which will allow the United States the necessary breathing room and tactical mobility in a post-Iraq war world, should not be discarded with ease. Certainly not at the behest of allies, be they Saudi Arabia or even America's best friend in the region, Israel. America must make this difficult decision, and brace for this dilemma on its own terms and for its own sake. In the end, one must be convinced that a stronger United States, holding the strategic upper hand at the turn of the twenty-first century, will benefit Israel, Saudi Arabia, and all other allies.

For America to successfully bring its allies on board, and for these countries to believe in America's commitment to their security, guarantees must be provided. For one, Israel should receive a clear, public, and unwavering commitment to its protection from any nuclear attack, similar to proclamations made on behalf of Europe during the Cold War. "A nuclear attack on Israel will be considered a nuclear attack on the United States," is not a phrase attributed to any U.S. president. It should be now. This kind of unequivocal security guarantee would allow Israel some space to reconsider its fear of Iranian nukes, while it would not amount to direct confrontation with Iran, leaving ample room for negotiations. Making further statements that Iran will not be allowed under any circumstances to develop nuclear fuel is not only counterproductive from a negotiating perspective—as it allows little face-saving maneuvering on the other side—but it also reeks of empty promises, similar to those uttered before North Korea detonated a weapon in its arsenal. More of those unkept promises will only lead to a further deterioration of America's prestige and will serve to weaken alliances.

When dealing with Saudi Arabia, the guarantee cannot be made public, since this would not likely help the Kingdom, whose population is already scathingly anti-American. Saudi Arabia is a friend so long as the Saudi monarchy is in place, and there is no guarantee that this reality will last forever. Should Wahhabis become stronger, Saudi Arabia could conceivably become an enemy of the United States. The real question is whether America should gamble on a friend ruling over a population of enemies, as is the case with the Saudis, or an enemy ruling over a population of friends, as we find in Iran. The method by which America can walk the tightrope of Iran's nuclear program may prove to be the gateway for a new Middle East, one more in line with the dreams that President Bush, and most Americans, honestly held for Iraq.

Chapter 10

HEGEMONS UNITE: A GLIMPSE INTO THE FUTURE

We covet no one else's territory; we seek no dominion over any other people; we seek the right to live in peace, not only for ourselves but for all the peoples of this earth.
    —President Richard M. Nixon, addressing the people of the Soviet Union (1972)[1]

We are content with our territory and do not seek to expand.... We have stated that we will not attack any other member of the United Nations.
    —Javad Zarif, Iranian ambassador to the UN, addressing a group of American students (2006)[2]

On September 11, 2001, the United States of America woke up to a different world. No longer could the country nestled by the Pacific and Atlantic Oceans be considered safe within its own borders; the Twin Towers of the World Trade Center (WTC), a symbol of American enterprise and prosperity lay in rubble, and the Pentagon, the heart and soul of America's defense infrastructure took a direct hit from a hijacked airplane that had been turned into a potent cruise missile.

Not hours after the attacks, Americans understood that al-Qaeda could not be ignored as an imminent threat to the United States. But al-Qaeda was not a new name, it had been responsible for the bombings of American embassies in Kenya and Tanzania in 1998, the USS Cole off the coast of Yemen in 2000, and a previous attempt to topple the WTC in 1993. Now al-Qaeda would become synonymous with a new war, a hot war between the United States on one side, and Islamist terrorism on the other. During the 1990s, Americans had become accustomed to the relative calm of a post-Cold War era. In this new world, nations would reap the benefits of globalization and economic interdependency, and the sole superpower, the United States, would assist emerging states in their quest for independence, and the ethnic and religious conflicts that accompanied them. The wars in Bosnia and Kosovo, associated with the breakup of a former communist Yugoslavia, and not the prospects of nuclear war, would be the greatest concern to the Western world during this decade.

Nine days after the attacks of 9/11, President George W. Bush stood before a joint session of Congress and gave the nation an unusual moment of greatness—a speech that would have elicited envy from the master John F. Kennedy himself. It was unusual from a man known more for his candor than his mastery of words. But the president held the nation together and established a new way forward. By the end of the address, the country would be set on a "war on terror," and the first target would be Afghanistan, the host nation of Osama bin Laden and other masterminds of the 9/11 attacks. But that would just be the beginning. This war would be fought in order to make terrorism itself obsolete as a practice, not altogether different from the abolishment of slavery, and those surrounding the president thought this could be done.

But systemic problems with the war on terror—the "Long War," as the Department of Defense officially came to call it in 2006—would be profound. Not only was the grand strategy faulty at the core, but its endgoal was based on an utter misunderstanding of terrorism. Perhaps even more disturbing was that the psychological impact of the September 11 attacks precluded most people from asking the most simple, yet painfully callous questions: Are terrorist groups truly the greatest strategic threat to America? Even if armed with the most powerful weapon—a nuclear device—could a terrorist group make America obsolete? Upon examining these questions carefully, the answers would have been negative. Yet since these questions were never asked, a follow-up never surfaced, which might have asked what in fact would be the greatest existential threat to the United States in the twenty-first century. These matters have not been truly debated by the American public since.

But the Long War marched forward, based on a puzzling combination of idealism and callousness. One the one hand, democracy was recognized as the central goal of the war on terror, but amazingly it would be sought through the unprovoked invasion of Iraq. Expedient loopholes would be found to cleverly circumvent the longest living democratic document in the world, the U.S. Constitution, as terror suspects would be held indefinitely without charges, military tribunals would handle secret evidence, and prisoners of war would be arguably subjected to torture. American soft power declined sharply around the world, as allies lost faith in a system that was anything but accommodating, with Bush declaring to friend and foe alike that "you are either with us, or you are with the terrorists."

The Middle East, the focal point of the war on terror, became increasingly hostile to America, as approval rates dropped, cynicism grew, and opportunities for dialogue disappeared en masse. The war on terror itself would come to represent the essential problems of the Iraq war on a macro scale: a faulty idea, and an even more faulty strategy to carry it out. American power has diminished manifold, as credibility has faded, and military readiness hurt by an overstretched military committed to Iraq. But the questions that weren't asked on September 11 remain unanswered today.

A NEW STRATEGY

The United States must continue to fight a war against those who attempt to harm it. Today, a significant number of Muslim extremists conspires to bring mass death to American citizens. This is an issue that must be tackled with conviction and might. But conviction does not translate to the abandonment of soft power politics. Soft power can be especially useful in this war on terror, as America depends on law enforcement officers from around the world, and the continuous goodwill of foreign populations, to ultimately diminish the threat posed by extremist groups like al-Qaeda. America needs to deal with the problem systemically. This does not mean refraining from killing terrorists, or keeping off the table the military option at any time. It simply means formulating a coherent strategy to deal with the root causes of terrorism for the long term, while maintaining the necessary tactical tools to battle enemies in the present.

For America to be prepared for the existential challenges of the twenty-first century, policymakers must show vision, and maintain a long-term outlook. It is a daunting task, as politics increasingly becomes dominated by twenty-four-hour news cycles and the worries *du jour*. But the United States, like all other great powers before it, is by definition at risk of falling from grace. As commitments around the world increase, and interests become synonymous with every region of the world, America must be ready to deal with challenges to its dominant, hegemonic position from potential rivals. These rivals could be single countries or alliances. Friends today can be foes in the future, and competitors today can turn into mortal enemies. But perhaps the better way to prepare for the unforeseen is to maintain a deterrent capability, along with a coherent system of order in the world, based on American hegemony, but not exclusive of other nations' interests to the point of precipitating rivalries.

The Nixon Doctrine, which allows regional leaders to play an active role in securing their own domains, allows America to exploit the strength of regional powerhouses, thus permitting the United States to make its influence less blunt, less present, and more connected to soft power. Other nations are better poised to provide security in their respective regions, and this can allow for more local prestige, a vague concept that has unfortunately escaped numerous policymakers, not the least of whom were the masterminds of the Iraq occupation. Prestige is critically tied to sovereignty, and unprovoked occupation, whether in the proud Middle

East or elsewhere, has throughout history proven a grindingly challenging enterprise at best, and a total fiasco at worst.

The Nixon Doctrine, if applied toward forming a systemic balance in the world, can and should begin with the critical region of the Middle East. Demand for the region's oil, natural gas, and petrochemicals supplies will not recede any time soon. And Islamist terrorism, which is likely to gain greater strength and become a heavier burden on America and its allies, cannot be altogether divorced from U.S. considerations.

Because soft power will continue to play a critical role in the new Nixon Doctrine world, the need to form alliances on the basis of mutually favorable political ideologies like democracy will only increase in importance. Islamic terrorism, along with the greater questions surrounding the acceptance of America's position as global leader, cannot be faced merely with bullets and tanks. Ultimately, terrorist activities are only vindicated by a response that is perceived to be overtly violent in nature. This is the dilemma that has plagued any nation seeking to stomp out an insurgency or terrorist campaign. The harder one pushes back with brute force, the more difficult the problem becomes. In fact, the limited but growing analytical literature on terrorism that is available agrees perhaps on only one thing: one of the main, immediate goals of any terrorist attack is to invite a brutal response by the target government. This game of dare is deadly, and should be approached with caution and farsightedness, and not with emotion or impulses of revenge.

Democracy, which provides an avenue for voicing political grievances, and thus mitigates the need for terrorism to arise, requires institutionalism, and cannot be dictated by an outside power or even a benevolent leader. Democracy must come from within, and some institutional memory of it must exist within the countries that are to experience it. Germany and Japan both had, to varying degrees, an institutional memory of democratic practice, and thus it was not impossible to see them become democracies after their devastating defeats of World War II. Eastern European nations too, had witnessed homegrown, pro-American democratic movements several years before the fateful end of communism in 1989. Those countries that had more experience with democratic currents tended to fare much better after the massive political changes took place.

In the Middle East, Iran is a country moving in the direction of democracy. With a trajectory of independence spanning centuries, and its experience with multifaceted, politics-based competition (as opposed to ethnic-based differences), national elections, and constitutional referenda, the nation is far ahead of most of its neighbors. The Arab world, which has experienced a long history of colonialism at the hands of early Muslim armies, the Ottoman Empire, and most recently Europe, has had difficulty adjusting to the era of sovereign nation-states. Constant divisions and a lack of nationalist clarity have mired the region. Sectarian and tribal conflict remains part and parcel of regional tensions, from overt conflicts in Iraq and Lebanon, to those brewing just beneath the surface in places like Bahrain and Saudi Arabia.

The Islamic Republic of Iran, the quintessential anti-American supporter of terrorism, must be engaged through serious dialogue, but only once U.S. policymakers have come to realize the true nature of Iran's trajectory, and whether in the long term, Iran is to be considered a threat or an ally. Already, policymakers in the last four administrations have perceived Iran's trajectory of independence, and have counseled against a total embargo or the use of force. These brave individuals in government, tasked with providing the hardest realities of all—those that defy popular convention, and which appear on the surface to run counter to American interests—have shown a willingness to think on grand strategic terms, and put the future of America before anything else.

Formulating a coherent, successful policy for the United States of America will take the collaboration of countless people who are committed to furthering the security of their country. It will also take a population informed in the nuances of U.S.-Iranian relations to provide support and ideas toward this aim. This can begin with more responsible, in-depth news coverage, and more careful rhetoric on the part of elected political leaders. The next section discusses a policy proposal to deal with the current political crisis with Iran. It takes into account the points that have been made in this book, and seeks to marry the critical, immediate concerns of policymakers, with a grand strategic outlook of Iran, and its likelihood to play the role of an ally to the United States.

POLICY PRESCRIPTIONS

As with any policy, a certain set of assumptions must be initially laid out. The first assumption made here is that the current anti-America rhetoric by Iran is a reflection of the political identities of certain key actors, and not Iranian strategic intentions toward the United States in the long run. Iran's cult of anti-Americanism is part of the regime's narrative, and it is connected to the rulers' legitimization of power, rather than to the actual designs of a state seeking total war with a much more powerful rival. Another assumption is that Iranian power is growing, and will not be easily contained over the long term. That is, while sanctions and even military action can set back Iran's nuclear project and other aims at increasing its military industrial capabilities, over the long term Iran is poised to reemerge as the powerhouse of the Middle East. A last, but crucial assumption, which is based not only on available statistics, but on an ocean of anecdotal support, is that Iran's new generation is significantly pro-American, much more so than that found in most other nations in the region, or even the world.

With these assumptions in mind, we can make the following policy recommendations. For the Executive Branch of the United States of America: (a) Provide an unequivocal, public security guarantee to Israel, along the lines that "an attack by any state against Israel utilizing unconventional weapons of any kind, will be taken as an attack on the United States"; (b) Privately and conditionally bring Saudi Arabia under America's security umbrella, and otherwise create incentives to keep the GCC from developing or procuring a nuclear arsenal. This will be critical in avoiding an arms race in the region. Arab nations' concerns about a rising Iran must be taken into account, and assurances should be made that America understands their security outlook; (c) Establish and maintain efficient communication channels with stable regime elements in Iran, including the Islamic Revolutionary Guard Corps (IRGC), the office of the supreme leader, and the executive branch. This does not mean rushing to hold presidentto-president talks, or president-to-supreme leader talks. It merely means keeping the lines of communication open, as America did with the Soviet Union during the Cold War, in order to avert a potential crisis borne out of a misunderstanding. To be sure, Iran's communication approach can be puzzling to Americans, but letters sent by the president of Iran to the White House should not be dismissed as mere "rants," as was the case when President Ahmadinejad sent a letter to President Bush in 2006. More importantly, America must be willing to de-link the nuclear issue from areas of potential cooperation, such as the stabilization of Iraq and Afghanistan. Talks on any subject will help rebuild a relationship that has been strained by the hostage crisis and the Iranian regime's harsh rhetoric. But the improvement of overall relations will take time, and perhaps a new generation will have to come to power before the Iranian government can completely back down from its anti-American identity.

For the Legislative Branch of the United States of America: (a) Maintain a narrow and flexible scope for sanctions on Iran, allowing for specific, face-saving steps that the regime can take in order to further ease the economic pressures. This means a path toward slow rapprochement, without expecting a declaration to the tune of an apology, or a retreat. This would be impossible, and expecting such a move by Iran is negligently misguided, given the serious, immediate need to improve the political climate in the Middle East; (b) Cease all support, rhetorical or otherwise, for Iranian opposition groups, especially the Mojahedeen, or National Council of Resistance of Iran (NCRI), which the State Department has listed as a terrorist organization off and on since 1997. Some members of Congress, unfortunately, are not following the State Department's line and make it a point to support the organization, whose help of Saddam Hussein during the eight-year Iran-Iraq war gained it universal repudiation inside Iran. Just as it ended up a catastrophic mistake for high-ranking U.S. administration officials to associate with, and gain (nonfactual) information from Iraqi dissident Ahmad Chalabi and his associates leading up to the Iraq war of 2003, the Mojahedeen cannot be allowed to court American policymakers into making potentially damaging decisions regarding Iran. Even nonviolent groups such as monarchists, however, should be kept at arm's length. And while the U.S. government should not seek to restrict the broadcasting of promonarchy messages into Iran, it should also clearly maintain that it does not encourage them. While most Iranians hold a high degree of contempt toward the Islamic regime, the answer will not be to encourage nondemocratic or extremist groups to impact Iranian politics; (c) Establish long-term, wide-ranging academic programs to bring large numbers of Iranian students to the United States, as well as significant numbers of American students and researchers to Iran. This has been one of the few critical channels of communication between the two countries following the revolution, and the more mutual information that exits, the clearer the overall picture is about the other society and its possible intentions. Any security-related limits on Iranian students coming to the United States, such as those temporarily imposed after the attacks of September 11, are misdirected and counterproductive, especially given the rarity of international terrorist acts actually committed by Iranian nationals; and, finally, (d) allow for, and encourage joint U.S.-Iranian enterprises in filmmaking, publishing, crafts, and other Iranian cultural exports and sources of independent thought and national pride. Iranian filmmaking has been an oasis of expression in Iran, and has lifted the image and prestige of Iran, not only in the United States, but around the globe. Such expressions are important, not only in providing a better glimpse of Iranian culture to Americans, but because such joint efforts could further build trust at the ground level, and improve the position of democratically minded Iranians, who often utilize these media as a form of political and social expression. Cinema, like poetry, has an impact on Iranian society that cannot be overestimated.

CONCLUSION

Perhaps because of the problems presented by the Iraq occupation, or simply because cooler heads have prevailed, or even perhaps because Iran was never a target, President Bush in his 2006 State of the Union address made it clear that regime change would not be on his agenda for Iran. In a way, Bush echoed previous statements made by Iranian President Khatami, when he said:

> Democracies in the Middle East will not look like our own, because they will reflect the traditions of their own citizens. Yet liberty is the future of every nation in the Middle East, because liberty is the right and hope of all humanity. . . . [Let] me speak directly to the citizens of Iran: America respects

you and we respect your country. We respect your right to choose your own future and win your own freedom. And our nation hopes one day to be the closest of friends with a free and democratic Iran.[3]

This proclamation did not make news for long, as the rhetoric between Tehran and Washington escalated over the coming months in relation to Iran's nuclear program. But the war of words, as both sides (but mostly Iran) have played it, belies a deeper fact that countless studies and intelligence reports provide. That Iran and America are inherent allies, cheated of this position by myopic mistakes of previous administrations and unnuanced Iranian rulers. Today, Iran is considered one of the biggest foes of America, but only ironically, because in many ways, it is one of its biggest friends in the making.

Some have traced the revolution and the cult of anti-Americanism to the overthrow of Mohammad Mosaddeq in 1953. In many ways, this incident brought out the worst in Iran's desire for independence, as moderate options seemed to have proved futile in the face of great power greed and ignorance. But Iran's trajectory of independence did not begin there, and it certainly faced other obstacles prior to Mosaddeq. The Tobacco Protest of 1890 proved to the world that Iran was not willing to be bought, even if its leaders were willing to sell it. The Constitutional Revolution of 1905–1911 gave Iranians hope that Europe could export its methods of democratic government to their country, while leaving its commercial interests at home. Brave Iranian leaders sought an end to systemic corruption, often at their own peril. Even Reza Shah, who ridiculously sought to adopt European dress by force while missing the point of *freedom* of dress in Europe, ultimately longed for an independent Iran.

Religious forces in Iran have also not remained monolithic, despite every attempt by the regime to prove otherwise. Shi'i dynamism has proven to be an important part of the trajectory of independence, not only in relation to the practice of ijtihad, and the personal freedom to choose a mujtahid, but also surrounding the epic battles between more liberal, rationalist elements of Islamic jurisprudence, and those of a more rigid strain. Even mainstream conservative clerics, however, have differed on the notions of Islamic government and the role of the mosque within the state. Most have opted to minimize the role of religion in government, and they continue to remain the face of Iranian Shi'ism, despite calls by the ruling clerics to toe the theocratic line.

The Iranian Revolution brought out the dark side of nonalignment. It sought to expel foreign influences, and unnecessarily used the United States as a scapegoat for every slight on Iranian pride. It established a cult of anti-Americanism and saw manifestations of America's impact on Iranian culture as a direct attack on Islamic values. When expedient, the revolution jettisoned those ideas it had ardently espoused, such as popular will, and even shari'ah. In its consolidation of power and its halting of political development, it was aided by Saddam's invasion of 1980, which brought hundreds of thousands of deaths to Iran, but also allowed the state to reach a level of primacy that would have otherwise been unattainable through the mere machinations of Khomeini and his associates.

But the 1980–1988 war did something else. It showed Iran to be a truly independent country, no longer beholden to outside powers. With some notable exceptions, the region ganged up on Iran, and Iran was able to survive and come out of the conflict determined to be smarter, less idealistic, and more powerful. Today, as American commentators speak of a "defiant" Iran, unwilling to offer widespread concessions in relation to its nuclear program or support for Hezbollah, we must remember the price that Iran was willing to pay in order not to be managed by outside actors. Iran, in its own eyes, earned the right not to be dictated terms, to be "defiant," as it survived a war that the international community was collectively wishing it would lose. Negotiations between Iran and the United States then, will have to respect Iran's sovereignty, and will have to see Iran as a product of its own systems. If leaders such as Ahmadinejad, who are elected by the people, direct pointed, anti-Semitic comments at Israel, Iranians themselves will have to deal with the consequences. Should Israel decide to attack Iran because of recent statements and actions, it would be understandable, but not necessarily in the best interest of America and the region.

Former NATO Supreme Commander General Wesley Clark, who is no stranger to the effective application of military power, has rightly cautioned that we should take a more tactful approach in dealing with "a region struggling to regain its pride after centuries of perceived humiliation by the West." To encourage the kinds of governments we want to see in the Middle East, Clark believes, we must "act indirectly and patiently—even while we take the specific actions truly necessary for our self-defense."[4] This outlook goes to the heart of this nascent century, and the challenges that America will continue to face in the Middle East and around the world. A more nuanced approach to politics can only be fruitful. If America can balance today's world with tomorrow's goals, the payoff will be significant. At the end of the day, Iran's regional hegemony might be the best recipe for maintaining the American kind. But that chapter in history has yet to be written.

NOTES

INTRODUCTION

1. Max Weber, *The Theory of Social and Economic Organization* (New York: Oxford University Press, 1947), p. 152. Quoted in Peter M. Blau, *Exchange and Power in Social Life* (New York: Wiley, 1964), p. 115.

2. "[A] 2002 review ... was commissioned by national security adviser Stephen J. Hadley, who was then deputy adviser, to assess the possibility for 'regime change' in Iran. Those findings described the Islamic republic on a slow march toward democracy and cautioned against U.S. interference in that process." See "Iran Is Judged 10 Years from Nuclear Bomb," *The Washington Post* (August 5, 2005). For an argument in favor of "hegemonic peace," see William C. Wohlforth, "The Stability of a Unipolar World," *International Security*, 24(1) (Summer 1999): 5–41.

3. Colin S. Gray, *The Geopolitics of Super Power* (Lexington: The University Press of Kentucky, 1988), p. 15.

4. Robert A. Pape, "The Strategic Logic of Suicide Terrorism," *The American Political Science Review*, 97(3) (August 2003): 348; also see Robert A. Pape, *Dying to Win: The Strategic Logic of Suicide Terrorism* (New York: Random House, 2005).

5. A former deputy undersecretary of defense, Jed Babbin is a frequent cable news talk show guest who has spoken of President Ahmadinejad and Osama bin Laden as "ideological buddies," and suggested that Ahmadinejad spoke of wiping Israel off the map as an attempt to bring on Armageddon ("Heartland," *Fox News*, February 4, 2006). Such viewpoints ignore basic differences between extreme Sunnis like bin Laden, who consider Shi'is to be infidels, and even the most radical of Iranian Shi'is. The fact that Jerusalem houses the third holiest site in Islam seems to escape many commentators who are quick to link Iran's anti-Israeli and anti-Semitic rhetoric with Iran's nuclear program. In great contrast, conservative commentator and former presidential candidate Pat Buchanan has maintained a more realistic line regarding Iranian power and President Ahmadinejad's intentions and abilities ("Scarborough Country," *MSNBC*, December 21, 2006).

6. W. Montgomery Watt, *Muhammad: Prophet and Statesman* (Oxford, UK: Oxford University Press, 1961), p. 228. For a good overview of Shi'i Islam, see Moojan Momen, *An Introduction to Shi'i Islam: The History and Doctrines of Twelver Shi'ism* (New Haven, CT: Yale University Press, 1987).

7. *BBC News*, "Profile: Iran's Dissident Ayatollah" (January 30, 2003), online: http://news.bbc.co.uk/2/hi/middle_east/2699541.stm

CHAPTER 1

1. Quoted in Lindsay Allen, *The Persian Empire: A History* (London: British Museum Press, 2005), p. 43.

2. J. M. Cook, *The Persian Empire* (London: J. M. Dent & Sons, 1983), pp. 41–42.

3. J. R. Perry, "Justice for the Underprivileged: The Ombudsman Tradition of Iran," *Journal of Near Eastern Studies*, 37(3) (July 1978): 204. On the perception of Iran's natural boundaries, see Firoozeh Kashani-Sabet, "Fragile Frontiers: The Diminishing Domains of Qajar Iran," *International Journal of Middle East Studies*, 29(2) (May 1997): 205–209.

4. Matthew W. Stolper, *Entrepreneurs and Empire: The Murasu Archive, the Murasu Firm, and Persian Rule in Babylonia* (Leiden, the Netherlands: Nederlands Instituut voor het Nabije Oosten, 1985), p. 41.

5. Richard N. Frye, *The Golden Age of Persia: The Arabs in the East* (London: Weidenfield, 1993), p. 5.

6. On the decline of women's education, see Frye, *The Golden Age of Persia*, pp. 20–21. For statistics related to female participation in higher education, see "The Gender and Citizenship Initiative: Country Profiles," *The United Nations Development Programme*, online: http://gender.pogar.org/

7. Alice C. Hunsberger, *Nasir Khusraw, The Ruby of Badakhshan: A Portrait of the Persian Poet, Traveller and Philosopher* (London: I.B. Tauris, 2003), p. 4. On the tumultuous period of eight- and ninth-century Baghdad and Qom, see Andrew J. Newman, *The Formative Period of Twelver Shi'ism: Hadith as Discourse between Qum and Baghdad* (Richmond, UK: Curzon, 2000); Hossein Modarressi, "Rationalism and Traditionalism in Shi'i Jurisprudence: A Preliminary Survey," *Studia Islamica*, 59 (1984): 141–158; Joseph Eliash, "Misconceptions Regarding the Juridical Status of the Iranian 'Ulama,'" *International Journal of Middle East Studies*, 10(1) (February 1979): 9–25; Said Amir Arjomand, "The Consolation of Theology: Absence of the Imam and Transition from Chiliasm to Law in Shi'ism," *The Journal of Religion*, 76(4) (October 1996): 548–571. On the Usuli/Akhbari controversy, see Andrew J. Newman, "The Nature of the Akhbari/Usuli Dispute in Late Safavid Iran, Part 1: 'Abdallah al-Samahiji's 'Munyat al-Mumarisin,'" *Bulletin of the School of Oriental and African Studies, University of London*, 55(1) (1992): 22–51.

8. Andrew J. Newman, *Safavid Iran: Rebirth of a Persian Empire* (London: I.B. Tauris, 2006), Chapter 2.

9. Lawrence Potter, "An Introduction to the Gulf Region," *The Gulf/2000 Project*, online: http://gulf2000.columbia.edu/country.shtml

10. Perry, "Justice for the Underprivileged," p. 204.

11. J. R. Perry, *Karim Khan Zand: A History of Iran, 1747–1779* (Chicago, IL: University of Chicago Press, 1979), p. 288.

12. Kamran Ekbal, "Ein britischer Plan zur Restauration der Zand-Herrschaft aus dem Jahre 1807," *Die Welt des Islams*, New Ser., Bd. 22, Nr. 1/4 (1982): 37–50.

CHAPTER 2

1. Quoted in relation to Iranian Prime Minister Mohammad Mosaddeq's hunger strikes, in Farhad Diba, *Mossadegh: A Political Biography* (London: Croom Helm, 1986), p. 24.

2. Mansoor Moaddel, "Shiʻi Political Discourse and Class Mobilization in the Tobacco Movement of 1890–92," in John Foran (ed.), *A Century of Revolution: Social Movements in Iran* (Minneapolis: University of Minnesota Press, 1994), p. 8.

3. See Nikki Keddie, *Modern Iran: Roots and Results of Revolution* (New Haven, CT: Yale University Press, 2003), pp. 48–49. On the influence of the Ottoman Empire over Amir Kabir's reforms, including the greater inclusion of Christians, see Anja Pistor-Hatam, *Iran und die Reformbewegung im Osmanischen Reich: Persische Staatsmänner, Reisende und Oppositionelle unter dem Einfluß der Tanzimat* (Berlin: Klaus Schwarz Verlag, 1992), pp. 38–48.

4. Abbas Amanat, *Resurrection and Renewal: The Making of the Babi Movement in Iran, 1844–1850* (Ithaca, NY: Cornell University Press, 1989), p. 298. On more of the development of Qurrat-ul-ʻayn, see Chapter 7. For more on the tenets of the Baabis, see Peter Smith, *The Babi and Bahaʼi Religions: From Messianic Shiʻism to a World Religion* (Cambridge, UK: Cambridge University Press, 1987).

5. Ann K. S. Lampton, *Theory and Practice in Medieval Persian Government* (London: Variorium Reprints, 1980), p. 20, quoted in Moaddel, "Shiʻi Political Discourse and Class Mobilization in the Tobacco Movement of 1890–92," p. 7.

6. See Keddie, *Modern Iran*, Chapters 3–4.

7. A. Reza Sheikholeslami, *The Structure of Central Authority in Qajar Iran: 1871–1896* (Atlanta, GA: Scholars Press, 1997), p. 164; on Kamran Mirza's dual office, see p. 161.

8. Moaddel, "Shiʻi Political Discourse and Class Mobilization in the Tobacco Movement of 1890–92," p. 11.

9. Hamid Dabashi, *Authority in Islam: From the Rise of Muhammad to the Establishment of the Umayyads* (New Brunswick, NJ: Transaction Publishers, 2002), p. 104.

10. Ervand Abrahamian, "Oriental Despotism: The Case of Qajar Iran," *International Journal of Middle East Studies*, 5(1) (January 1974): 12.

11. Janet Afary, "Social Democracy and the Iranian Constitutional Revolution of 1906–11," in John Foran (ed.), *A Century of Revolution: Social Movements in Iran* (Minneapolis: University of Minnesota Press, 1994), p. 21.

12. Afary, "Social Democracy," p. 23. On the formation of the first secret *anjuman*, see Janet Afary, *The Iranian Constitutional Revolution, 1906–1911: Grassroots Democracy, Social Democracy & the Origins of Feminism* (New York: Columbia University Press, 1996), pp. 42–43; on the Naus controversy, see p. 51.

13. W. Morgan Shuster, *The Strangling of Persia: Story of the European Diplomacy and Oriental Intrigue That Resulted in the Denationalization of Twelve Million Mohammedans—A Personal Narrative (1912)* (New York: Greenwood, 1968), p. 191.

14. Afary, *The Iranian Constitutional Revolution*, p. 55. For more on liberal-minded and Western-influenced clergy (most notably personified by Sayyid Mohammad Tabatabaʼi), see Vanessa Martin, *Islam and Modernism: The Iranian Revolution of 1906* (London: I.B. Tauris, 1989), especially pp. 30 and 59, and Chapter 3. For

an excellent overview of women's contribution to the Constitutional Revolution, see Chapter 7 in Afary, *The Iranian Constitutional Revolution*.

15. Afary, *The Iranian Constitutional Revolution*, p. 63.

16. Quoted in Shuster, *The Strangling of Persia*, p. xxx.

17. Afary, pp. 317–323.

18. Stephanie Cronin, *The Army and the Creation of the Pahlavi State in Iran, 1910–1926* (London: Tauris Academic Studies, 1997), pp. 19–20.

19. Shuster, *The Strangling of Persia*, pp. 203–204.

CHAPTER 3

1. "Mr. Truman & the Shahinsah," *Time* (November 28, 1949).

2. Stephanie Cronin, *The Army and the Creation of the Pahlavi State in Iran, 1910–1926* (London: Tauris Academic Studies, 1997), p. 85. For more on the Reza Khan-British alliance, see Michael P. Zirinsky, "Imperial Power and Dictatorship: Britain and the Rise of Reza Shah, 1921–1926," *International Journal of Middle East Studies*, 24(4) (November 1992).

3. In 1924, Reza Khan engaged in a campaign to dismiss the sitting, figurehead king, Ahmad Shah, who at the time was in Europe, and place in his stead a republican form of government. Given his overt control over the military and his reputation as a power hungry individual, Reza Khan's opponents feared that his support for republican governance was a diversion intended to open the way for his own ascension to the throne. Some have suggested that the religious establishment feared the kind of forced secularization that republican leader Atatürk had instilled in Turkey. However, opposition to forming a republican government at the time was voiced even by secular nationalists like Mohammad Mosaddeq, who was then a majles deputy. Vanessa Martin seeks to dispel the connection between Turkey's republicanism and opposition to Reza's bill in the majles, by maintaining that broad-based opposition to the motion existed and very limited contemporary accounts are given in the Persian literature to support the widely held claim of a Turkish connection. See Vanessa Martin, "Mudarris, Republicanism and the Rise to Power of Riza Khan, Sardar-I Sipah," *British Journal of Middle Eastern Studies*, 21 (2) (1994).

4. FO248/1106: "Cowan, Qazvin, to Marling" (November 20, 1915), quoted in Stephanie Cronin, "An Experiment in Revolutionary Nationalism: The Rebellion of Colonel Muhammad Taqi Khan Pasyan in Mashhad, April–October 1921," *Middle Eastern Studies*, 33(4) (October 1997): 697.

5. Cronin, "An Experiment in Revolutionary Nationalism," p. 698.

6. Cronin, *Creation of the Pahlavi State*, p. 104.

7. H.E. Chehabi, "The Banning of the Veil and Its Consequences," in Stephanie Cronin (ed.), *The Making of Modern Iran: State and Society under Riza Shah, 1921–1941* (London: Routledge, 2003), p. 202 (emphasis mine). Recounted by his widow is Reza Shah's motivation for the unveiling of women, and how the king would have preferred to die than to "show his wife bare-headed to strangers, but he had no choice, as otherwise Iranians will be thought to be savage and backward": 'Alinaqi 'Alikhani (ed.), *Yaddashta-ye 'Alam*, Vol. 4, 1353 (Bethesda, MD: IBEX Publishers, n.d), p. 298, quoted in Chehabi, "The Banning of the Veil and Its Consequences," p. 200.

8. Nikki Keddie, *Modern Iran: Roots and Results of Revolution* (New Haven, CT: Yale University Press, 2003), p. 87; on military expenditures, see p. 91.

9. Ibid., p. 94.

10. Ibid., p. 101.

11. See Farhad Diba, *Mohammad Mossadegh: A Political Biography* (London: Croom Helm, 1986), Chapter 1.

12. Diba, *Mohammad Mossadegh*, pp. 83–84.

13. Despite average increases in exports and production of 42 percent between 1926 and 1931, "Iran's share of revenue fell by 22 per cent over the same period." In 1931, Iran's oil income fell to a low between 307,000 and 310,000 pounds sterling, while Great Britain took in one million pounds sterling in taxes from the AIOC. See Parviz Daneshvar, *Revolution in Iran* (London: Palgrave Macmillan Press, 1996), p. 14.

14. File 120.4382/3-1551: Agreed Conclusions and Recommendations of the Conference of Middle Eastern Chiefs of Mission, Istanbul, February 14–21, 1951, *Foreign Relations*, 1951 (Vol. V), p. 71.

15. McGhee Files: Lot 53 D 468, "Petroleum," *Foreign Relations*, 1951 (Vol. V), pp. 309–315.

16. Sepehr Zabih, *The Mossadegh Era: Roots of the Iranian Revolution* (Chicago, IL: Lake View Press, 1982), pp. 88–126.

17. Daneshvar, *Revolution in Iran*, p. 38; for more on the SAVAK, Army Counter-Intelligence, and the "two-party" system, see pp. 39–40.

18. Quoted in Misagh Parsa, "Mosque of Last Resort: State Reform and Social Conflict in the Early 1960s," in John Foran (ed.), *A Century of Revolution: Social Movements in Iran* (Minneapolis: University of Minnesota Press, 1994), p. 144.

19. Hussein Sirriyeh, *U.S. Policy in the Gulf, 1968–1977: Aftermath of British Withdrawal* (London: Ithaca Press, 1984), p. 62.

20. Ali M. Ansari, *Iran, Islam and Democracy: The Politics of Managing Change* (London: The Royal Institute of International Affairs, 2000), p. 53. On the White Revolution vote, see Parsa, "Mosque of Last Resort," p. 145. On the migration of farmers to urban areas, see Ali Farazmand, *The State, Bureaucracy, and Revolution in Modern Iran: Agrarian Reforms and Regime Politics* (Westport, CT: Praeger, 1989), pp. 139–140.

21. Zabih, *The Mossadegh Era*, p. 155.

CHAPTER 4

1. *Central Intelligence Agency*: Research Study, "Elites and the Distribution of Power in Iran" (Secret, February 1976).

2. Sayid Saffari, "The Legitimation of the Clergy's Right to Rule in the Iranian Constitution of 1979," *British Journal of Middle Eastern Studies*, 20(1) (1993): 80.

3. Baqer Moin, *Khomeini: Life of an Ayatollah* (New York: St. Martin's Press, 2000), Chapter 1.

4. Robin Wright, *In the Name of God: The Khomeini Decade* (New York: Simon & Schuster, 1989), pp. 52–53.

5. Ayatollah Ruhollah Khomeyni, *Islamic Government*, National Technical Information Service, Translations on Near East and North Africa, No. 1897 (U.S. Department of Commerce, January 19, 1979), p. 7.

6. Parviz Daneshvar, *Revolution in Iran* (London: Palgrave Macmillan Press, 1996), pp. 101–102.

7. Cheryl Bernard and Zalmay Khalilzad, *The Government of God: Iran's Islamic Republic* (New York: Columbia University Press, 1984), pp. 41–42.

8. Gary Sick writes about this cyclical pattern in *All Fall Down: America's Tragic Encounter with Iran* (New York: Random House, 1985).

9. Hamid Dabashi, "By What Authority?: The Formation of Khomeini's Revolutionary Discourse, 1964–1977," *Social Compass*, 36(4) (1989): 522.

10. On the Jaleh Square massacre, see Daneshvar, *Revolution in Iran*, p. 106; on General Nassiri and the shah's freeing of political prisoners, see p. 108.

11. Quoted in Daneshavar, *Revolution in Iran*, p. 131.

12. Bahman Baktiari, *Parliamentary Politics in Revolutionary Iran: The Institutionalization of Factional Politics* (Gainesville: University Press of Florida, 1996), pp. 78–80.

13. Robert D. McFadden, Joseph B. Treaster and Maurice Carrol, *No Hiding Place: The New York Times Inside Report on the Hostage Crisis* (New York, Times Books, 1981), p. 40.

14. Abol Hassan Bani-Sadr, *My Turn to Speak: Iran, the Revolution & Secret Deals with the U.S.* (Washington, DC: Brassey's, 1989), p. 31.

15. For an overview of the mission, see Gary Sick, "Military Options and Constraints," in Paul H. Kreisberg (ed.), *American Hostages in Iran: The Conduct of a Crisis* (New Haven, CT: Yale University Press, 1985). See also McFadden, Treaster, and Carrol, *No Hiding Place*, p. 201.

16. David C. Rapoport, "A Comparative Theory of Military Types," in Samuel Huntington (ed.), *Changing Patterns of Military Politics* (New York: Free Press of Glencoe, 1962), p. 79.

17. Shahram Chubin and Charles Tripp, *Iran and Iraq at War* (Boulder, CO: Westview Press, 1988), p. 33.

18. Quoted in Chubin and Tripp, *Iran and Iraq at War*, p. 50.

19. *Defense Intelligence Agency*: "The Iran-Iraq War: A Reference Aid (U), Defense Research Reference Series (August 8, 1988), Secret.

20. Dabashi, "By What Authority?" p. 535.

CHAPTER 5

1. Alexander Bligh, "The Saudi Religious Elite (Ulama) as Participant in the Political System of the Kingdom," *International Journal of Middle East Studies*, 17(1) (1985): 40. For historical analysis, see Joseph A. Kechichian, "The Role of the Ulema in the Politics of an Islamic State: The Case of Saudi Arabia," *International Journal of Middle East Studies*, 18(1) (1986); on the compromise between modernity and fundamentalism, see p. 54.

2. Ayman Al-Yassini, *Religion and State in the Kingdom of Saudi Arabia* (Boulder, CO: Westview Press, 1985), p. 29.

3. Ghassane Salameh and Vivian Steir, "Political Power and the Saudi State," *MERIP Reports*, No. 91, Saudi Arabia on the Brink (October 1980), p. 42; on

the clergy's exile in Egypt, see p. 38, and on the influence of ARAMCO, see p. 6.

4. Frank E. Vogel writes, "Saudi Arabia also has a dual legal system, but the relative roles of the two sides are reversed. The Islamic component of the legal system is fundamental and dominant." Frank E. Vogel, "Islamic Governance in the Gulf: A Framework for Analysis, Comparison, and Prediction," in Gary G. Sick and Lawrence G. Potter (eds.), *The Persian Gulf at the Millennium: Essays in Politics, Economy, Security, and Religion* (New York: St. Martin's Press, 1997), p. 276.

5. *U.S. Department of State*, "International Religious Freedom Report for 2005, Saudi Arabia," online: http://www.state.gov/g/drl/rls/irf/2005/51609.htm

6. A useful analysis of *Kashf al-Asrar* is found in Vanessa Martin, "Religion and State in Khumaini's Kashf Al-Asrar," *Bulletin of the School of Oriental and African Studies, University of London*, 56(1) (1993).

7. George N. Sfeir, "The Saudi Approach to Law Reform," *The American Journal of Comparative Law*, 36 (4) (Autumn 1988): 730.

8. Al-Yassini, *Religion and State in the Kingdom of Saudi Arabia*, p. 29.

9. Nikki Keddie, *Modern Iran: Roots and Results of Revolution* (New Haven, CT: Yale University Press, 2003), pp. 16–17.

10. Ibid., p. 40.

11. Norman Calder, "Judicial Authority in Imami Shi'i Jurisprudence," *Bulletin (British Society for Middle Eastern Studies)*, 6(2) (1979): 105.

12. Aharon Layish, "Saudi Arabian Legal Reform as a Mechanism to Moderate Wahhabi Doctrine," *Journal of the American Oriental Society*, 107(2) (1987): 281.

13. Ibid., p. 282.

14. The council wasn't operational until 1958. Koury, *The Saudi Decision-Making Body: The House of Al-Saud* (Hyattsville, MD: Institute of Middle Eastern and North African Affairs, 1978), p. 37.

15. Kechichian, "The Role of the Ulema in the Politics of an Islamic State," p. 60. Mentioned is al-Qahtani's direct lineage to the former Ikhwan, as well as a connection to the Prophet Muhammad's lineage. A detailed account of the seizure of the Grand Mosque appears in pp. 58–63.

16. Ibid., p. 61.

17. Sami Zubaida, "An Islamic State? The Case of Iran," *Middle East Report*, No. 153, Islam and the State (July–August 1998), p. 6.

18. Azadeh Nikham, "The Islamization of Law in Iran: A Time of Disenchantment," *Middle East Report*, No. 212, Pushing the Limits: Iran's Islamic Revolution at Twenty (Fall 1999), p. 20.

19. Kechichian, "The Role of the Ulema in the Politics of an Islamic State," p. 57. See also Stéphane Lacroix, "Between Islamists and Liberals: Saudi Arabia's New 'Islamo-Liberal' Reformists," *The Middle East Journal*, 58(3) (2004): 364.

20. Salameh and Steir, "Political Power and the Saudi State," p. 9.

21. Bligh, "The Saudi Religious Elite," p. 42.

22. Patrick Clawson, "The Paradox of Anti-Americanism," *Middle East Review of International Affairs*, 8 (1) (March 2004), online: http://meria.idc.ac.il/journal/2004/issue1/jv8n1a2.html. It is important to note that the poll, conducted during a time when reformists enjoyed sufficient parliamentary strength, landed the pollsters in jail. For the Saudi poll, see "Impressions of America 2004: How

Arabs View America; How Arabs Learn about America," A Six-Nation Survey Commissioned by the Arab American Institute and Conducted by *Zogby International* (September 2005), online: http://www.comm.cornell.edu/als481/readings/Impressions%20of%20America%202004.pdf

23. Vogel, "Islamic Governance in the Gulf," p. 283.

CHAPTER 6

1. Cicero, *On Duties*, M.T. Griffin and E. M. Atkins (eds.) (Cambridge, UK: Cambridge University Press, 1991), p. 71.

2. Transcribed in President Mohammad Khatami, *Dialogue among Civilizations: A Paradigm for Peace*, Theo Bekker and Joelien Pretorius (eds.) (Pretoria, South Africa: Pretoria University, 2001), p. 14.

3. *Iran Times* (May 30, 1997), quoted in David Menashri, *Post-Revolutionary Politics in Iran: Religion, Society and Power* (London: Frank Cass, 2001), p. 87.

4. Menashri, *Post-Revolutionary Politics in Iran*, p. 86.

5. "Arab Attitudes toward U.S. Grow More Negative: Poll," *Reuters* (December 14, 2006). The statistics are from a Zogby Poll of 2006, performed in Saudi Arabia, Egypt, Morocco, Jordan, and Lebanon. The sample size "ranged from 600 to 800 in each country, and the margin of error for each sample was between 3.5 percent and 4.7 percent." As of January 2007, Egypt was still carrying a popular Iraqi insurgent channel on satellite television, which showed Americans being targeted by Sunni extremists. This, despite calls by the United States and the Iraqi government to pull the station. See "Why Is Egypt Airing Insurgent TV from Iraq?" *The Christian Science Monitor* (January 17, 2007).

6. Ali M. Ansari, *Iran, Islam and Democracy: The Politics of Managing Change* (London: The Royal Institute of International Affairs, 2000), p. 52.

7. Ali Gheissari and Vali Nasr, *Democracy in Iran: History and the Quest for Liberty* (Oxford, UK: Oxford University Press, 2006), p. 123. For a glimpse into Rafsanjani's ambitious infrastructure projects, see "Rafsanjani's Iran," *GCSS Staff Report*, V (June 1994–April 1996): 27–67. On the bank embezzlement scandal, see Menashri, *Post-Revolutionary Politics in Iran*, p. 112.

8. Menashri, *Post-Revolutionary Politics in Iran*, pp. 82–83. A young, Danish student provides a look into Western influence over Iran—*"tabajom-e farhangi"*— in Claus V. Pedersen, "Youth Culture and Official State Discourse in Iran," in Jorgen Baek Simonsen (ed.), *Youth and Touth Culture in the Contemporary Middle East* (Aarhus, Denmark: Aarhus University Press, 2005).

9. Gheissari and Nasr, *Democracy in Iran*, p. 129.

10. "Could Iran Help the US Stabilize Iraq?" *The Christian Science Monitor* (December 15, 2006).

11. The quote is "Hey, Jay, you want to do Iran?" Quoted in Bob Woodward, *State of Denial* (London: Simon & Schuster, 2006), p. 224.

12. Comments made during a lecture at Columbia University (December 6, 2006).

13. Blog: "On Faith: A Conversation on Religion with Jon Meacham and Sally Quinn," "Absolute Truth Manifests Itself in Diverse Ways," posted by Sayyed Mohammad Khatami, (November 15, 2006): http://newsweek.washingtonpost.com/onfaith/. Masoumeh Ebtekar served as Iran's first female vice president and

later went on to serve in the Tehran city council. Although a reformer, she is known in the West as the spokesperson for the U.S. embassy hostage-takers of 1979.

14. "Could Iran Help the US Stabilize Iraq?" (December 15, 2006).

15. Farideh Farhi, "The Antinomies of Iran's War Generation," in Lawrence G. Potter and Gary G. Sick (eds.), *Iran, Iraq and the Legacies of War* (New York: Palgrave Macmillan, 2004), p. 107.

16. "Investigation of Holocaust Also Raises Questions about Zionist Regime: FM," *Tehran Times* (December 12, 2006).

17. "Iranian Jews in U.S. Grapple with Crisis," *Associated Press* (August 7, 2006). On the derogatory term for Jews in Palestine, see Benny Morris, *Righteous Victims: A History of the Zionist-Arab Conflict 1881–2001* (New York: Vintage Books, 2001), p. 10.

18. "Iran ruft zu Waffenlieferungen an die Hizbullah auf," *Frankfurter Allgemeine Zeitung* (August 1, 2006).

19. Interview with the author (January 26, 2007). On Iran putting Arab regimes on notice, see "In Mideast Tumult, Iran's Clout Rises," *The Christian Science Monitor* (July 31, 2006); see also "Ahmadinejad Calls for Lebanon Cease-fire," *Associated Press* (July 26, 2006). Iran's clout rose in large part because of U.S. and Israeli miscalculations. The initial response from the United States at the beginning of hostilities was full support for Israel, and UN Resolution 1559, which calls for the disarmament of Hezbollah. Miscalculating that Israel would be able to significantly set back the Lebanese militia, Secretary of State Condoleezza Rice said she had "no interest in diplomacy for the sake of returning Lebanon and Israel to the status quo ante." In the end, a cease-fire was brokered, and Hezbollah's popularity (along with Iran's) increased. See "U.S. Plan Seeks to Wedge Syria From Iran," *The New York Times* (July 23, 2006).

20. See "Arab Attitudes toward U.S." Also mentioned are residents' negative opinions related to "the Iraq war and the Palestinian conflict, but also ... the United States' policy on Lebanon, its promotion of democracy in the region."

21. "What Iran Vote Says about Ahmadinejad's Support," *The Christian Science Monitor* (December 18, 2006). For Internet stats, see "Internet Usage in the Middle East (Middle East Internet Usage & Population Statistics)," *Internet World Stats*, online: http://www.internetworldstats.com/stats5.htm

22. See Gerardo L. Munck and Carol Skalnik Leff, "Modes of Transition and Democratization: South America and Eastern Europe in Comparative Perspective," in Lisa Anderson (ed.), *Transitions to Democracy* (New York: Columbia University Press, 1999).

23. Ibid., p. 201.

24. Ibid., p. 199.

CHAPTER 7

1. 3:16, translation by Thomas Hobbes (1628).

2. "Geopolitics Casts Pall on Hobbled Iranian Economy," *USA Today* (September 5, 2006).

3. Interview with Lawrence G. Potter (December 6, 2006). Ali Ansari puts it thus: "The war with Iraq encouraged authoritarianism but prevented the resolution of the many contradictions inherent in the political structure. In effect, the government was granted extraordinary powers as factions set aside their disputes to focus their attentions on the invader." Ali M. Ansari, *Iran, Islam and Democracy: The Politics of Managing Change* (London: Royal Institute of International Affairs, 2000), p. 49.

4. Farideh Farhi writes, "[The] IRGC [was] initially organized to fight against domestic opponents in Kurdistan, Khuzistan, Torkaman Sahra, and other areas." See Farideh Farhi, "The Antinomies of Iran's War Generation," in Lawrence G. Potter and Gary G. Sick (eds.), *Iran, Iraq and the Legacies of War* (New York: Palgrave Macmillan Press, 2004), p. 106. Khuzestan, a largely Arab province in the south of Iran, continues to act as a source of unrest. See "Iran to Hang Six Men Publicly," *AFP* (July 30, 2006).

5. Anthony H. Cordesman, *The Military Balance in the Middle East* (Westport, CT: Praeger, 2004), p. 264.

6. Ibid., p. 266.

7. Ibid., p. 6; on Saudi expenditures, see p. 315.

8. David C. Rapoport, "A Comparative Theory of Military Types," in Samuel Huntington (ed.), *Changing Patterns of Military Politics* (New York: Free Press of Glencoe, 1962), pp. 90–91.

9. *Al-Ahram* (March 6, 1969), quoted in Benny Morris, *Righteous Victims: A History of the Zionist-Arab Conflict 1881–2001* (New York: Vintage Books, 2001), p. 348. On Iran's rising population, see *World Population Prospects, The 2002 Revision* (New York: United Nations, ESA/WP 180 February 26, 2003), quoted in Cordesman, *The Military Balance in the Middle East*, p. 51.

10. David C. Rapoport sees religious terrorism, such as that of al-Qaeda, as part of a greater trend in history's mutation of terrorism. For this theory of the "Four Waves of Terrorism," the last of which is religious, see "The Fourth Wave: September 11 in the History of Terrorism," *Current History*, 100(650) (2001): 419–424.

11. "Iran Seeks to Become Major Mideast Player," *Associated Press* (July 20, 2006).

12. Ibid.

13. Richard L. Russell, *Weapons Proliferation and War in the Greater Middle East* (New York: Routledge, 2005), p. 21.

14. Farhi, "The Antinomies of Iran's War Generation," p. 107.

15. See "EXCLUSIVE: Iranian Weapons Arm Iraqi Milita," *ABC News* (November 30, 2006), online: http://abcnews.go.com/International/IraqCoverage/story?id=2688501. On Syrian support of Kurdish guerrillas fighting Turkey, see "Mubarak in Syria to Defuse Tension with Turkey," *CNN* (October 4, 1998), online: http://www.cnn.com/WORLD/meast/9810/04/syria.turkey/

16. "Country Analysis Brief: Saudi Arabia," *Energy Information Administration, The U.S. Department of Energy* (August 2005), online: http://www.eia.doe.gov/emeu/cabs/saudi.html. On Bahrain's uprisings, see Vali Nasr, *The Shia Revival: How Conflicts within Islam Will Shape the Future* (New York: W.W. Norton & Company, 2006), pp. 234–236.

17. "Iran Is Seeking More Influence in Afghanistan," *New York Times* (December 27, 2006). For viewpoints on the rising Shi'i in the Middle East, see Vali Nasr's

"When the Shiites Rise," *Foreign Affairs* (July/August 2006) and *The Shia Revival.* Also see Yitzhak Nakash, *Reaching for Power: The Shi'a in the Modern Arab World* (Princeton, NJ: Princeton University Press, 2006).

18. See Morris, *Righteous Victims*, Chapter 9.

19. Interview with the author (December 18, 2006).

20. *Central Intelligence Agency* (Memo): "Profile of Iranian President Bani-Sadr," CONFIDENTIAL (Issue Date: February 5, 1980; Date Declassified: January 13, 2000), Sanitized; Complete.

21. Discussion with Iranian male (late 20s) in Tehran (May 12, 2007).

22. Russia has been a main provider of know-how in relation to Iran's nuclear program, and China continues to receive oil shipments from Iran. Their support for Iran during Security Council deliberations on Iran's nuclear program has in the past allowed Iran to escape official UN condemnation of its proliferation activities. See "Security Council Reaches Accord on Iran," *Associated Press* (July 28, 2006).

CHAPTER 8

1. Data from The World Bank: www.worldbank.org

2. The public campaign to wage a war against Iraq and overthrow Saddam Hussein's regime began in earnest during the mid-1990s. Among the leader neo-conservative forums for support of the war during Clinton's presidency were the think tank The American Enterprise Institute (AEI) and *The Weekly Standard*: see "How to Attack Iraq" (November 16, 1998), and Robert Kagan, "Saddam Wins—Again" (January 4, 1999); Also see a "Letter to the Editor" on Iraq by Stephen J. Solarz and Paul Wolfowitz in the mainstream *Foreign Affairs*, 78(2) (March/April 1999). Wolfowitz would become Deputy Defense Secretary in the Bush administration and wage an internal campaign to attack Iraq.

3. From a lecture at Columbia University: "States and Citizens: How the World Came to Be the Way It Is" (September 19, 2005).

4. See Samuel P. Huntington, *The Clash of Civilizations and the Remaking of the World Order* (New York: Simon & Schuster, 1998). For a facts-based approach to the question of suicide terrorism, see Robert A. Pape, *Dying to Win: The Strategic Logic of Suicide Terrorism* (New York: Random House, 2005).

5. Richard Perle, who sat on the Defense Advisory Board Committee during the first term of the Bush administration, and David Frum, Bush speechwriter and author of the term "axis of evil" (originally. "axis of hatred"), coauthored a book that only perpetuates the notion of a monolithic enemy: *An End to Evil: How to Win the War on Terror* (New York: Ballantine, 2003), Chapter 3 ("The New Axis"). In an interview with *CNN* on September 10, 2002, Vice President Dick Cheney said, "We have to worry about the possible marriage, if you will, of a rogue state like Saddam Hussein's Iraq with a terrorist organization like al-Qaeda." See "Cheney: Saddam Working on Nuclear Weapons," *CNN* (Online): http://archives.cnn.com/2002/ALLPOLITICS/09/09/cheney.interview/index.html. On Vietnam as an extension of an anticolonial campaign, see Robert McNamara, *In Retrospect: The Tragedy and Lessons of Vietnam* (New York: Random House, 1995), pp. 30–33.

6. From a lecture at Columbia University: "Policy, Strategy and Operation: Integrating Political Ends and Military Means" (October 12, 2005).

7. For a helpful introduction to this question, see Robert Jervis, "Theories of War in an Era of Leading-Power Peace: President Address, American Political Science Association, 2001," *American Political Science Review*, 96 (1) (March 2002). On Lippmann, see Robert S. Litwak, *Détente and the Nixon Doctrine: American Foreign Policy and the Pursuit of Stability, 1969–1976* (Cambridge, UK: Cambridge University Press, 1984), p. 16. For a liberal but more idealistic view of a "Concert of Democracies," see Ivo Daalder and James Lindsay, "Democracies of the World, Unite," *American Interest* (January/February 2007). Kenneth N. Waltz reminds us that the Weimar Republic, which led to Nazi Germany, was a democracy. For Waltz' refutation of the "democratic peace" argument, see "Structural Realism After the Cold War," *International Security*, 25(1) (2000): especially pp. 6–8.

8. From the lecture *"Politik als Beruf, "* given at the Freistudentischen Bund in Munich (1918–1919).

9. Litwak, *Détente and the Nixon Doctrine*, p. 103. For Henry Kissinger, the Nixon Doctrine was meant to deal with peripheral conflicts such as Vietnam, and obviously not direct superpower rivalry. See Henry Kissinger, *Diplomacy* (New York: Simon & Schuster, 1994), pp. 708–709. On the question of the later-mentioned threat of pan-Arabism as an impetus for the "twin pillar policy," see Bruce R. Kuniholm, *The Persian Gulf and United States Policy: A Guide to Issues and References* (Claremont, CA: Regina Book, 1984).

10. Litwak, *Détente and the Nixon Doctrine*, p. 87

11. Quoted in "Study Calls Iran 'Biggest Beneficiary' of US War on Terror," *The Christian Science Monitor* (August, 25, 2006). Also see "Sadr's Militia Regrouping, Rearming," *The Christian Science Monitor* (July 15, 2004).

12. See Stephen D. Biddle, *American Grand Strategy After 9/11: An Assessment*, Strategic Studies Institute, United States War College (2005). See Interview with Robert A. Pape, "The Logic of Suicide Terrorism," *The American Conservative* (July 18, 2005). On the "balance of weakness," see Jalil Roshandel, "Towards Cooperative Security in the Persian Gulf," in Bjorn Moller (ed.), *Oil and Water: Cooperative Security in the Persian Gulf* (London: I.B. Tauris, 2001), and "Iran's Foreign and Security Policies: How the Decision-making Process Evolved," *Security Dialog*, 31(1) (March 2000).

13. Kenneth N. Waltz, "Globalization and American Power," *The National Interest* (Spring 2000). See also "Rice: U.S. Concerned about Rising China," *Associated Press* (November 17, 2006). On China's growth, see "China's Economy to Grow 8% Annually from 2006 to 2010," *China Daily* (March 21, 2005). Also see "China," *CIA Factbook*, https://www.cia.gov/cia/publications/factbook/geos/ch.html#Econ; Also, "China, Shy Giant, Shows Signs of Shedding Its False Modesty," *The New York Times* (December 9, 2006).

14. Colin S. Gray, *The Geopolitics of Super Power* (Lexington: The University Press of Kentucky, 1988), p. 18.

15. Paul Kennedy, *The Rise and Fall of the Great Powers: Economic Change and Military Conflict from 1500 to 2000* (New York: Vintage Books, 1989), p. 515.

16. Quoted in J. Patrice McSherry, *Predatory States: Operation Condor and Covert War in Latin America* (Lanham, MD: Rowman & Littlefield Publishers, 2005), p. 27. On the IEDs, see "Quadrennial Defense Review," *Department of Defense* (February 6, 2006): 63–64.

CHAPTER 9

1. There is a wealth of declassified information surrounding China's entrance into the nuclear club, available online through George Washington University: "The United States and the Chinese Nuclear Program 1962–1964," William Burr and Jeffrey T. Richelson (eds.) (January 12, 2001): http://www.gwu.edu/~nsarchiv/NSAEBB/NSAEBB38/#docs. Especially poignant are the following memoranda: Robert H. Johnson, State Department Policy Planning Council, "A Chinese Communist Nuclear Detonation and Nuclear Capability: Major Conclusions and Key Issues," October 15, 1963, Secret (Source: Policy Planning Council Records, 1963–64, box 275, S/P Papers Chicom Nuclear Detonation and Nuclear Capability, Policy Planning Statement, October 15, 1963); Memorandum, Robert H. Johnson, Department of State Policy Planning Council, "The Chinese Communist Nuclear Capability and Some 'Unorthodox' Approaches to the Problem of Nuclear Proliferation," June 1, 1964, Secret (Source: RG 59, Policy Planning Council Records, 1963–64, box 264, 1964—Johnson Chron File Bulky Reports).

2. Sun-Tzu, *The Art of Warfare: The First English Translation Incorporating the Recently Discovered Yin-ch'ueh-shan Texts*, Translated, with an Introduction and Commentary, by Roger T. Ames (New York: Balantine Books, 1993), p. 132.

3. Thomas C. Schelling, *Arms and Influence* (Westport, CT: Greenwood Press, 1966), pp. 44–45. For the record, Cortés did not actually burn his ships. See Winston A. Reynolds, "The Burning Ships of Hernán Cortés," *Hispania*, 42(3) (September, 1959): 317–324.

4. Quoted in "Iran Must Not Be Allowed to Develop Nuclear Weapons -Bush-UPDATE," *AFX News* (via *Forbes*) (March 1, 2006).

5. "Iran's Nuclear Threat," *Rasmussen Reports* (September 15, 2006). The telephone survey polled 1,000 American adults, and had a margin of error of ±3 percentage points, with a 95% confidence interval.

6. International Monetary Fund, IMF Country Report No. 06/154, "Islamic Republic of Iran: 2005 Article IV Consultation—Staff Report; Staff Statement; Public Information Notice on the Executive Board Discussion; and Statement by the Executive Director for the Islamic Republic of Iran" (April 2006), p. 13. Oil consumption is "inelastic"—that is, its demand is not easily managed through price manipulation and therefore increasing the price would not necessarily stave off demand. This is yet another argument in favor of energy diversification. See "Iranian People's Behavior in Gasoline Consumption," *Iranian Trade Association*, online: www.iraniantrade.org

7. There were several press reports in January 2006 surrounding the alleged sale of fake nuclear "blueprints" to the Iranians, whose credibility has come to be questioned. Notwithstanding, there are ample reasons to believe that Iran would consider such weapons to be in its strategic interest. See *The Guardian*, "George Bush insists that Iran must not be allowed to develop nuclear weapons ..." (January 5, 2006).

8. Mahan Abedin, "Iranian Public Opinion and the Nuclear Stand-Off," *Mideast Monitor*, 1(2) (April/May 2006).

9. Case in point is a declassified Defense Intelligence Agency report outlining what it calls "Major Instances of Chemical Weapons Use" in the Iran-Iraq war. Of the twelve such incidents mentioned (mostly committed by Iraq), it cites only one

time in which the use of such weapons "stopped the Iranian advance." Mostly, their use was labeled as having "little effect," "no effect on the battle," "little effect on either side," etc. On one occasion (April 1987, East of Basra), Iran's use of chemical weapons is considered to have created "[f]ew Iraqi casualties; probable psychological effect on Iraqi military." Defense Intelligence Agency, "The Iran-Iraq War: A Reference Aid (U), Defense Research Reference Series (August 8, 1988), Secret.

10. Interview with the author (December 18, 2006).

11. Scott Sagan, "How to Keep the Bomb from Iran," *Foreign Affairs* (September/October 2006): 55.

12. Scott D. Sagan and Kenneth N. Watlz, *Nuclear Weapons: A Debate Renewed* (New York: W.W. Norton & Company, 2003), p. 37.

13. Sagan, "How to Keep the Bomb from Iran, p. 58. On the A. Q. Khan connection to Iran, see "Iran Claims Nuclear Steps in New Worry," *The New York Times* (April 17, 2006).

14. Guy Ronen, "Appeasement 2006," *Yedioth Ahronoth* (April 23, 2006). Online: ynetnews.com

15. Michael Ledeen, "Active Appeasement," *National Review Online* (October 9, 2006).

16. Quoted in Benny Morris, *Righteous Victims: A History of the Zionist-Arab Conflict 1881–2001* (New York: Vintage Books, 2001), p. 515. While Arafat's PLO was originally involved in several acts of nonsuicide terrorism, including hijackings and assassinations, Israeli President Begin ironically is one of the few Israeli figures credited with belonging to a self-proclaimed terrorist organization—the Irgun, which operated in pre-Independence Israel. On a refutation of Arab attacks on Israelis using comparisons to Hitler, see "When They Say Hitler—What Do They Mean," *Israeli Ministry of Foreign Affairs* (November 3, 1996), online: www.israel-mfa.gov.il, taken from *Haaretz* (November 3, 1996).

17. Ahmadinejad's political support is not unconditional. Following a December 2006 defeat of his supporters at the voting booth, reformists were gaining ground. See "In Iran Kritik an Ahmadineschad," *Frankfurter Allgemeine Zeitung* (December 29, 2006).

18. Judith S. Yaphe and Charles D. Lutes, "Reassessing the Implications of a Nuclear-Armed Iran," McNair Paper 69, *Institute for National Strategic Studies* (Washington, DC: National Defense University, 2005), p. 41.

19. Robert A. Pape of Chicago University carried out a comprehensive study of all suicide terrorist bombings that have been documented. His findings suggest that suicide terror is not merely a Muslim concept and that the majority of operations have involved the secular Marxists Tamil Tigers of Buddhist Sri Lanka. See Robert A. Pape, *Dying to Win: The Strategic Logic of Suicide Terrorism* (New York: Random House, 2005); The answer to whether states seek to maximize their power (Mearsheimer) or merely their survival (Waltz) is in the eye of the beholder. See John J. Mearsheimer, *The Tragedy of Great Power Politics* (New York: W.W. Norton & Company, 2001) and Kenneth N. Waltz, *Theory of International Politics* (Reading, MA: Addison-Wesley, 1979).

20. Barry R. Posen, "We Can Live With a Nuclear Iran," Op-Ed, *The New York Times* (February 27, 2006). On the length of time it might take for Iran to build a bomb, see "Iran Is Judged 10 Years from Nuclear Bomb," *The Washington Post*

(August 2, 2005). On Israel's alleged plan, see "Revealed: Israel Plans Nuclear Strike on Iran," *The Sunday Times* (January 7, 2007). On the GCC, see "Arab States Study Shared Nuclear Program," *Associated Press* (December 10, 2006).

21. "Stalled Enrichment Prompts Concern, Hope," *Associated Press* (January 12, 2007). On the raid of the Iranian post in Irbil, see "Bush Approved Raids on Iranians in Iraq," and "Iraq FM Defends Detained Iranians," *Associated Press* (January 13, 2007). David Frum, a neoconservative who supported the Iraq war, maintains that no one "ever anticipated a ground invasion of either Iran or North Korea . . . ." Rather, air strikes would be the option, but only "as a last resort." Comments made on "Late Edition with Wolf Blitzer," *CNN* (November 19, 2006). Regarding the chain of events leading to the reactor bombing in Iraq, see Richard Wilson, "Nuclear Proliferation and the Case of Iraq," *Journal of Palestine Studies*, XX(3) (Spring 1991): 10. Wilson is of the belief that Israel should not have bombed the Osirak reactor, while this author disagrees.

CHAPTER 10

1. Radio and Television, Address to the People of the Soviet Union, May 28, 1972, in Nixon Papers, 1972 vol., p. 630, quoted in Henry Kissinger, *Diplomacy* (New York: Simon & Shuster, 1994), p. 706.

2. Columbia University (December 6, 2006).

3. "President Bush's State of the Union Address," TQ Transcript Wire, *The Washington Post* (January 31, 2006).

4. Wesley Clark, "Broken Engagement: The Strategy that Won the Cold War Could Help Bring Democracy to the Middle East—If Only the Bush Hawks Understood It," *Washington Monthly* (May 2004).

SELECTED BIBLIOGRAPHY

Abrahamian, Ervand. "Oriental Despotism: The Case of Qajar Iran." *International Journal of Middle East Studies*, 5(1) (January 1974).

Afary, Janet. "Social Democracy and the Iranian Constitutional Revolution of 1906–1911," in John Foran (ed.), *A Century of Revolution: Social Movements in Iran* (Minneapolis: University of Minnesota Press, 1994).

———. *The Iranian Constitutional Revolution, 1906–1911: Grassroots Democracy, Social Democracy, & the Origins of Feminism* (New York: Columbia University Press, 1996).

Allen, Lindsay. *The Persian Empire: A History* (London: British Museum Press, 2005).

Amanat, Abbas. *Resurrection and Renewal: The Making of the Babi Movement in Iran, 1844–1850* (Ithaca, NY: Cornell University Press, 1989).

Ansari, Ali M. *Iran, Islam and Democracy: The Politics of Managing Change* (London: The Royal Institute of International Affairs, 2000).

Arjomand, Said Amir. "The Consolation of Theology: Absence of the Imam and Transition from Chiliasm to Law in Shi'ism." *The Journal of Religion*, 76(4) (October 1996).

Baktiari, Bahman. *Parliamentary Politics in Revolutionary Iran: The Institutionalization of Factional Politics* (Gainesville: University Press of Florida, 1996).

Bani-Sadr, Abol Hassan. *My Turn to Speak: Iran, the Revolution & Secret Deals with the U.S.* (Washington: Brassey's, 1989).

Bernard, Cheryl and Zalmay Khalilzad. *The Government of God: Iran's Islamic Republic* (New York: Columbia University Press, 1984).

Biddle, Stephen D. *American Grand Strategy After 9/11: An Assessment*, Strategic Studies Institute, United States War College (2005).

Blau, Peter M. *Exchange and Power in Social Life* (New York: Wiley, 1964).

Bligh, Alexander. "The Saudi Religious Elite (Ulama) as Participant in the Political System of the Kingdom." *International Journal of Middle East Studies*, 17(1) (1985).

Calder, Norman. "Judicial Authority in Imami Shi'i Jurisprudence." *Bulletin (British Society for Middle Eastern Studies)*, 6(2) (1979).

Chehabi, H. E. "The Banning of the Veil and Its Consequences," in Stephanie Cronin (ed.), *The Making of Modern Iran: State and Society under Riza Shah, 1921–1941* (London: Routledge, 2003).

Chubin, Shahram and Charles Tripp. *Iran and Iraq at War* (Boulder, CO: Westview Press, 1988).

Clark, Wesley. "Broken Engagement: The Strategy That Won the Cold War Could Help Bring Democracy to the Middle East—If Only the Bush Hawks Understood It." *Washington Monthly* (May 2004).

Clawson, Patrick. "The Paradox of Anti-Americanism." *Middle East Review of International Affairs*, 8(1) (March, 2004), online: http://meria.idc.ac.il/journal/2004/issue1/jv8n1a2.html.

Cook, J. M. *The Persian Empire* (London: J. M. Dent & Sons, 1983).

Cordesman, Anthony H. *The Military Balance in the Middle East* (Westport, CT: Praeger, 2004).

Cronin, Stephanie. *The Army and the Creation of the Pahlavi State in Iran, 1910–1926* (London: Tauris Academic Studies, 1997).

———. "An Experiment in Revolutionary Nationalism: The Rebellion of Colonel Muhammad Taqi Khan Pasyan in Mashhad, April–October 1921." *Middle Eastern Studies*, 33(4) (October 1997).

Daalder, Ivo and James Lindsay. "Democracies of the World, Unite." *American Interest*, (January/February 2007).

Dabashi, Hamid. "By What Authority? The Formation of Khomeini's Revolutionary Discourse, 1964–1977." *Social Compass*, 36(4) (1989).

———. *Authority in Islam: From the Rise of Muhammad to the Establishment of the Umayyads* (New Brunswick, NJ: Transaction Publishers, 2002).

Daneshvar, Parviz. *Revolution in Iran* (London: Palgrave Macmillan Press, 1996).

Diba, Farhad. *Mohammad Mossadegh: A Political Biography* (London: Croom Helm, 1986).

Ekbal, Kamran. "Ein britischer Plan zur Restauration der Zand-Herrschaft aus dem Jahre 1807," Die Welt des Islams, New Ser., Bd. 22, Nr. 1/4 (1982).

Eliash, Joseph. "Misconceptions Regarding the Juridical Status of the Iranian 'Ulama.'" *International Journal of Middle East Studies*, 10(1) (February 1979).

Farazmand, Ali. *The State, Bureaucracy, and Revolution in Modern Iran: Agrarian Reforms and Regime Politics* (Westport, CT: Praeger, 1989).

Farhi, Farideh. "The Antinomies of Iran's War Generation," in Lawrence G. Potter and Gary G. Sick (eds.), *Iran, Iraq and the Legacies of War* (New York: Palgrave Macmillan Press, 2004).

Frum, Richard N. *The Golden Age of Persia: The Arabs in the East* (London: Weidenfield, 1993).

Frum, David and Richard Perle. *An End to Evil: How to Win the War on Terror* (New York: Ballantine, 2003).

Gheissari, Ali and Vali Nasr. *Democracy in Iran: History and the Quest for Liberty* (Oxford, UK: Oxford University Press, 2006).

Gray, Colin S. *The Geopolitics of Super Power* (Lexington: The University Press of Kentucky, 1988).

Hunsberger, Alice C. *Nasir Khusraw, The Ruby of Badakhshan: A Portrait of the Persian Poet, Traveller and Philosopher* (London: I.B. Tauris, 2003).

Huntington, Samuel P. *The Clash of Civilizations and the Remaking of the World Order* (New York: Simon & Schuster, 1998).

Jervis, Robert. "Theories of War in an Era of Leading-Power Peace: President Address, American Political Science Association, 2001." *American Political Science Review*, 96(1) (March 2002).

Kashani-Sabet, Firoozeh. "Fragile Frontiers: The Diminishing Domains of Qajar Iran." *International Journal of Middle East Studies*, 29(2) (May, 1997).

Kechichian, Joseph A. "The Role of the Ulema in the Politics of an Islamic State: The Case of Saudi Arabia." *International Journal of Middle East Studies*, 18(1) (1986).

Keddie, Nikki. *Modern Iran: Roots and Results of Revolution* (New Haven, CT: Yale University Press, 2003).

Kennedy, Paul. *The Rise and Fall of the Great Powers: Economic Change and Military Conflict from 1500 to 2000* (New York: Vintage Books, 1989).

Khatami, Mohammad. *Dialogue among Civilizations: A Paradigm for Peace*, Theo Bekker and Joelien Pretorius (eds.) (Pretoria, South Africa: Pretoria University, 2001).

Khomeyni, Ayatollah Ruhollah. *Islamic Government*, National Technical Information Service. Translations on Near East and North Africa, No. 1897 (U.S. Department of Commerce, January 19, 1979).

Kissinger, Henry. *Diplomacy* (New York: Simon & Schuster, 1994).

Koury, Envery M. *The Saudi Decision-Making Body: The House of Al-Saud* (Hyattsville, MD: Institute of Middle Eastern and North African Affairs, 1978).

Kuniholm, Bruce R. *The Persian Gulf and United States Policy: A Guide to Issues and References* (Claremont, CA: Regina Book, 1984).

Lacroix, Stéphane. "Between Islamists and Liberals: Saudi Arabia's New 'Islamo-Liberal' Reformists." *The Middle East Journal*, 58(3) (2004).

Layish, Aharon. "Saudi Arabian Legal Reform as a Mechanism to Moderate Wahhabi Doctrine." *Journal of the American Oriental Society*, 107(2) (1987).

Litwak, Robert S. *Détente and the Nixon Doctrine: American Foreign Policy and the Pursuit of Stability, 1969–1976* (Cambridge, UK: Cambridge University Press, 1984).

Martin, Vanessa. *Islam and Modernism: The Iranian Revolution of 1906* (London: I.B. Tauris, 1989).

———. "Religion and State in Khumaini's Kashf Al-Asrar." *Bulletin of the School of Oriental and African Studies, University of London*, 56(1) (1993).

———. "Mudarris, Republicanism and the Rise to Power of Riza Khan, Sardar-I Sipah." *British Journal of Middle Eastern Studies*, 21(2) (1994).

McFadden, Robert D., Joseph B. Treaster, and Maurice Carrol. *No Hiding Place: The New York Times Inside Report on the Hostage Crisis* (New York: Times Books, 1981).

McNamara, Robert. *In Retrospect: The Tragedy and Lessons of Vietnam* (New York: Random House, 1995).

McSherry, Patrice. *Predatory States: Operation Condor and Covert War in Latin America* (Lanham, MD: Rowman & Littlefield Publishers, 2005).

Mearsheimer, John J. *The Tragedy of Great Power Politics* (New York: W. W Norton, 2001).

Moaddel, Mansoor. "Shi'i Political Discourse and Class Mobilization in the Tobacco Movement of 1890–1892," in John Foran (ed.), *A Century of Revolution: Social Movements in Iran* (Minneapolis: University of Minnesota Press, 1994).

Modarressi, Hossein. "Rationalism and Traditionalism in Shi'i Jurisprudence: A Preliminary Survey." *Studia Islamica*, (59) (1984).

Moin, Baqer. *Khomeini: Life of an Ayatollah* (New York: St. Martin's Press, 2000).

Momen, Moojan. *An Introduction to Shi'i Islam: The History and Doctrines of Twelver Shi'ism* (New Haven, CT: Yale University Press, 1987).

Morris, Benny. *Righteous Victims: A History of the Zionist-Arab Conflict 1881–1821* (New York: Vintage Books, 2001).

Munck, Gerardo L., and Carol Skalnik Leff, "Modes of Transition and Democratization: South America and Eastern Europe in Comparative Perspective," in Lisa Anderson (ed.), *Transitions to Democracy* (New York: Columbia University Press, 1999).

Nakash, Yitzhak. *Reaching for Power: The Shi'a in the Modern Arab World* (Princeton, NJ: Princeton University Press, 2006).

Nasr, Vali. "When the Shiites Rise." *Foreign Affairs* (July/August 2006).

———. *The Shia Revival: How Conflicts within Islam Will Shape the Future* (New York: W.W. Norton, 2006).

Newman, Andrew J. "The Nature of the Akhbari/Usuli Dispute in Late Safavid Iran, Part 1: 'Abdallah al-Samahiji's 'Munyat al-Mumarisin.'" *Bulletin of the School of Oriental and African Studies, University of London*, 55(1) (1992).

———. *The Formative Period of Twelver Shi'ism: Hadith as Discourse between Qum and Baghdad* (Richmond, UK: Curzon, 2000).

———. *Safavid Iran: Rebirth of a Persian Empire* (London: I.B. Tauris, 2006).

Nikham, Azadeh. "The Islamization of Law in Iran: A Time of Disenchantment. *Middle East Report*, No. 212, Pushing the Limits: Iran's Islamic Revolution at Twenty (Fall 1999).

Pape, Robert A. "The Strategic Logic of Suicide Terrorism." *The American Political Science Review*, 97(3) (August, 2003).

———. *Dying to Win: The Strategic Logic of Suicide Terrorism* (New York: Random House, 2005).

Parsa, Misagh. "Mosque of Last Resort: State Reform and Social Conflict in the Early 1960s," in John Foran (ed.), *A Century of Revolution: Social Movements in Iran* (Minneapolis: University of Minnesota Press, 1994).

Pedersen, Claus V. "Youth Culture and Official State Discourse in Iran," in Jorgen Baek Simonsen (ed.), *Youth and Touth Culture in the Contemporary Middle East* (Aarhus, Denmark: Aarhus University Press, 2005).

Perry, J. R. "Justice for the Underprivileged: The Ombudsman Tradition of Iran." *Journal of Near Eastern Studies*, 37(3) (July 1978).

———. *Karim Khan Zand: A History of Iran, 1747–1779* (Chicago, IL: University of Chicago Press, 1979).

Pistor-Hatam, Anja. *Iran und die Reformbewegung im Osmanischen Reich: Persische Staatsmänner, Reisende und Oppositionelle unter dem Einfluß der Tanzimat* (Berlin, Germany: Klaus Schwarz Verlag, 1992).

Posen, Barry R. (op-ed) "We Can Live With a Nuclear Iran." *The New York Times* (February 27, 2006).

Potter, Lawrence. "An Introduction to the Gulf Region." *The Gulf/2000 Project*, on-line: http://gulf2000.columbia.edu/country.shtml.

"Rafsanjani's Iran," *GCSS Staff Report*, Volume V (June 1994–April 1996).

Rapoport, David C. "A Comparative Theory of Military Types," in Samuel Huntington (ed.), *Changing Patterns of Military Politics* (New York: Free Press of Glencoe, 1962).

———. "The Fourth Wave: September 11 in the History of Terrorism." *Current History*, 100(650) (2001).

Reynolds, Winston A. "The Burning Ships of Hernán Cortés." *Hispania*, 42(3) (September 1959).

Roshandel, Jalil. "Iran's Foreign and Security Policies: How the Decision-Making Process Evolved." *Security Dialog*, 31(1) (March 2000).

———. "Towards Cooperative Security in the Persian Gulf," in Bjorn Moller (ed.), *Oil and Water: Cooperative Security in the Persian Gulf* (London: I.B. Tauris, 2001).

Russell, Richard L. *Weapons Proliferation and War in the Greater Middle East* (New York: Routledge, 2005).

Saffari, Sayid. "The Legitimation of the Clergy's Right to Rule in the Iranian Constitution of 1979." *British Journal of Middle Eastern Studies*, 20(1) (1993).

Sagan, Scott D. and Kenneth N. Watlz. *Nuclear Weapons: A Debate Renewed* (New York: W.W. Norton & Company, 2003).

Sagan, Scott D. "How to Keep the Bomb from Iran." *Foreign Affairs* (September/October 2006).

Salameh, Ghassane and Vivian Steir. "Political Power and the Saudi State." *MERIP Reports*, No. 91, Saudi Arabia on the Brink (October 1980).

Schelling, Thomas C. *Arms and Influence* (Westport, CT: Greenwood Press, 1966).

Sfeir, George N. "The Saudi Approach to Law Reform." *The American Journal of Comparative Law*, 36(4) (Autumn 1988).

Sheikholeslami, A. Reza. *The Structure of Central Authority in Qajar Iran: 1871–1896* (Atlanta, GA: Scholars Press, 1997).

Shuster, W. Morgan. *The Strangling of Persia: Story of the European Diplomacy and Oriental Intrigue that Resulted in the Denationalization of Twelve Million Mohammedans—A Personal Narrative* (1912) (New York: Greenwood, 1968).

Sick, Gary. *All Fall Down: America's Tragic Encounter with Iran* (New York: Random House, 1985).

———. "Military Options and Constraints," in Paul H. Kreisberg (ed.), *American Hostages in Iran: The Conduct of a Crisis* (New Haven, CT: Yale University Press, 1985).

Sirriyeh, Hussein. *U.S. Policy in the Gulf, 1968–1977: Aftermath of British Withdrawal* (London: Ithaca Press, 1984).

Smith, Peter. *The Babi and Baha'i Religions: From Messianic Shi'ism to a World Religion* (Cambridge, UK: Cambridge University Press, 1987).

Solarz, Stephen J., and Paul Wolfowitz. "Letter to the Editor." *Foreign Affairs*, 78(2) (March/April 1999).

Stolper, Matthew W. *Entrepreneurs and Empire: The Murasu Archive, the Murasu Firm, and Persian Rule in Babylonia* (Leiden, Netherlands: Nederlands Instituut voor het Nabije Oosten, 1985).

Sun-Tzu. *The Art of Warfare: The First English Translation Incorporating the Recently Discovered Yin-ch'ueh-shan Texts*. Translated, with an Introduction and Commentary, by Roger T. Ames (New York: Balantine Books, 1993).

Vogel, Frank E. "Islamic Governance in the Gulf: A Framework for Analysis, Comparison, and Prediction," in Gary G. Sick and Lawrence G. Potter (eds.), *The*

Persian Gulf at the Millennium: Essays in Politics, Economy, Security, and Religion (New York: St. Martin's Press, 1997).

Waltz, Kenneth N. *Theory of International Politics* (Reading, MA: Addison-Wesley, 1979).

———. "Globalization and American Power." *The National Interest* (Spring 2000).

———. "Structural Realism After the Cold War." *International Security*, 25(1) (Summer 2000).

Watt, W. Montgomery. *Muhammad: Prophet and Statesman* (Oxford, UK: Oxford University Press, 1961).

Wilson, Richard. "Nuclear Proliferation and the Case of Iraq." *Journal of Palestine Studies*, XX(3) (Spring 1991).

Wohlforth, William C. "The Stability of a Unipolar World." *International Security*, 24(1) (Summer, 1999).

Woodward, Bob. *State of Denial* (London: Simon & Schuster, 2006).

Wright, Robin. *In the Name of God: The Khomeini Decade* (New York: Simon & Schuster, 1989).

Yaphe, Judith S., and Charles D. Lutes. "Reassessing the Implications of a Nuclear-Armed Iran." McNair Paper 69, *Institute for National Strategic Studies* (Washington, DC: National Defense University, 2005).

Al-Yassini, Ayman. *Religion and State in the Kingdom of Saudi Arabia* (Boulder, CO: Westview Press, 1985).

Zabih, Sepehr. *The Mossadegh Era: Roots of the Iranian Revolution* (Chicago, IL: Lake View Press, 1982).

Zirinsky, Michael P. "Imperial Power and Dictatorship: Britain and the Rise of Reza Shah, 1921–1926." *International Journal of Middle East Studies*, 24(4) (November 1992).

Zogby International. "Impressions of America 2004: How Arabs View America; How Arabs Learn about America," A Six-Nation Survey Commissioned by the Arab American Institute.

Zubaida, Sami. "An Islamic State? The Case of Iran." *Middle East Report*, No. 153, Islam and the State (July–August, 1998).

NEWS AND PERIODICALS

ABC News
AFP
The American Conservative
Associated Press
BBC News
China Daily
The Christian Science Monitor
CNN
Forbes
Fox News
Frankfurter Allgemeine Zeitung
Guardian of London
Haaretz

Mideast Monitor
MSNBC
National Review Online
The New York Times
Rasmussen Reports
Reuters
The Sunday Times
Tehran Times
Time
USA Today
The Washington Post
The Weekly Standard
Yedioth Ahronoth

INTERVIEWS AND PRIMARY SOURCES

Anderson, Lisa: "States and Citizens: How the World Came to Be the Way It Is," Lecture, Columbia University: (September 19, 2005).

Betts, Richard: "Policy, Strategy and Operation: Integrating Political Ends and Military Means," Lecture, Columbia University (October 12, 2005).

Central Intelligence Agency: Research Study, "Elites and the Distribution of Power in Iran" (secret, February 1976).

Central Intelligence Agency: (Memo) "Profile of Iranian President Bani-Sadr," Confidential (Issue Date: February 5, 1980; Date declassified: January 13, 2000), sanitized, complete.

CIA Factbook: "China," online: https://www.cia.gov/cia/publications/factbook/geos/ch.html#Econ.

Defense Intelligence Agency: "The Iran-Iraq War: A Reference Aid (U), Defense Research Reference Series (August 8, 1988), Secret.

Foreign Relations, 1951 (Vol. V): File 120.4382/3-1551: Agreed Conclusions and Recommendations of the Conference of Middle Eastern Chiefs of Mission, Istanbul, February 14–21, 1951.

———. McGhee Files: Lot 53 D 468: "Petroleum" (1951).

George Washington University: "The United States and the Chinese Nuclear Program 1962–1964," William Burr and Jeffrey T. Richelson (eds.) (January 12, 2001): http://www.gwu.edu/~nsarchiv/NSAEBB/NSAEBB38/#docs; Memoranda: Robert H. Johnson, State Department Policy Planning Council, "A Chinese Communist Nuclear Detonation and Nuclear Capability: Major Conclusions and Key Issues," October 15, 1963, secret (Source: Policy Planning Council Records, 1963–64, box 275, S/P Papers Chicom Nuclear Detonation and Nuclear Capability, Policy Planning Statement, 10/15/63); Memorandum, Robert H. Johnson, Department of State Policy Planning Council, "The Chinese Communist Nuclear Capability and Some 'Unorthodox' Approaches to the Problem of Nuclear Proliferation," June 1, 1964, secret (Source: RG 59, Policy Planning Council Records, 1963–1964, box 264, 1964—Johnson Chron File Bulky Reports).

International Monetary Fund: IMF Country Report No. 06/154: "Islamic Republic of Iran: 2005 Article IV Consultation—Staff Report; Staff Statement; Public

Information Notice on the Executive Board Discussion; and Statement by the Executive Director for the Islamic Republic of Iran" (April, 2006).

Internet World Stats: "Internet Usage in the Middle East (Middle East Internet Usage & Population Statistics)," online: http://www.internetworldstats.com/stats5.htm.

Iranian Trade Association: "Iranian People's Behavior in Gasoline Consumption," online: http://www.iraniantrade.org.

Khatami, Mohammad: "Absolute Truth Manifests itself in Diverse Ways," *On Faith: A Conversation on Religion with Jon Meacham and Sally Quinn* (November 15, 2006, 5:00 p.m.), online: http://newsweek.washingtonpost.com/onfaith/.

Linnington, Abigail (Major, U.S. Army): Interview with the author (January 25, 2007).

Potter, Lawrence G. Interview with the author (December 6, 2006).

The United Nations Development Programme: "The Gender and Citizenship Initiative: Country Profiles," online: http://gender.pogar.org/.

U.S. Department of Defense: "Quadrennial Defense Review" (February 6, 2006).

U.S. Department of Energy: *Energy Information Administration*, "Country Analysis Brief: Saudi Arabia," (August 2005), online: http://www.eia.doe.gov/emeu/cabs/saudi.html.

U.S. Department of State: "International Religious Freedom Report for 2005, Saudi Arabia," online: http://www.state.gov/g/drl/rls/irf/2005/51609.htm.

The World Bank: Data, online: http://www.worldbank.org.

Wrona, Richard (Major, U.S. Army). Interview with the author (January 27, 2007).

Zarif, Javad: Lecture, Columbia University (December 6, 2006).

INDEX

About the Author

NATHAN GONZALEZ is founder of *NationandState.org*, an open-source foreign policy think tank. He has published several academic papers on U.S.-Iranian relations and is a regular contributor to various blogs and opinion publications. In 2002, he received a prize from the University of California, Los Angeles for his research on Iraq, through which he predicted that a U.S. invasion would bring about massive sectarian strife, pervasive anti-Americanism in Iraq, and a stronger Iran. The author holds a bachelor's degree in political science from UCLA, and a master of international affairs from Columbia University.